D0765220

The WESTERN

Parables of the American Dream

The **WESTERN**

Jeffrey Wallmann

Foreword by

Richard S. Wheeler

Texas Tech University Press

This book was set in Goudy Oldstyle. The paper used in this book meets the minimum requirements of ANSI/NISO Z39.48-1992 (R1997). ∞

Design by Tamara Kruciak

Printed in the United States of America

Library of Congress Cataloging-in-Publication Data
  Wallmann, Jeffrey M.
      The western : parables of the American dream / Jeffrey
  Wallmann ; foreword by Richard S. Wheeler.
          p.   c.m.
      Includes bibliographical references and index.
      ISBN 0-89672-423-9 (alk. paper)
      1. Western stories—History and criticism. 2. American
  fiction—West (U.S.)—History and criticism. 3. Western
  television programs—History and criticism. 4. Frontier and
  pioneer life in literature. 5. Western films—History and criticism.
      6. West (U.S.)—In literature. I. title.
  PS374.W4W27   1999
  813'.087409—dc21   99-39869
                                                          CIP

99 00 01 02 03 04 05 06 07 / 9 8 7 6 5 4 3 2 1

Texas Tech University Press
Box 41037
Lubbock, Texas 79409-1037 USA

800-832-4042

ttup@ttu.edu

Http://www.ttup.ttu.edu

To all my saddlepards at the University of Nevada, Reno, and the Western Writers of America

Contents

Foreword

This is an important book. It fills, at last, an odd lacuna in American letters, and is destined to become a watershed in literary criticism.

The Western: Parables of the American Dream is simply the first comprehensive, rigorous, sophisticated study of the American Western, and Jeffrey Wallmann's findings will fascinate and inform both the critics and defenders of the genre. No future study of the Western can possibly be undertaken without referencing this seminal work.

The silence surrounding the Western is one of the great mysteries of American literature. Here we have a genre that comprised, in its heyday, a large portion of all of American fiction, and yet few scholars have made any effort to discern what the genre is all about, and those who have tackled it have done so with axes to grind, *a priori* conclusions they wished to support, almost always negative. What is even odder, this silence embraces a genre that has won at least three Pulitzer Prizes: *The Way West*, by A. B. Guthrie, *The Travels of Jaimie McPheeters* by Robert Lewis Taylor, and *Lonesome Dove*, by Larry McMurtry. One might also add *Laughing Boy* by Oliver La Farge.

Plainly, something curious has been going on for most of a century. The commonly adduced reason for this, of course, is that Western writing is junk. That is an oddly dismissive notion. No one doubts that most Western novels and short stories are indeed junk. Surely ninety percent of all those thousands of stories are junk. But so is ninety percent of every other genre, and ninety percent of all mainstream novels. And yet mysteries and science fiction have received massive scholarly attention, while Westerns have been scorned.

Clearly, something odd is going on. Perhaps some of it is simply academic snobbery: Westerns are written for *hoi polloi*, but one can find serious examination of the human condition in other genres of entertainment fiction. Or perhaps the vast popularity of Westerns, both fictional and film, was all it took to drive elitist scholars away.

Even odder is the notion that an entire genre, consisting of many thousands of novels and countless short stories, is essentially identical material, expressing a few easily discerned points of view. This sort of presumption is apparent in William Kittredge's dismaying assertion that Westerns are "racist, sexist, and imperialist." This sort of blanket indictment of a massive body of literature would be reckless in any circumstance, simply because so many Western authors, over so many decades, wrote about so many facets of the American migration westward. But it is all the more reckless when unsupported by anything but a few ephemeral notions of what a Western is.

What Jeffrey Wallmann has done in this remarkable study is show how complex the genre really is, and how difficult it is to categorize the literature of the westward expansion in any simplistic way. He has examined many hundreds of novels, spanning two centuries, decade by decade, without prejudice and with the purpose of reaching truth and understanding about this neglected body of American literature. As would be expected, he has found that *none* of the clichés casually assumed by academics and critics is valid. The body of Western fiction is much too complex to reduce itself to simplistic notions such as that all Westerns are racist, or sexist, or imperialist. Many Westerns actually deplore racism, sexism, or imperialism. One of Wallmann's discoveries is that the Western has tended to support whatever were the national social concerns of the time.

What's more, as Wallmann points out, Westerns expressed no particular values at all other than those common to all literature, such as hope, or courage, or faith in the future. The stories were expressions of their times, and the authors who wrote them were simply writing according to their lights, expressing the contemporary virtues. It is arrogant for later generations to condemn such literature for not measuring up to current notions of virtue.

Even the idea that Westerns were mythological and at odds with the "real" West—an idea much favored by the historical revisionist—is itself simplistic. The revisionists, so absorbed with negative aspects of the expansion, don't have it right, either. One way in which Western fiction is closer to actuality than the revisionist historians is simply in the expression of optimism. Most Westerns are optimistic; most Westering people brimmed with optimism and good cheer and joy, even though the odds of success were slim. The revisionists, with their sour view of the expansion, have blinded themselves to that.

Jeffrey Wallmann has made a major contribution to American letters. His work largely invalidates the *a priori* material published before, and provides a sound basis for future study that will, at last, seriously examine and celebrate the diverse, complex, and remarkable body of America's most beloved fiction.

Richard S. Wheeler

The WESTERN

Barkin' at the Knot

The western seems to explain to us something about ourselves and our dreams, on both a personal and a national level.
John Milton

This book is about popular western fiction, covering not only how westerns dramatize personal relationships, but also how they incorporate cultural factors that determine belief, identity, and status, and thus rhetorically reflect the issues of their day. Such a survey occurred to me in late 1992, when I happened to read Richard Wheeler's "Commentary" in the then-current issue of *The Roundup*, the journal of the Western Writers of America. Entitled "Grace Under Pressure: A Beleaguered Literary Genre," the piece declares that "no disciplined, scholarly, unbiased research dealing broadly with the values, themes, ideals, plots and characters in westerns, decade by decade, from 1900 to the present, has ever been done" (p. 19).

Wheeler is right. Until recently, academics have tended to dismiss western fiction as lowbrow entertainment that, unlike other popular genres such as mysteries and science fiction, lacks sufficient merit for serious attention. Fortunately, contemporary scholars of American history and literature as well as western writers themselves have been more willing to consider the role of westerns in our culture. A growing number of quite insightful articles and books have appeared, usefully emphasizing important aspects of the western but to varying degrees limited in scope. I have drawn on many of these works, and mentioning a few of the more influential texts is warranted here, if only to acknowledge my debt to them.

Certainly a basic source for western criticism has been John G. Cawelti in his two books *The Six-Gun Mystique* (1971; revised 1977) and *Adventure, Mystery and Romance: Formula Stories as Art and Popular Culture* (1976). Defining westerns as both "a form of adolescent fantasy" (*Adventure*, p. 211) and "structures of narrative conventions which carry out a variety of cultural functions in a unified way" (*Six-Gun*, p. 60), Cawelti characterizes westerns as happening when lawlessness is retreating yet still challenging the forces of law and order, which to him means the frontier period from the end of the Civil War to just past the turn of the century. This same framework was employed earlier by Henry Nash Smith in his seminal work *Virgin Land: The American West as Symbol and Myth* (1950), which in a multidisciplinary approach examines the history of westward expansion and the texts resulting from it. Whereas Smith relies heavily on the dime novel for his conclusions, and Cawelti ignores dime novels in favor of James Fenimore Cooper as the progenitor of westerns, they both fail to see that the frontier is a concept not bound by time or place, and thus overlook western fiction dating back to Revolutionary days—although Cawelti allows in his introduction to the second edition of *Six-Gun* that Richard Slotkin in *Regeneration Through Violence: The Mythology of the American Frontier, 1600–1860* (1973) "demonstrates that many of the mythical patterns important to the nineteenth and twentieth century Western originated not with Cooper . . . but in the Captivity and Indian War narratives of the seventeenth and eighteenth centuries" (p. 7). Notwithstanding, *Virgin Land, Six-Gun,* and *Adventure* remain standards for those searching for models to follow in studying westerns.

Western criticism confines itself not only to specific periods and regions, but also to specific topics. For example, I am indebted to excellent studies on particular writers, such as Robert Emmet Long's *James Fenimore Cooper* (1990), John L. Cobbs's *Owen Wister* (1984), Ann Ronald's *Zane Grey* (1975), and *The New West of Edward Abbey* (1982); on minority and women writers, such as William Loren Katz's *The Black West* (1973), Norris Yates's *Gender and Genre* (1990), and Rachel DuPlessis's *Writing Beyond the Ending: Narrative Strategies of Twentieth-Century Women Writers* (1983); and on subgenres, such as Daryl Jones's *The Dime Novel Western* (1978), John Dinan's *The Pulp Western: A Popular History of the Western Magazine in America* (1983), J. Fred Mac-Donald's *Who Shot the Sheriff?: The Rise and Fall of the Television Western* (1987), and Philip French's *Westerns: Aspects of a Movie Genre* (1977) and Jim Hitt's *The America West from Fiction (1823–1976) into Film (1909–1986)* (1990). As well, western criticism can explore certain aspects of the genre, such as the collection of essays in *The Frontier Experience and the American Dream,* which "reconsiders the American literary tradition from colonial times to the present by focusing on the imaginative impact of the frontier experience" (p. 3), or can be included in studies about the real West, such as the chapter "The West as Utopia and Myth, 1890–1990" in Gerald D. Nash's *Creating the West* (1991), necessary because "the American West has embodied much of the American Dream, and the disentanglement of myth from reality has been difficult at best" (p. x).

Moreover, criticism may be limited to express points of view. Historian Bernard DeVoto equates westerns with the cattle trade, "the only

American business which has evoked a literature, a mythology, and graphic symbolism of its own" (p. 8). So does Douglas Branch, who in *The Cowboy and His Interpreters* (1926) suggests that Owen Wister's *The Virginian* (1902) is not a western because "there is not one scene set on the range among cattle" (p. 107). In *The Return of the Vanishing American* (1986), Leslie Fielder argues that our culture is mired in racial and ethnic conflict, and thus westerns are "not quite Westerns . . . when no Indian . . . appears in them" (p. 27). On the other hand, many if not most recent assessments emphasize the mythic quality inherent in western fiction, particularly since the close of the frontier circa 1890. Western historian Robert Athearn's posthumous *The Mythic West* (1986) presents a thoughtful discussion of "the day-to-day scene and the make-believe or fantasized world that has, for a great many people, actual substance. And there is no real conflict between the two" (p. 332). Other critics, notably Richard Etulain in "The Historical Development of the Western," take a more dismal view of myth; it arises in westerns, Etulain claims, from the "desire to avoid a depressing present and the increasing tendency to escape into the past [that] is much with us today" (p. 719). Wilson Clough, in *The Necessary Earth: Nature and Solitude in American Literature* (1968), feels that myth should be rejected: "A sentimental nostalgia for this elemental past is of little use to those seeking esthetic maturity" (p. 158). But then, still other critics scoff at westerns altogether. *The Columbia History of the American Novel* (1991) dismisses westerns as merely the "formulaic version" of the novel of the West (p. 437); and Wallace Stegner disdains westerns for being "petrified," made of "interchangeable parts" in "fiction factories" (p. 190).

I am equally indebted to scholars whose focus is on the ideological agenda of New Western Historianism—sometimes called "revisionist historianism" or "revisionism." A development of roughly the last two or three decades, revisionism is by and large an overdue and well-intentioned focus on the greed, genocide, and environmental destruction that attended our pioneering movement, in an effort to counter a culturally ingrained vision of virile heroes winning the West for Truth, Justice, and the American Way. Beyond that generalization, revisionism has become so multidisciplinary and diverse that, as best-selling author John Jakes observes, "I don't know what exactly what's meant by 'revisionism' in writing about the West, but if it means western fiction is becoming more mature, honest, factual, faithful to the record—the frontier experience as it really was—then I suppose I've been a 'revisionist' ever since I started writing historical novels" (p. 16). Most contemporary western writers, I contend, would concur with Jakes and point to their work as proof. An example of responsible revisionist criticism is William Deverell's article "Fighting Words: The Significance of the American West in the History of the United States" in *The Western Historical Quarterly* (Summer 1994). Deverell suggests that the West, especially the Old West, is a factor in determining our nation's present and future, and thus we cannot allow mythic stereotypes to represent factual history. Instead, he proposes that historians and fiction writers alike have a duty to remove the blinders and uncover the truths, even while acknowledging the legendary status of the West in the American psyche.

There is merit in his thesis, and Deverell's article is illustrative of the thought-provoking, balanced approach taken by the more tempered and rigorous revisionists.

At times, however, the revisionist viewpoint has led to some rather radical perceptions. For instance, in her *Legacy of Conquest* (1986), Patricia Nelson Limerick is right to point out that the pioneer West was scarcely a golden age of heroes, and that western history and fiction should be more inclusive of women and minorities. Limerick is wrong, however, to imply that avaricious European men have conspired to squelch the fact that pioneering was fraught with injustice and failure, and to silence any differing viewpoints by women and non-white racial and cultural groups. Histories and literature by women and minorities are readily available, and many are reprints of books dating back generations. Similarly, Richard Slotkin in his exhaustive trilogy *Regeneration Through Violence: The Mythology of the American Frontier 1600-1860* (1973), *The Fatal Environment: The Myth of the Frontier in the Age of Industrialization, 1800-1890* (1985), and *Gunfighter Nation: The Myth of the Frontier in 20th-Century America* (1992) perceives westerns as variations of primal myths—myths that if Indian are "genuine," and if European are "spurious"—which create a frontier whereon the only governing principles are savage war and bonanza politics, with the destruction of people and natural resources lending to the destroyer a moral and spiritual "regeneration." William Kittredge—who once wrote westerns under the name Owen Roundtree—claims in works such as *Hole in the Sky* (1992) that western heroes are akin to modern-day psychotics, driven by violent acts and inured to their moral horrors in stories that are "racist, sexist and imperialist." And Jane Tompkins not only agrees in *West of Everything: The Inner Life of Westerns* (1992) but argues that the western "doesn't have anything to do with the West as such. It is about men's fear of losing their mastery and hence their identity, both of which the Western tirelessly reinvents" (p. 45).

I do not wish to dwell at length on revisionist and other critics; they are included in the text where appropriate, but this book is not intended to be an analysis of western criticism. Still, the more extreme variety of revisionism has become rather the academic rage and currently is enjoying a certain Politically Correct panache, and since my views about westerns often run counter to extreme revisionism, an expanded word here strikes me as fitting. From my perspective, on the whole, two problems mar the arguments of the more extreme revisionists. First, they ignore or reject the tenet that westerns, particularly westerns written years ago, are neither Politically Correct nor Incorrect, but simply the products and reflections of other times, other issues, other values. Traditionally, westerns revolve around such conflicts as good folk fighting bad folk, like lawmen chasing outlaws; or little folk overcoming big folk, like farm widows resisting cattle barons; or enterprising folk battling the environment, like traildriving a herd or founding a stagecoach line. Revisionist concerns about race or gender are only incidental. There are exceptions, of course, and current political and social concerns are providing increasing numbers of plot conflicts and motivations nowadays—as well they should. Yet too often in their criticism, revisionists like Tompkins impose their own contemporary mores on the Old West rather than engage with the culture in which westerns are set. Second, the source material they cite as evidence is highly selective, which either exposes their ignorance of westerns in general or betrays a conscious picking of only those works that buttress their preconceived notions. As reviewer Robert Murray Davis commented about *West of Everything*, "one could wish it less sloppy in emotion and scholarship and more conscious of the distinction between art—especially popular art—and real human behavior" (p. 241). Perhaps a more notable illustration of selectivity is the trilogy by Slotkin. Unlike other revisionists who cite meagerly few westerns relative to their blanket allegations, Slotkin's books are meticulously researched with extensive source material supporting his thesis—but only his thesis, regardless of other works, themes, or historical trends. Thus, while Slotkin is right that the frontier, as the founding myth of the American nation, has served the cause of racism and imperialism, he seems blind to the fact that the frontier has been enlisted for other purposes and persuasions, including the cause of liberty and equality. The only alternative Slotkin sees is a "populist" nostalgia for an agrarian past that cannot be recaptured; consequently, he ignores innumerable westerns like *Shane*, whose progressive populism looks forward rather than backward, and whose heroes win by taking effective action rather than lamenting a lost cause. Similarly, Slotkin in *Regeneration* thoroughly examines how early colonialists held opposing visions of the New World—as a diabolical wilderness whose natives need subjugation if not annihilation, versus a Garden of Eden whose natives are closer to nature and thus to God—but after discussing the advent of the "Vanishing [Native] American" in literature, he simply dispenses with the Garden of Eden motif as though it had no further influence on western fiction. Not only is this incorrect, but Slotkin's one-sidedness detracts from his compelling argument, and implies that he is unaware of the crucial role played by dualities in American life and literature. A result of such bias is that extreme revisionists simply replace one questionable legend with another that is equally dubious. For instance, most stories about Wyatt Earp are based on Stuart N. Lake's eulogizing biography *Wyatt Earp: Frontier Marshal* (1931), but many other versions like Frank Waters's *The Earp Brothers of Tombstone* (1960) portray Earp as a pathological scoundrel; and although the revisionist take on Earp may seem more credible to our contemporary sensibilities, there is no reliable way to judge its accuracy because the events of the Old West were not recorded very scrupulously, which leaves the "truth" about Wyatt Earp with roughly the same status as the "truth" about King Arthur. Paul Hutton makes the same point about General Custer: "As the American view of militarism and Indians changed, so . . . from a symbol of courage and sacrifice in the winning of the West, Custer's image was gradually altered into a symbol of arrogance and brutality displayed in the white exploitation of the West. The only constant factor in this reversed legend is a remarkable disregard for historical fact" (p. 45). It is one thing to criticize the frontier myth and censure westerns that have gratuitous violence or sex, or foster exploitation of women, minorities, or the land; it is quite another to condemn on the basis of ideology and preferred examples an entire genre as corrupt, lacking any redeeming value.

Of course, the choosing of sufficient, relevant, and representative examples of westerns is not a problem confined to extreme revisionists. The genre is so vast and varied that even listings by categories such as plot, period, or main characters necessitates severe selectivity. Hence, a major work like James K. Folsom's *The American Western Novel* (1966), which focuses on plots and themes with little appraisal of their merit or meaning, discusses only the most basic and prevalent divisions in a quite generalized manner. Enforced sampling can be to the good, though, for many if not most westerns are poorly written pulp yarns and quickie formula movies. To paraphrase Theodore Sturgeon's famous dictum about science fiction, "Ninety percent of westerns is crap. Ninety percent of everything is crap." Much of such crap can safely be left buried and forgotten, of no useful purpose save as archeological digs for zealous literary historians. The bottom line, then, is that it is virtually impossible to fulfill Dick Wheeler's wish for a comprehensive study of the values, themes, ideals, plots, and characters of westerns up to the present. That is why I call this chapter "Barkin' At the Knot," which is an old cowboy expression for attempting the impossible.

Because I, too, must restrict the scope of my inquiry, I think it appropriate to begin by discussing the western's fundamentals and suggesting a working definition. Consequently, Chapter 2 is called "Brandin' and Cullin'," another cowboy term that refers to marking cattle that belong to a herd and removing those that belong elsewhere. For the most part, westerns derive from the Myth of the New World, which drew the first European explorers to the western hemisphere, fusing the earlier utopian dreams into the expectation of a new land where everything could begin anew, and thus where new communities could form, rather than where old communities would simply be reestablished. I do not mean myth in the sense of quaintly parochial stories like fables and fairy tales, but rather in the more profound sense as the spiritual and intellectual explanations of a culture's values—of how the people of a culture view themselves and how their culture fits into the world. This form of mythology is integral to every culture, including America, and is expressed through storytelling in literature and now in such media as film and television. So in this context, "the frontier mythology created and ironically examined in our imaginative literature provides the symbolic language with which we continue to debate Crèvecoeur's question, 'What is an American?'" (Mogen, Busby, and Bryant, p. 21). For a long time, the frontier experience was a physical reality as pioneers spread westward, and as mentioned above, it was envisioned either puritanically as a wicked land of savages bent on destruction, or as a Garden of Eden whose natives had a special affinity with nature and an innate sense of honesty, mercy, and fidelity. Both visions required that the New World be tamed by courageous persons paradoxically seeking independence while simultaneously establishing communities, and the frontier formed a boundary line that suggests transitional possibilities, people forced to move forward or backward but not to stay put. So one defining element of westerns is that they are about character, about the makeup of people, the testing of their mettle, the realization of who fundamentally they are and what ultimately they stand for. Because the frontier serves as the symbolic "cutting edge" of American civilization and progress, there is no specific region or time period, and consequently there are westerns set on the Canadian frontier, the Alaskan frontier, the Spanish and Mexican frontiers, even the pseudo-North American frontier of the Australian frontier, such as *Quigley Down Under* (1990). And because the frontier is the place in which opposites and cultures meet and conflict, westerns are adventures. Revisionists such as Tompkins and Slotkin indict westerns as violent, but actually our national willingness, even desire, to believe that important events are the results of the acts of courageous individuals has produced histories and stories that accentuate memorable names, rousing clashes, and more than a little braggadocio. Naturally, writers and filmmakers have dramatized fact and fiction the way the public wants it—full of action. Not necessarily violence, but exciting, moving action. So for the purposes of this study, westerns are considered to be adventure stories, set on a frontier, about personal character striving to overcome perilous circumstances.

Chapter 2 stands apart as a discussion of the composition of westerns and the foundation for their historical development. That development, in terms of how westerns have affected and been affected by American culture, is the subject of the next four chapters. Although this requires a clearly outlined chronology, it cannot be one that confines the literary and social forces into a precise cause-and-effect structure which their very existence denies. History is messy, after all. Thus the chronological limits and the kind of evaluation that I present are intended to make for explanations of an open, flexible sort. Chapter 3 is called "Trailblazin'," the forging of a new path through wilderness country. It sketches the antecedents and origins of the western, such as Indian War narratives and colonial travelogues, and traces the development of new forms of literary fiction brought on by the Enlightenment, the Great Awakening, and the Revolution. The first example of an adventure set on a frontier about personal character striving to overcome perilous circumstances was *Life and Adventures of Col. Daniel Boone,* an appendix to *The Discovery, Settlement, and Present State of Kentucke,* written in 1784 by land promoter John Filsen. As dramatized, Boone is a scout and woodsman who makes the Indian's way of life his own without becoming barbarous; as such, Boone is the ancestor of James Fenimore Cooper's Deerslayer figure and innumerable other western heroes—an idealized half-savage, half-civilized protector of the weak and avenger of injustice. Like the better westerns to follow, *Boone* comments not only on personal character but on the character of the nation. At the time, fledgling America was gripped by a fervor to cultivate the wilderness, and *Boone* is a paean to Manifest Destiny. This national passion to cultivate had produced problems by James Fenimore Cooper's era; in keeping with the then-popular democratizing spirit of Jacksonian America, Cooper tempered his faith in advancing progress and cautioned against East spoiling a pastoral West.

Cooper's literary romanticism evolved into works by Emerson, Melville, and Poe. The focus of Chapter 3, though, is on how Cooper's bitter view of nature in conflict with civilization went on to be expressed in simplistic, stereotypical "dime novels." As the wilderness shrank and American society experienced a tremendous industrial and urban growth, the dime novelists expanded the woodsman-scout hero to include gunfighters, farmers, railroaders, stagecoach drivers, gamblers, and most important, cowboys. This profusion of characters and settings by writers seeking popular success is why Chapter 4 is called "Brush Bustin'," because riders who chouse cattle through brush country have to dodge every which way to avoid getting thorn-torn and trapped.

Chapter 5 covers the first three decades of this century, a time when, generally speaking, western stories were simplistic entertainments emphasizing heroic private virtues such as courage, honor, and integrity, the values that fostered the independent man or woman. Production was high and hasty, an avalanche of westerns flowing from prolific yarnsters like Charles Seltzer and W. C. Tuttle and low-budget movie studios like Selig and First National—which is why the chapter is named "Highballin' Camp," meaning a busy camp in which everyone works at top speed. However, the bulk of the chapter is devoted to Owen Wister and Zane Grey, the two most prominent and critically acclaimed practitioners of the western at the time and perhaps even today. Their protagonists are typical of dime westerns—tough, resourceful individualists who uphold decency and ethical codes in the face of nonexistent, ineffective, or corrupt legal institutions—and in this they copy Filsen's archetypal hero, who had resolved the duality of man as civilized or savage. But by 1900 the duality of the frontier as a wilderness or a garden had widened and polarized. On the wilderness side, Wister's Virginian is a lineal descendent of Filsen's Daniel Boone, living on a relatively socialized frontier and fighting its savage elements for the sake of settlement and civilization. On the garden side, Grey's heroes are akin to Cooper's Natty Bumppo, operating on a largely preindustrial frontier where civilization is an encroachment; indeed, the more developed Eastern society becomes, the more it corrupts the healthy vistas of the open West. These two differing views of the West, then, are modifications of the original opposing visions of the New World as a Hell on Earth or a Garden of Eden, only altered over time and by Wister and Grey to reflect their contemporary cultural and market circumstances.

Chapter 6 traces the fate of western fiction from its halcyon popularity during the Depression to the late 1960s and its current deep decline, which is why the chapter is called "Runaway Buckin' to Bitin' the Dust." A runaway bucker is a horse that as soon as mounted breaks into a gallop for fifty yards and then leaps four or five feet high and lands stiff-legged. The fast-forward motion ceases so abruptly that many a rider has been jack-knifed off, "biting the dust" spread-eagled and knocked out of breath. As well as slang for spilling from a horse, "biting the dust" can also mean getting killed. Whether the western is dead or merely winded is discussed in the last chapter. Through the formulas popularized by dime novelists, Wister, and Grey, the frontier myth effected by Filsen proved highly popular during the Depression and continues to this day to provide the underlying metaphors and imagery for traditional western fiction. As well, by World War II western writers were improving the quality of their dialogue, their literate style, the drawing of characters and the accuracy of their setting. A better balance between white males and minorities and women began to be portrayed, and characters became inward-looking, frequently having to face personal crises before confronting the villain, and community as a place gave way to community as a spirit. Paralleling our changing morals, westerns grew in scope and intensity through the 1960s as writers increasingly examined sexual struggles and psychological weaknesses of their characters. Throughout the 1960s, moreover, the romance of older stories gave way to existentialism, as exemplified by the tragic perspective of E. L. Doctorow's *Welcome to Hard Times* (1960; film, 1967). And, as the disillusionment of the Vietnam War and Watergate gathered momentum on through the 1980s, westerns reflected the prevailing attitudes of Americans, depicting scenes of blight, bigotry, addiction, sexism, imperialism, wanton violence, and explicit sexuality. Half-breeds were popular, for they were cut off from society, and in a unique position to deliver scathing criticism; and replacing individual villains as the enemy was corrupt society with its weak laws, racism, and prejudice. Into the early 1990s, these brutally sardonic formulas degenerated even further into pastiches, self-parodies, and other desperate gimmicks of writers who have found themselves proficient at telling an obsolete story. In this regard, the chapter title could just as well have been "Merry-go-roundin'," which is the term cowboys use to describe cattle milling in water, heading nowhere but becoming hopelessly massed and often drowning.

Chapter 7 is less a conclusion than a speculation on the future of the western. And there is a future—the western may have fallen off badly, but it persists in getting up and back in the saddle, which is why the chapter is called "Ridin' It Out," a cowboy expression for staying with a bucking horse until it is broken. The cynical, selfish trend has about spent itself, I believe. The nation is no longer a melting pot, if it ever was one, and in response to current issues of survival in a fragmenting society, there is a reviving public effort to build and sustain secure communities through the fostering of understanding and tolerance of cultural and ethnic diversity. Westerns, in reflecting these issues, are increasingly relating stories through a multiplicity of viewpoints, dramatizing personal histories through the eyes of protagonists, emphasizing narrative truth over historical accuracy. Whatever the future holds, westerns will comment on and make meaning of American culture, as always, as adventures set on a frontier about personal character striving to overcome perilous circumstances. As Jeni Calder states, a bit cynically, the western "enriches a brief past for the benefit of a possibly barren present. . . . As long as it is acknowledged that the Western cannot imitate history and should not, the myth will survive" (pp. 215, 218).

Finally, having covered content, I should add a word about terminology and style. Many critics and writers—including Richard S. Wheeler in his foreword to this book—capitalize western as Western. I do not, believing that as a genre it should be written in the lower case just as other genres, such as romance, science fiction, and mystery, are. Because the relationship of westerns to myth and culture is so complex, I have also tried to write as simply and engagingly as the subjects allow—to strike a balance between being direct to avoid the dense "academese" beloved by scholars, and by being insightful to avoid the breezy "journalese" that lacks depth or anything else that might tax a reader. If successful, my survey of western fiction will not be taken as a dogmatic examination, but rather as an overview of relevant connections that is academically sound yet readily understood by the general public, generating, I hope, critical discussion and further inquiry.

Brandin' and Cullin'

Our national mythology based on frontier experience is the vehicle with which we examine the ironies and contradictory values expressed in that curious phrase, "The American Dream"—which, after all, has been the implicit subject of many of our best writers since our diverse ancestors arrived on their many different errands into the wilderness.
David Mogen

Westerns are beef cows. Since their inception, they have been market-driven, produced for mass consumption, and bred and crossbred to feed shifting public tastes—the literary equivalent of Angus, Brahma, Herefords, hothouse stock, longhorn, magpies, Mexican buckskin, open-faced, shorthorn, Sonora reds, spraddle horns, whitefaces, yellow-bellies, and zorillas. Naturally, there have been some odd mavericks that prove to be the exception, and questionable borderline strays that can be fudged as belonging or not belonging depending on the opinion of the fudger, and a few whose claims for inclusion are patently fraudulent:

> Paloo groaned. "If there's a worse chore than snakin' ladino stock from brush thickets, I dunno what it is!"
>
> "You ought to try busting sea cows down in the Gulf Coast country like I once did," Ki claimed deadpan. "Those sea-lion cows grow fins on their hocks, and when you daub a loop on 'em, they raise a foot and saw the rope in half with a fin."
>
> "Son," Paloo replied severely, "lyin' to a gent my age ain't decent. Them sea-lions don't wear fins on their hoofs, but on the end o' their tails. They cut the twine by wrappin' their tail around it and giving it a quick jerk. You stick to truths hereafter and folks'll think better of yuh . . . " (Wesley Ellis, *Lone Star and the Phantom Gunmen*, pp. 105–106)

Understandably, determining what constitutes essential "western-ness" as distinct from the natures of other genres is a hard, sometimes arbitrary, and occasionally hazardous task. It is necessary nonetheless. Akin to the roundup Paloo and Ki are on, the purpose of this chapter is to begin stamping a brand on what is, and culling out what is not, a western. For starters, though, it is worth pointing out that one element westerns have in common with other genres is that they are mythic. Myth in this context does not mean fictitious accounts about imaginary people or things, like fables and fairy tales, but rather in the more profound sense as the spiritual and intellectual images of a culture's values—of how the citizens of a culture view themselves and view how they as a culture fit into the world (see Campbell, Gerstner and Cords, Dundes, Frazer, Frye, Hatab, Kirk, Knight, Leeming, and Lévi-Strauss). As a result, Henry Nash Smith notes,

The experience of sharing these images expresses value-judgments that everyone is expected to endorse. A symbol of this kind does much more than convey a simple declarative statement concerning the past . . . It suggests to the members of the social group a special conception of themselves, and tends to impose on them very definite notions of what is good and what is desirable in social policy. (pp. 30, 31)

Integral to every culture, including American culture, this form of mythology is expressed through storytelling in literature and now in media like film and television. Indeed, without mythology there could be no literature. Myths "are taken with particular seriousness by [a] society," Northrop Frye rightly points out, "because they express something deep in that society's beliefs or vision of its situation and destiny. Myths, unlike other types of stories, stick together to form a mythology. . . . Literature as we know it, as a body of writing, always develops out of a mythical framework of this kind" (p. 110). The cultural mythology underlying westerns is the American Dream, which for the most part derives from the Myth of the New World. The Myth of the New World is the inspiration that drew the first European explorers to the Western hemisphere, fusing all the earlier utopian dreams such as Arcadia and New Atlantis into the expectation of a new land where everything could begin afresh, and thus where new communities could form, rather than where old communities would simply be reestablished. Not surprisingly, the American Dream that evolved is above all the dream of seeking happiness in self-realization. To do so requires that collectively the general welfare be promoted, and that individually one's talents can be pursued with vigor and imagination, thereby realizing everyone's inborn physical and spiritual endowments. The American Dream is no less a mythic perspective, remaining internalized in our national psyche; the influence of the American Dream, as Frederick Carpenter states, "has usually been indirect and unconscious . . . but the vague idea has *influenced* the plotting of our fiction and the imagining of our poetry. Almost by inadvertence our literature has accomplished a symbolic and experimental projection of it" (p. 3).

Being expressions of this myth, westerns are fundamentally allegories of the American Dream. "[W]e define ourselves most fundamentally by reference to our frontier heritage, which symbolically represents the ambiguous implications of our belief in limitless possibilities," writes David Mogen (Mogen, Busby, and Bryant, p. 26). As such, westerns contain many of the characteristics associated with myths. Perhaps the most important trait has to do with the fact that myths are almost always stories that everyone already knows. For example, the myth of St. George and the dragon is constantly retold, even though in the end the knight will always rescue the damsel. It is immaterial how trite or silly the myth might be, or that in reality the damsel may well own a dragon farm; the very repeating of the myth serves to reaffirm some underlying cultural value or collective aspiration. That is the function of myth. Similarly, that is the function of westerns.

Of course, each western is superficially unique, with its own mix of characters and events. The knight errant St. George becomes the gunfighter Shane, the damsel becomes a nester family, and the dragon becomes an outlaw spewing bullets or a banker spewing foreclosures instead of flame and smoke. In literature, Frye points out, "everything is new, and yet recognizably the same kind of thing as the old, just as a new baby is a genuinely new individual, although it's also an example of something very common, which is human beings, and also it's lineally descended from the first human beings there ever were" (pp. 45–46). For instance, westerns about competition between brothers, such as *Gunsmoke in Tucson* (1958), which pits outlaw brother against lawman brother, or conflicts between fathers and sons, such as *Gunman's Walk* (1958), in which the father kills his son, are simply revampings of relationships that can be traced back to traditional mythological sources. Certainly the major themes with which Shakespeare dealt so artistically and with commercial success are still the major western themes today: hatred, love, greed, mercy, envy, loyalty, and so on. Othello is convinced by his unscrupulous courtier Iago that his wife Desdemona has been unfaithful, with fatal results for Othello. So in Delmer Daves's *Jubal* (1956), rancher Shep Hogan (Ernest Borgnine) is convinced by his spurned foreman Pinky (Rod Steiger) that his wife May (Valerie French) has been unfaithful with ranch hand Jubal Troop (Glenn Ford), with fatal results for Hogan. Both stories revolve around the thwarted passions and insane jealousy of those supremely loved, exemplifying how human nature remains unchanged—or at least in evolutionary terms changes so slowly as to be virtually ingrained—and only the characters of the people involved and the societal strictures placed on them alter according to time and place. Westerns, then, continue to focus on the more permanent values and aspirations of the essential human dilemmas by reflecting the more transitory assumptions and prejudices of human cultural identity. Consequently, Earl Pomeroy remarks, "every generation seems to define the West anew" (p. 30). Moreover, westerns not only reflect their contemporaneous culture, but they can also affect the culture. The fictive society of a western cannot help but be compared and contrasted with the existing one, even if the comparison may be very overt or barely implied, or left to the sharpness of the reader's insight. In either case, by concentrating on specific evils or graces in the social system, the western in effect holds up a mirror which intensifies and purifies and universalizes the readers' own lives, which lets them see themselves and respond. More than simple diversion, J. Fred MacDonald observes, "the Western as a cultural construct also operates as an educative conduit through which important social and personal lessons are disseminated. In this way the Western is parabolical. Set primarily in the past where history may be manipulated to serve contemporary purposes, the genre is filled with symbols and symbolic actions relating directly to the popular mentality of the society accepting" (p. 78).

Because westerns refer to and attempt to deal with their period of history, their storylines become old and obsolete. Back in the thirties, there was a kind of western plot that went like so: a widower and his daughter, battling a ruthless despot after their business property, are rescued through the intervention of a vagabond expert in their particular trade, who then settles down, marrying the daughter and assuming control of the business. The plot was told involving ranches, mines, stage depots, timber, steamboats, oil drilling rigs, etc., and it remained valid throughout the Depression, connecting with the reality of its era. It also made a brief reappearance in 1946–1948, when all the war veterans left the services with their mustering-out pay. But the time came when the story was used up, past its time, and pretty much ceased to be told. "Fiction in any form," Raymond Chandler states, "has always intended to be realistic. Old-fashioned novels which now seem stilted and artificial to the point of burlesque did not appear that way to the people who first read them" (p. 177). Aside from certain postmodern and other conscious literary attempts to discombobulate the reader, on the whole

Chandler is correct: stories that seem natural at one time become fanciful, even laughable, at another; and writers, especially of this century, are challenged to develop an authentic approach to their material and to the society in which they reside. To the extent westerns are mythic, however, their verisimilitude resides less in factual veracity than in their interpretive and rhetorical power, their ability to capture and structure the imagination of their audience. Observes James K. Folsom,

> The apparent realism of some Western fiction has caused unwary critics to assume that the genre is, or ought to be, a realistic one, and to attribute the weakness of inferior Western fiction to the fact that the writer does not know enough about the facts of Western life; actually, the success of any particular Western is much better assessed on the basis of how well the conventions which surround the story's protagonist serve to deepen and intensify the meaning of the parable. (p. 102)

The West of the western, then, is a blend of the mythic and the authentic; as C. L. Sonnichsen writes, "the two Wests can and do exist side by side in our minds, influencing each other and overlapping each other, without causing us any discomfort" (p. 12). Of course, the authenticity of westerns is predicated upon the historical facts of America's settlement, independence, and expansion. After colonists had settled along the Eastern seaboard, their only direction for movement was West, and movement was necessary for both economic and social reasons. They were on the move for the dream of more furs beyond the next river basin, for the promise of better soil over the next rise of hills, for the lure of gold or silver buried in the next mountain range, or for the sheer adventure they were sure to meet beyond the limits of civilization. But first and last they were on the move, meaning that the frontier of fact was less a geographical region than a process, relating to the growth that was occurring around a particular border area. This is opposed to the European meaning of frontier, which "is something fixed. It is the sharp edge of a sovereign State," whereas in America it is "the advancing fringe of a dynamic society" (Hancock, pp. 2–3). Similarly, Frederick Jackson Turner called the European frontier "a fortified boundary line running through dense populations" (p. 41) in contrast to how "in American thought and speech the term 'frontier' has come to mean the edge of settlement" (p. 3).

In reflecting the restless nature of American culture, westerns dwell on movement around a frontier, whether it be by settlers, troopers, wagon trains, or roaming cowboys. The frontier of fiction, like the frontier of fact, cannot be defined in European terms of static geographical limits, as when Philip French labels westerns as occurring "west of the Mississippi, south of the 49th parallel and north of the Rio Grande" (p. 24), or Norris Yates locates them in "the area west of the Missouri, south of the tundra, and north of the Sierra Madre" (p. 6). After all, the original frontier was not even the Eastern seaboard colonies, but the wilderness of the explorer, the scout, and the trapper. Accordingly, such trapper adventures as Harvey Fergusson's *Wolf Song* (1927), A. B. Guthrie, Jr.'s *The Big Sky* (1947), Vardis Fisher's *Mountain Man* (1965), and William Heuman's "The Fur Brigade" ("A blizzard-hearted wench set off the spark. A reckless trapper fanned it to flame-pitch" [p. 72]) should be classified as westerns. Later, when permanent settlements were established, colonialists emigrated for virgin land still well east of the Appalachians. During this period, Maine, Georgia, and Vermont were every bit as much frontiers as Colorado or Arizona would become. And John Ford's *Drums Along the Mohawk* (1939), King Vidor's *Northwest Passage* (1937), and John Murray Reynolds's "Tomahawk Valley" ("A brutal wilderness was Tyron County of New York in the year 1781" [p. 21]) are every bit as much westerns as Ed Earl Repp's *West of Cheyenne* (1938) or Elmore Leonard's *3:10 to Yuma* (1957). The frontier of James Fenimore Cooper's Leatherstocking Tales is the woodlands of upstate New York. There have been westerns set on the Canadian frontier, the Alaskan frontier, the Spanish California and Mexican frontiers, even the lookalike Australian frontier—certainly *North to Alaska* (1960), *King of the Royal Mounted* (1940), *The Mark of Zorro* (1924), *Vera Cruz* (1954), and *Quigley Down Under* (1990) count as westerns.

In effect, fictional frontiers serve less as specific locations than they do as transitory borders demarcating a relationship between settled society and primitive territory. Of course, westerns cite places as well as dates for verisimilitude, as in this passage from Ernest Haycox's *Return of a Fighter* (1929):

He left the train the following morning at the Dalles and took a feeder south to Bend. Late in the afternoon he walked through the streets that once had been familiar and now were changed. Bend had grown some—its streets ran farther into the sagebrush, its stores made a greater showing. It had lost some of its frontier atmosphere; there weren't so many horses hitched to the racks. (p. 7)

But the description of Bend, Oregon, is not so unique that it couldn't also fit Fallon, Nevada, or Caldwell, Idaho, or almost any other expanding community in sagebrush country. The western frontier, representing the symbolic "cutting edge" of American civilization, is more of a mythic setting that provides transitional possibilities—as Edwin Fussell notes, "an imaginary line between civilization and nature, or the uncreated future" (p. 273)—where individuals are forced to move forward or backward but cannot remain static. Thus, the stories that develop are about the testing of mettle, the realization of who individuals fundamentally are and what ultimately they stand for. Westerns, then, are about personal character —not the piety of values, but the mix of temperament, chemistry, behavior, and environment that molds one's character. *Dances With Wolves* (1990), for example, examines the character of Lieutenant John J. Dunbar, his loyalty to a nation versus his revulsion at the Civil War, and his need for psychic rejuvenation as a white versus his desire for inclusion into the Sioux culture, the film also exploring the character of America, the barbarous madness of its civilization versus the benign nature of its subjugated native population. In Frank Waters's *The Man Who Killed the Deer* (1942), the Pueblo Indian tribe is at a frontier, a border that somehow must be confronted, and the protagonist is at a similar crossroads concerning his personal character. "A man can't run all of the time," Randolph Scott declares in *Man in the Saddle* (1951), "he has to fight sooner or later."

The testing of character requires the challenge of adventures, the transcending of perilous circumstances. Westerns, after all, are the legacy of an intrepid immigrant stock who swiftly learned that not all Indians were docile, that the land was often as much rock as soil, that winters were harsher than those in England, and that illness and feuding were ever-present. Only the hardy and strong were able to survive. Their constant moving and struggling, and the mixing of a nation in the making, provide the opportunities for worthy adversaries, physically or emotionally mortal jeopardy, and the narrative requirements of conflict and growth necessary for adventure stories. However, such action does not mean that westerns are inherently violent, contrary to the accusations by media critics such as then Federal Communications Commission chairman Newton Minow, who in 1961 assailed television's "procession of violence, sadism, murder, western badmen, western good men" (p. 207), and revisionist historians such as Jane Tompkins, who claims that "a movement toward death . . . marks the western and sets it off from other genres" (p. 358). For character to be tested requires a balance between vulnerability and endurance, and endurance requires toughness —a toughness, according to Rupert Wilkinson in *American Tough* (1984), ambivalent in that it is admirable when asserted by heroes and despicable when displayed by villains. Traditionally, the action taken by heroes is justified, a forced response to the violence begun by the villains, and characters who cannot or will not act in their own defense are implicitly weak. In *Shane* (1949; film, 1953), the hapless sodbusters are protected from the big rancher's hired killer by Shane, who believes "a gun is just a tool . . . as good—or as bad—as the man who carries it" (pp. 139–140). Hence, traditional western action is somewhat contradictory, "detrimental to society in general" while "it tests a man's true worth, both morally and competitively" (Hamilton, p. 10). Because the aim is testing through the means of action, traditional westerns avoid lingering on the effects of fistfights, horse-draggings, gunshot wounds, and the like— unless the plot calls for developments such as a funeral or an injured man to be nursed—to the extent that no matter how many brawls Roy Rogers is in, his hat never gets dislodged. Over the past three decades, however, westerns have become considerably more graphic in showing the physical and psychological consequences of violence. Throughout Clint Eastwood's *The Unforgiven* (1992), for example, the violence is queasily realistic, spliced with reaction shots of protagonist Will Munny, other characters, and the townsfolk registering disgust at the acts of murder and mayhem. In one scene, the wannabe gunman Kid kills his first victim and instead of elation experiences extreme remorse: "It don't seem real. He ain't never going to breathe ever again," the Kid grieves, to which Munny replies, "Hell of a thing, killing a man. You take away all he's got and all he's ever gonna have." As Scott Emmert observes, "It may not be an overstatement to suggest that Westerns which find ways to repudiate the connection between violence and progress, a connection which permeates American history, may serve positive societal as well as thematic ends" (p. 45). Granted, during the same thirty years there have been a number of horrifically barbarous westerns, such as *Gentleman Killer* (1969) and *Requiem for a Bounty Hunter* (1970; rereleased in 1978 with explicit sex scenes as *Porn Erotic Western*), in which the violence is for violence's sake, lacking justification, ending not in the resolution of a conflict but when all the characters have expired. As we will see in Chapter 5, though, stories that dispense with the conventions and limitations of the western and depend on savagery for their *raison d'être* cannot rightly be called westerns, even if they have a frontier setting as their backdrop, lacking as they do any shred of the moral core necessary for development of character. Violence has no genre. When in the late 1960s the persistent criticism of violence led to the replacement on television of action-oriented westerns with domestic-style westerns like *Bonanza* and *The Big Valley*, violence persisted in police, detective, and other dramas. "As late as November 1984 one interest group, the National Coalition on TV Violence, could claim that video violence had risen 75 percent since 1980 and was now at record levels" (MacDonald, p. 100). Moreover, there has been and continues to be more graphic and gratuitous violence in mysteries, science fiction, even women's romances:

> Simone remained serene in her bath, refolding her hands in her lap with indifference. The metal sides grew hot and steam began wafting from the perfumed water. Regardless, her bath stayed cold. Cold as the mind which regarded it, solid and blank as a cake of ice. She sat in her cold bath as the water started boiling, the metal steadily reddening. The tub became a cauldron hissing and sputtering over the blazing fire of the wood floor. (Douglass, pp. 203–204)

Increased violence is a sign of the times featured in all genres, and cannot be taken as an attribute of westerns alone. Some revisionists, taking a different tack, allege that westerns are violent because frontier America was violent. Richard Slotkin, for instance, argues that "the first colonialists saw in America an opportunity to regenerate their fortunes, their spirits, and the power of their church and nation; but the means of regeneration ultimately became the means of violence, and the myth of regeneration through violence became the structuring metaphor in the American experience" (*Regeneration*, p. 5). But the charge that the frontier was an unrelentingly violent place is not historically accurate. In a well-documented chapter of *The Wister Trace* (1987), Loren Estleman recounts how there was more violence in some of the established Eastern cities and many more lynchings in the South than in the regional West; how the dustup at the O. K. Corral accounted for Tombstone's worst year, in which only five people total were killed; how the same number were killed in Dodge City's worst year, and only four died in Deadwood, South Dakota's most violent year; and how records indicate that gunslingers consciously avoided one another, drawing more notoriety than blood—Billy the Kid shot three people, not the twenty-one of legend; Bat Masterson killed three, not twenty-something; Wild Bill Hickok's score was just three; and Buffalo Bill Cody flat lied and never shot down anyone—and that no gunmen of equal caliber ever had a facedown gunfight, and that nobody ever was killed in a shoot-out at high noon (pp. 15–20). Sonnichsen allows that violence was present in the West, but was not present all the time. "The moving-picture West is made up of selected bits of reality, but the implication that the Violent West is the true and complete West is all wrong. Most of the troubles of the pioneer Westerners were nonviolent: isolation, loneliness, boredom, back-breaking toil, mortgages, grasshoppers, blizzards, drouths, sickness, and old age and death. Only a small percentage of them died of lead poisoning" (pp. 11–12). Besides, Eastern civility quickly tamed the Wild West. "For one thing, too many men burned too many beans," narrator Gary Cooper drawled in *The Real West* television documentary of March 29, 1961. "The winters seemed longer, and the lonesome seemed thicker. So they wrote home for Mary Ann. And when she arrived—by the thousands— respectable and strong-willed . . . the West knew it was going to have to start shaving on Sunday and stop wearing its galluses looped across its butt." To their credit, the better, more acclaimed writers of westerns have refused to produce stories which bolster the cliché of callous violence. Instead, they have been "keeping alive both the fact and the fiction of the way it was out there along the wild frontier," where the pioneers "were the most extraordinary people who ever built a nation anywhere" (Henry, p. 36). As author Bill Turner has long maintained, "the western story is an adventure story and its truth is the truth of action and open country and the possibility of a man rising above himself and acting heroically. Because of its roots in American history and tradition it has an essential relationship to the American spirit and hence a potential that has not been fully realized. It surely needs writers who see this relationship and articulate it for the modern reader" (p. 64). Turner need not worry; the vast majority of writers and filmmakers have continually striven to articulate western fact and fiction the way the public wants it—full of dramatic narrative action only occasionally marked by violence.

Adventure stories about the character of individuals striving to transcend perilous circumstances are the stuff of which heroes are made. Heroes come in many varieties. There are the willing heroes, self-motivated and committed to adventure, like those played by John Wayne, who seem always to be on hand, always prodding ahead bravely and without doubts. Other heroes are more reluctant, needing to be motivated. Major Thomas Thorn in Glendon Swarthout's *They Came to Cordura* (1958) turns coward in battle, only to be assigned the duty of leading a group of Medal of Honor winners out of hundreds of miles of enemy territory. As is customary with reluctant heroes, once committed they are determined to follow through to finally learn the meaning of courage. Group-oriented heroes act in concert, such as members of a cavalry troop, an outlaw gang, or a cattle outfit. B. M. Bower, for example, wrote sixteen westerns about the Flying U ranch, which for all practical purposes operates like an extended family. More common is the loner hero, such as Clint Eastwood's Preacher in *Pale Rider* (1985) and Amos Edwards in Alan LeMay's *The Searchers* (1954). In the filmed version of *The Searchers* (1956), the last scene shows Edwards (John Wayne) unable to enter a cabin, his silhouette framed in its doorway, capturing symbolically the outsider who is permanently exiled from family life. Often the loners are catalyst heroes, who may act heroically but do not change much internally, their main function being to cause transformation in others. Catalyst heroes are especially useful in series or episodic stories, such as *The Lone Ranger*, but they also come in handy in westerns that end with heroes riding off into the sunset, waving goodbye as they disappear. Thus Natty Bumppo can avoid coming to terms with the exigencies of the heart or of society, and with irrevocable determination can retreat to the woods with his Indian friend, Chingachgook.

As well, there are antiheroes, who are not necessarily the opposite of heroes; after all, they have to be sympathetic characters to gain an audience. Generally, they either behave like conventional heroes but are cynical and emotionally wounded, like the ostracized John Russell in Elmore Leonard's *Hombre,* or they are roguish outlaws and villains who rebel against social proscriptions, much like Ringo in *Stagecoach* (1939) or Paul Newman and Robert Redford's comic crooks in *Butch Cassidy and the Sundance Kid* (1969). Americans tend to love such antiheroes because they are enviably independent, on the move, and able to thwart authority.

Whatever the type, heroes can be men or women. Although westerns predominantly have male heroes, to assert that the females have "always played an inconsequential role" (Nancy Cook, p. 222) or that westerns "either push women out of the picture completely or assign them roles in which they exist only to serve the needs of men" (Tompkins, *West of Everything,* p. 372) is to do great injustice to the extensive body of stories focusing on, sympathetic to, and headlined by women. Female heroes valiantly protect their homes and families from raiding hostiles, such as Olga and daughter Christmas in Tom Roan's "The Devil Comes Back to Forty Mile" ("A blue-eyed fighting hell-cat, Olga Songbird killed them through the cracks in the door, and a fighting girl, with china-blue eyes glittering like fire, dropped another man who was trying to flee back to the cottonwoods out front" [p. 23]). As well as keeping hearth and heart together while their men are away, they single-handedly manage against spooked horses, stampeding cattle, storms, draught, sickness, pursuit, and ambush. They initiate action out of economic necessity, like Kate Prentiss in Caroline Lockhart's *The Fighting Shepherdess* (1919); or out of self-defense, like Cat Ballou in *Cat Ballou* (1965); or out of vengance, like Belle Dawson in Vingie E. Roe's *Black Belle Rides the Uplands* (1935) and Hannie Caulder in Burt Kennedy's film *Hannie Caulder* (1972). They civilize and reform violent male characters, as Faith does with gunman Blaze Tracey in *Hell's Hinges* (1916) and the Eastern schoolmarm Clementine does with the uncultured Wyatt Earp in *My Darling Clementine* (1946). They courageously go to the rescue, like Stacey Ann Walton in Edgar L. Cooper's "Queen of

Gunsmoke Range" ("Into the wild passes of Gimlet Brakes she rode, a girl on a golden horse, bringing hope to a hard-cased rannie who knew but one faith—gunsmoke!" [p. 3]). They loyally stand by their men during battle, even those women who are less than pristine pure—such as Judith in James Fenimore Cooper's *The Deerslayer* (1841), mistress of a military officer, yet in her own right able to deal with hardship and danger. And more than a few female heroes are so far from being mere accessories or occasions for men's actions that they display more testosterone than their male counterparts, like the "She-Wolf of the Rio Grande" ("The Angel they called her, and her Owlhoot crew laughed. Quirt-swinging spitfire was more like it, they avowed, yet they followed her reckless rustler-trail across the Rio and back 'til every cattleman north of the border prayed for the day she'd eat lead" [Cushman, p. 74]).

Westerns, then, exemplify the heroic questing and internal growth that comes with *human* development and change. Indeed, the recognition that intelligence, self-reliance, multiple skills, and physical fitness and prowess are human attributes allows women to be just as heroic as men. Such would not be the case if a society defined heroism solely in terms of brute strength and force, for then the society would limit women's capacities and exclude them from heroic roles. As evinced by diaries, letters, and autobiographies, pioneer women no less than men were bold, daring, strong-willed, determined individualists, their plain and robust behavior reflecting their austere life close to the earth. "Such women were as tough as the trails they rode," reports historian Stan Steiner. "And many men might have been somewhat intimidated by the boldness and prowess of their new style of femininity, which was as uniquely and distinctively Western as the men" (p. 85). If frontier adventures are important for what they relate about knowledge and survival, then any action—guarding ranches, seeking fortunes, enforcing justice, reforming love—is potentially heroic. Heroism in westerns should thus be read and understood as a human necessity, capable of being present in both genders.

Of course, differences between the sexes have been a perennial source of plot conflict and motivation since Adam and Eve. It is unfortunate that the last two generations have experienced, first, a surfeit of juvenile-oriented westerns in which heroes kiss only their horses and sidekicks flee from "widder ladies"; and second, an increasing disrespect for women bordering on contempt that parallels the rise in violence toward women in our contemporary society. Historically, American culture and literature have valued monogamy and matrimony, and certainly on the frontier in fact and fiction women, especially eligible women, were highly prized and treated with an almost chivalric honor. Writes Walt Coburn,

> Women were sacred. Texas did not yet have too many of them, not yet enough to go around. The border out here was their paradise. Anything in skirts could find a husband overnight—unless she was so fat a man could not get her in a covered wagon or so ungodly ugly her face and figure would burst a muley bull's gall bladder! Even then she had to be protected, just for the sake of the breed if nothing more. Hell, that was just plain common sense! (p. 26)

Because of the western's propensity for much action at a fast clip, fictive romances tend to start with "love at first sight" by one or both parties and swiftly escalate through a series of misunderstandings and adventures to a climactic declaration of devotion. The quickened pace may be fantasy, but in reality romances happened between pioneer men and women who worked together, their love bound by their mutual survival and strengthened by their shared hardships. In westerns, similarly, marriage symbolizes a triumph over adversity, and whereas the singular quest in a romance heroine's life is to find Mr. Right and marry him, the quest in westerns is love between individuals, love that occurs only when both parties participate. Moreover, westerns reflect frontier courtship in the way women had the right to choose their partners, their independence providing such plot complications as obstinate parents and unsuitable suitors. Married, women expected companionship rather than domination, and despite the stigma attached to divorce, wives who were mistreated could leave with their children, for example, as "grass roots widows" seeking respectable employment elsewhere. Bad marriages, brutal husbands, harpy wives, the struggle to start fresh and elude stalking spouses, have long been material for western plots and subplots. Overall, perhaps the area of relationships and sexual tensions generates the widest scope for challenges in stories. As Margaret Fuller observes, "Male and female represent the two sides of the great radical dualism" (p. 176).

Dualism, or duality, is not confined to only male and female. It is difficult to think of a single significant idea or act that does not have its counterpart—for example, love-hate, folly-wisdom, despair-hope, bravery-cowardice—and much of American fiction including westerns mirrors the paradox of duality. Indeed, long before the formal study of human behavior revealed that we are all more or less confused and sometimes anguished by our dual natures, mythology recorded our awareness of this ironic aspect of our existential condition. Westerns, being mythic, rely largely on dualities for the tests, obstacles, and enemies that the heroes encounter. The duality most often associated with westerns is the conflict between good and evil. *Time* magazine once termed the western "The American Morality Play" in which the good guys and the bad guys are symbols, not people (March 30, 1969); and historian Alan Lovell suggests that westerns consist of "a virtuous hero in conflict with a wicked villain who menaces a virginal heroine" (p. 97). This is myth in action. In stark black and white, the forces of good confront the forces of evil in a contest of will—of free will, the innate power to choose one or the other, with wickedness ultimately vanquished. A superficial reading of westerns might indicate that they are all variations of the good versus evil theme, but it is not as simple as that. Our moods, attitudes, our very characters are based on other dualities as well.

For instance, a duality often encountered in westerns is that of West versus East. When in the early 1600s the Old World began to be wracked by recurrent, often violent, economic, political, and religious controversies, emigrants fled in desperation to leave the deteriorating conditions behind and in idealism to settle the rumored Eden ahead. Consequently, our New World culture was born of an exodus from oppression, famine, and poverty in the East to abundant land and quick riches in the West (see Baritz, Cary and Warmington, Elliott, and Patch). Initially, colonialist writings using this duality usually portrayed England and continental Europe as the villainous East, as illustrated by a poem chiseled on a rock in Monument Bay, which was quoted in 1807 as reading in part:

> The Eastern nations sink, their glory ends
> And Empire rises where the sun descends.

By the time westerns came into their own as a genre, western expansion had moved the concept of East along in its wake, broadening East to include the eastern seaboard, and within a few decades to mean a whole nebulous region called Back East. Fictionally, the eastern United States became a breeding ground for effete, corrupt, or decadent characters that only a good dose of western adventure could cure.

Another duality frequently applied in westerns is that of Justice and Injustice. Most of the time in westerns the distinction is clean-cut, with a sheriff or marshal introducing and enforcing institutional law. The entire *Gunsmoke* series is based on this premise. Here institutional law equals justice, in contrast to the personal law of gun, fist, or noose that, as in *The Ox-bow Incident* (1940), can result in injustice. What constitutes justice isn't always so clear, as in *Hang 'em High* (1968), when Clint Eastwood arrests two naive kids for rustling, which by the letter of the law requires them to be hanged. Commonly westerns reverse the pattern, and pit fallible institutional law against a higher moral law. Arthur Kimball points out that one of Noah Webster's definitions of "law" is "law of nature," which he quotes as "a rule of conduct arising out of the natural relations of human beings established by the Creator, and existing prior to any positive precept" (p. 232). Thus the plot of Ray Hogan's *Outlaw Marshal* (1958), in which young Clay Santell is falsely accused and arrested by the roughshod incompetent lawman, Marshal Decket, and the questioning of justice outside the law in Eugene Manlove Rhodes's short story "Pasó por Aquí" (1927). Westerns thrive on the duality of justice and injustice—on the issue of fairness, really—because the political structures of laws, regulations, and enforcement always inject tension, if only because of the diverse reactions to authority.

The Law of Nature versus the Law of Man is not only a variation of the Justice-Injustice duality, it also incorporates the duality of Individual and Community. American culture values early independence, encouraging self-reliance in infants, and tolerating adolescent rebellion well beyond the norm that prevails in other cultures. In the effort to be more fully one's own person, American culture cherishes three things in particular—mobility, privacy, and convenience—which are the very sources of a lack of community. In this case, community does not refer to a place, to the spot where we live, but to where we find "a sense of community" among people who know us, with whom we feel connected and safe. Therein lies the dilemma, because even while Americans crave to be independent, to be more true to themselves and less vulnerable to pressures and blandishments from others, they seek a society in which to be heard, respected and given the rewards that are their due. Even in the late 1830s, de Tocqueville anticipated our drive to associate growing inevitably out of our rootlessness and the lack of relatedness he considered inherent in a democratic society. A century and a half later, the wish for independence still leads man "to do what he alone considers most essential, regardless of the consequences; the wish for affirmation makes him sensitive to the responses of others and susceptible to their influence" (Levinson, p. 121). Such a duality is fertile ground for conflicts and motivations in westerns. Dynamic stories like Oakley Hall's novel *Warlock* (1958) and Cliff Huffaker's screenplay *Seven Ways to Sundown* (1960) grow from the struggles over position, authority, and responsibility that almost inevitably arise between the individual and the community. Stormy dramas like Frederick Faust's *The Untamed* (1919) and Tom Lea's *The Wonderful Country* (1952) develop when psychological and social needs for conformity and stability are attacking equally compelling needs for freedom and wandering.

Of all the dualities, the one that likely has had the most influence on westerns is that of the image of the New World as either a wilderness or a garden. The Puritans spiritualized the myth of the New World as an "errand into the wilderness," the building of virtuous communities in a wicked land full of savages bent on their physical and spiritual destruction. Indicative of this view are the captive narratives, which began with Mary Rowlandson's account of her kidnapping by Indians and eventual escape, *A True History of the Captivity and Restoration of Mrs. Mary Rowlandson* (1682); thereafter, captive narratives went on to become one of the most popular forms of colonial adventure story for well into the next century. These precursors of the western were written about, for, and often by women, and were meant as sermonizing tracts confirming Puritan Christianity and civilization, the heroines suffering a symbolic descent into hell when they are captured, and finding redemption through their resistance to the physical threats and spiritual temptations of the Indians.

To others, however, the New World was an idyllic garden whose natives had a special relationship with nature. Even in the early 1600s, colonial writers were publishing books and epic poetry extolling the Indians' natural affections, their honesty and fidelity, and their innate sense of mercy and justice. Perhaps the most famous is *The True Travels, Adventures, and Observations of Captain John Smith* (1730), which repeats the tale Smith first told in 1616, about Indian princess Pocahontas risking her life to save him, her beauty and compassion authenticating his chivalric heroism. In 1637, Thomas Morton became an extremely popular writer both in the colonies and in Europe with *New English Canaan or New Canaan,* in which he proposes the sexual union of Indian and Christian in order to renew the vigor, favor, and goodness in the social and religious life of the human race. The villains were the Puritans and pilgrims, whom Morton characterized as venal, hypocritical bigots. Whereas in 1638 Philip Vincent's *A True Relation of the Late Battell Fought in New-England* describes Boston as a bastion of order under siege by Indians and heretical chaos, that same year John Underhill's *News From America* portrays the New World as a Calvinist Garden of Eden populated by natives who are closer to nature and thus closer to God. By the next century, books like William Smith's *Historical Account of the Expedition Against the Ohio Indians* (1765) were suggesting that the Indians' patriotism, independence, and love of liberty make them the models of the ideal American.

In summary, right from this early period, published accounts and novels portrayed women as heroes and were contradictory in their treatment of Indians, reflecting the often discordant attitudes of the colonialists toward them. The duality of the Puritan wilderness and the Edenic garden, as well as the other dualities of Male-Female, Good-Evil, East-West, Justice-Injustice, seem to be irreconcilably opposed. Yet in both belief and practice, the New World version of colonization was from the beginning a unique process of entering new lands to create new societies, rather than simply to establish old social orders in new settings, as it was in Europe. Hence new forms and values and answers could emerge from the contrary pulls of these dualities, expressive of the new time and place, and indeed constituting them. The chronicle of how these forces have been resolved begins in the next chapter.

Whatever the duality encountered, though, America required taming by courageous persons of insight seeking independence, striving for a life that was peculiarly their own, even as it was linked to a community. In reflecting this drive to realize the American Dream, westerns are adventure stories set on a frontier about the character of individuals striving to transcend perilous circumstances.

Trailblazin'

Tourist: "I've never been in the West before. It's so big!"
Roy Rogers: "Yes, ma'am. It runs all the way to the East."
Tourist: "It does?"
"Don't Fence Me In" (1945)

Complicating the settling of America was the question of identity. During the eighteenth century in particular, massive waves of non-English immigrants flooded in, bringing such an ethnic diversity of languages, religions, and customs that no common American identity could readily form. The pace and scale of this population explosion created some alarm, and indeed, Benjamin Franklin in a 1751 essay expressed fear that cultural development and political development were at odds with one another. More prophetic was William Byrd, a Virginia planter whose *Westover Manuscripts* (1841)—comprising *The History of the Dividing Line, A Progress to the Mines,* and *A Journey to the Land of Eden, a.d. 1733*—is the first classic work by an American-born writer, a Southerner. Byrd argued that two forces, one intellectual and the other religious, inevitably were headed for a society-transforming clash. Ironically, although Byrd was correct about the two forces, now known as the Enlightenment and the Great Awakening, it was through their combining rather than colliding that many of the differences were resolved in the New World.

The Enlightenment changed the way educated colonists looked at the world, turning them from mystical theology toward natural science and moral naturalism as appropriate ways to interpret their American experience. Simultaneously, a devout spirituality was revived in the Great Awakening, but with a new emphasis that shifted religious debates from the nature of God to the nature of man and his capacity to receive salvation, which in the process helped provide colonists with a rationale for believing that the New World was morally superior to the Old. What emerged was American Protestantism in the form it would maintain into the twentieth century, promoting the work ethic, the right to private property, and the nation's Manifest Destiny to spread its European-derived civilization from sea to sea. In the words of Edward Winslow, "religion and profit jump together" (Arber, p. 596). As this set of beliefs gradually coalesced, colonists became increasingly aware that they had more in common with strangers from strange lands than they had with their countries of origin, thereby undercutting ethnic ties and forging a shared cultural identity. Not surprisingly, late colonial and early American literature was much concerned with developing traditions, democratic equality, and the unique experiences encountered in the new land. These themes prevail in numerous books such as Jefferson's *Notes* on the State of Virginia (1782), Crèvecoeur's *Letters from an American Farmer* (1782), and William Manning's 1798 essay "The Key of Libberty" [*sic*].

It is probably correct to say that together the Enlightenment and the Great Awakening were a primary cause of American independence, with its displacement of monarchs and surrogate deities by the common man, the individual. In turn, the resultant nation was not founded on laws and institutions too strong to resist change, but instead was built with sufficient checks to give growth and conflict the chance to create a balance between polarities, or dualities. The resolving of such tensions and the molding of public opinion were especially influenced by frontier pioneers. After all, in both belief and practice, the New World version of settlement was from the beginning a unique process of entering the new land to form new societies, rather than simply to establish old social orders in a new setting. Because the pioneers needed to be resourceful, self-sufficient, and trusting of their own judgment to survive, they needed to create fresh ways of perceiving and resolving major dualities such as civilization versus wilderness, and community versus the individual. In doing so they embodied the values and virtues that the public desired.

However much fault may now be found with the ethics and tactics of the Westward Movement, as individuals those pioneers were genuinely courageous and at the time were considered to be heroes, the populace—like all populaces—requiring heroes to give excitement to their routine lives and meaning to their politics and culture. Consequently, the adventures of heroic folk on the frontier became extremely popular reading, the mingling of fact and fiction firing the public's imagination as well as reflecting various new approaches to resolving dualities. Thus it is wrong to assert, as do revisionist critics such as Nancy Cook, that the mythic frontier is "a world of absolutes, where compromise is unnecessary, even undesirable" (p. 222). Quite the contrary. For example, the hunters and trappers known as Mountain Men opened the wilderness to the very civilization they supposedly sought to escape. Actually, instead of being misfit free spirits, they "lived for a chance to exchange their dangerous mountain careers for an advantageous start in civilized life" (Goetzmann, p. 405). Moreover, fur-trading and other exploitation of the inland were a large part of national mercantilism and thus patriotic, as illustrated by Benjamin Franklin's praise of George Rogers Clark's securing of the Old Northwest: "Young man, you have given an empire to the Republic" (Kennerly, p. 8). Such merging of community and the individual can be found in the glorified accounts of exploration and development leading to settlement, which often appeared in the many popular histories of the period, such as Robert Beverley's *History and Present State of Virginia* (1705), and Cadwallader Colden's *History of the Five Indian Nations* (1727). Also, a primary thrust of books by scouts and other travelers was to persuade pioneers that their fortunes as well as their duty lay in settling otherwise unknown regions. Typical is Jonathan Carver's *Travels through the Interior Parts of North America in the Years 1766, 1767, and 1768* (1778), in which he ballyhoos the natural resources in the Great Lakes area, claiming that along with "great numbers of excellent furs," there are "many small islands . . . covered with copper ore" and friendly Indians "who have gold so plenty among them that they make their most common utensils of it," and concludes that it is the obligation of Anglo-Americans to surpass the French in utilizing these bounties (pp. 527– 528). Similarly, in *Travels Through North and South Carolina, Georgia, East and West Florida* (1791), William Bartram exaggerates no less about "the fragrant, delicious fruit, welcomed by communities of the splendid meleagris, the capricious roebuck, and all the free and happy tribes, which possess and inhabit these prolific fields" and suggests the trapping of "crocodile alligators," the taming of chicken snakes to catch vermin, and the cultivation of "wax-trees" to make candles (pp. 204–205).

As well, views resolving the duality of wilderness and civilization began to develop in the pre- and post-Revolution exploits of soldiers, rangers, and other Indian fighters. Works like Major Robert Rogers's self-aggrandizing *Journals* (1765) about the last French and Indian war, Provost William Smith's military studies *Historical Account of the Expedition Against the Ohio Indians* (1765) and *Historical Account of Bouquet's Expedition Against the Ohio Indians* (1765), and James Smith's self-explanatory *An Account of the Remarkable Occurrences in the Life and Travels of Col. James Smith (Now a Citizen of Bourbon County, Kentucky,) During His Captivity with the Indians, in the Years 1755, '56, '57, '58, & '59 . . . as well as of the Different Campaigns Carried on Against the Indians to the Westward of Fort Pitt* (1799) are all filled with scenes of valiant derring-do for God and country against, as can be expected, Indian foes of exceptional hardiness, craftiness, ruthlessness, and skillfulness in woodlore. In William Smith's *Bouquet* account, for instance, a soldier and geographer named Thomas Hutchins portrays European conflict as "the exercise of a spirited and adventurous mind" compared to American campaigns, wherein "everything is terrible; the face of the country, the climate, the enemy. There is no refreshment for the healthy, nor relief for the sick. A vast unhospitable desert, unsafe and treacherous, . . . where victories are not decisive, but defeats are ruinous, and simple death is the least misfortune which can happen to them" (Slotkin, *Regeneration*, p. 232)

During this period, however, such Indian war narratives increasingly admired Indian methods and attitudes, and advocated their implementation to better assure victory. In his book, James Smith insists that his fellow countrymen implement the lessons he learned first as an Indian captive and then adopted tribal member; indeed, the middle segment of his massive title claims that "the Customs, Manners, Traditions, Theological Sentiments, Modes of Warfare, Military Tactics, Discipline and Encampments, Treatment of Prisoners, &c., Are Better Explained, and More Minutely Related, Than Has Been Heretofore Done, by Any Author on that Subject." Imitation of the Indian led quite naturally to identification with the Indian, though not to the extent "that white men became thorough Indians," Slotkin notes. "The white 'qualities' of intellect and sentiment are too precious to be sacrificed for mere prowess. But he [soldier-geographer Thomas Hutchins] does suggest an adaptation of the white, a disciplining to the Indian life as a means of hardening the European into a competent ranger" (*Regeneration*, p. 234). Slotkin's point could validly apply to Indian war narratives in general.

Absorbing wilderness ways to nurture civilization helped resolve another duality—the Indian as godless savage versus the Indian as idealized man in his natural state. Striking some sort of balance in between does not mean that the two sides were not used in stories. Writers are forever seeking new wrinkles, new twists, and to this day the opposing poles of every duality provide fodder for plots and characters. Accordingly, Indians continued to be portrayed as good because, as Rousseau and Romanticism argued, God is good, nature is good, and man's native goodness is corrupted by society, thus the Indian's pastoral lifestyle is virtuous in contrast to the corruption and tyranny of European regimes. A prime example is Robert Rogers's bizarre play *Ponteach: or the Savages of America* (1766), which is based on his mostly imaginative times with Chief Ponteach [Pontiac] that he had related in his book *A Concise Account of North America* (1765). Pontiac is presented as a generous, honorable defender of truth, justice, and liberty who is surrounded by the devious French and British, particularly the British who "are false, deceitful, knavish, insolent" (p. 33). In a passionate speech to his council, Pontiac declares, "Rouse, then, ye Sons of ancient Heroes, rouse, Put on your Arms, and let us act a Part Worthy of Sons of such renowned Chiefs" (p. 57)

Nor is it accidental that the profile of an Indian is on the famous old five-cent piece. To the degree that the Indian came to symbolize independence, courage, and defiance of authority, that profile is a literal token of respect, just as in a more entertaining tribute the American rebels dressed up as Indians when executing their Boston Tea Party, and the Whiskey Rebels of 1794 adopted war paint at their meetings and settled their grievances in mock "Indian treaties." Writers and poets like Philip Freneau waxed eloquent about the pure and virile Indian unsullied by society. In *The Indian Student, or Force of Nature* (1783), Freneau describes how Shalum of the Susquehanna tribe is cajoled by a missionary into attending Harvard, a move he soon laments:

> And why (he cried) did I forsake
> My native wood for gloomy walls;
> The silver stream, the limpid lake
> For musty books and college halls. (p. 70)

Conversely, the other side castigated the Indians as bloodthirsty heathens existing in Satanic savagery. This was the prevalent viewpoint after almost two centuries of battling the Eastern woodland tribes. The harsh attitude toward Indians has modified over time, though traditionally most historians and fiction writers have seen little fault in how the West was won and how the Indians and other minorities were treated. In recent years the revisionist historians have exalted the opposite, idyllic view of Indians, intimating that before the white European male arrived to ruin things, the Indian lived in peace and harmony. Political correctness aside, historical correctness indicates that Europeans did not introduce conquest, but arrived in the midst of tribal conflicts that had already been going on for eons. The larger, stronger tribes long had preyed on the smaller—the Iroquois, for example, terrorized the weaker natives in the Northeast—and braves of all tribes were raised to fight, their duties tied principally to hunting and warring. Colonial and early American settlers often found themselves hard-pressed if not out-matched, and reaching accommodation with the Indians proved diffi-cult and long in coming. Reflecting this state of affairs, Captive Narra-tives remained a staple source of Indian villains who scalped men, axed babies, and abducted women for fates worse than death. Novelist Charles Brockden Brown translated the European Gothic story into American form by replacing remote castles and brooding ruins with the wilderness, and treacherous inquisitors and lecherous noblemen with barbarous Indians. As Brown remarks in the preface to his novel *Edgar Huntly; Or, Memoirs of a Sleepwalker* (1799), "the incidents of Indian hostility, and the perils of the western wilderness are far more suitable; and, for a native of America to overlook these, would admit of no apology."

As time passed and conflicts with the tribes east of the Appala-chians dwindled, Americans started to view the Indian as a vanquished enemy threatened with racial extinction. This attitude was influenced by the Indians themselves, who perceived that their way of life was quickly disappearing. As the Seneca orator Red Jacket argued in an 1805 protest against the incursions of missionaries, "Our seats were once large, and yours were small. You have now become a great people, and we have got scarcely a place to spread our blankets. You have got our country, but you are not satisfied: you want to force your religion on us" (Washburn, p. 212).

Increasingly the populace grew convinced of the Indian's certain destruction, and expressed concern for the Indians' plight in tones of al-most nostalgic regret for the triumph of progress over savagery. Therein lay the resolution of the Indian duality. Public opinion, mellowing some-what toward the side of Rousseau and Romanticism, began regarding the Indian as the Noble Savage—as one of the Lost, a primitive figure who provided a link with pastoral nature, a reminder for militant vigilance, and a rationale for religious tolerance, civil liberty, and economic free-dom. A typical example of the Noble Savage theme is Benjamin Drake's *Life of Tecumseh* (1841), which depicts Tecumseh as a doomed hero; he and his Shawnee are victimized and slaughtered by "white devils" in divine retribution for past sins, though at the end, Tecumseh predicts tribal regeneration: "The Master of Life is about to restore to the Shawanoes both their knowledge and their rights" (quoted in Slotkin, *Regeneration*, p. 428). Even more illustrative is Henry Longfellow's famous epic *Hiawatha* (1855), which tells of a primitive people giving way to a stronger but not necessarily nobler race. Hiawatha is a boy of supernatural origin who grows into a wondrous youth able to outrace arrows and talk to animals. His father, the West-Wind, tells him to

> Cleanse the earth from all that harms it
> Clear the fishing-grounds and rivers,
> Slay all monsters and magicians. (p. 123)

After a series of mythic adventures, Hiawatha suffers tragic losses, capped by the death of his beloved wife Minnehaha and the arrival of white men in their "great canoes." Hiawatha, realizing that the whites are destined to rule the land, enjoins his people not to resist but to

> Listen to their words of wisdom,
> Listen to the truth they tell you,
> For the Master of Light has sent them
> From the land of light and morning! (p. 164)

Then, just as King Arthur in Tennyson's "Morte d'Arthur" leaves for Avalon to be healed of his grievous wound, "Hiawatha the Beloved" departs westward in his birch canoe:

> To the Islands of the Blessed,
> To the Kingdom of Ponemah,
> To the Land of the Hereafter! (p. 164)

In turn, the image of the Noble Savage helped crystallize the concept of frontier heroes as civilized men well versed in Indian discipline and tactics. To paraphrase Slotkin, a sense of shared sympathy and shared education with the Indian became a prerequisite of sorts for heroes (p. 329). They constitute the original "man in the middle," to use John Cawelti's definition of the western hero. "The hero, though a friend of the townspeople, has the lawless power of movement in that he, like the savages, is a horse-man and possesses skills of the wilderness experience" (*Six-Gun*, p. 67).

Although Longfellow, Drake, and a number of other writers used the concepts of "the man in the middle," the Noble Savage, and the wilderness in service of civilization, the first to incorporate them successfully in a frontier story was John Filsen, when he penned "The Adventures of Col. Daniel Boone; containing a Narrative of the Wars of Kentucke," which appeared as an appendix to his book *The Discovery, Settlement and Present State of Kentucke* (1784). Filsen has rarely been credited as author of the western prototype, the majority of critics and scholars claiming that this distinction belongs to either James Fenimore Cooper or Owen Wister. For example, Loren Estleman states that the western "sprang full-grown from the imagination of Owen Wister" (p. 25); literary critic Robert Murray Davis calls his chapter on Wister "*The Virginian*: Inventing the Westerner" (*Playing Cowboys*, p. 3); and Robert Edson Lee in *From West to East* buttresses his support for Wister by citing historian Bernard DeVoto's thesis that "Wister invented . . . the myth of the Old West" (p. 150). Among those arguing for Cooper are John Cawelti, who maintains that Cooper founded "the basic shape of the western formula" (*Adventure*, p. 192), and James K. Folsom, who asserts that Cooper is the discoverer "of a viable method for the interpretation of Western history" whose "every major theme . . . is picked up by later writers about the West" (p. 58). In turn, Filsen has been relegated to a secondary status as the first important biographer of Daniel Boone, who has "been assumed—for literary purposes at least—to be the epitome of the pioneer character" (Folsom, p. 58). Fortunately, Filsen is at last gaining some well-deserved recognition, beginning perhaps with the detailed study of his "Adventures" by Richard Slotkin, who concludes that "the Boone narrative, in fact, constituted the first nationally viable statement of a myth of the frontier" (*Regeneration*, p. 269).

To be sure, many of the qualities associated with literature are lacking in Filsen's writing, which may account for his not being taken as seriously as Cooper or Wister. Indeed, his intentions were not literary but promotional, for Filsen was a surveyor and land speculator who wanted to attract buyers for his several thousand acres of Kentucky real estate. Instead of claiming any literary artistry, he insisted that his "Adventures" appendix about Boone was autobiographical, "published from his own mouth," recorded because Boone "was earlier acquainted with the subject of this performance [the settlement of Kentucky] than any other now living, as appears by the account of his adventures, which I esteemed curious and interesting" (p. 6). Certainly the story of Kentucky's history is largely Boone's history, involving fights with Indians, captures by them and the British, audacious escapes, adoption by the Shawnees, later trial and acquittal for being too friendly with the Shawnees, subsequent promotion to major, and retirement with great honor. As for Filsen's "Adventures" being autobiographical, however, accuracy was not the primary ingredient. Apparently Boone liked Filsen's mingling of fact and fiction; according to Boone biographer John Bakeless, Boone "took an innocent joy in being written up" and declared more than once that Filsen's book was totally accurate (p. 395). Once again, a historical individual helps fashion mythic legend out of true history—a penchant Boone shares with Davy Crockett, Buffalo Bill, Wyatt Earp, and Wild Bill Hickok.

Like many frontier yarns of its time, "The Adventures" has a contrived plot, with many doubling structures and cliffhanging moments. Still, at its core is the western story's emphasis on the character of an individual overcoming perilous odds. Boone's civilized sensitivities are progressively compromised as he penetrates the wilderness:

> Curiosity is natural to the soul of man, and interesting objects have a powerful influence on our affections. Let these influencing powers actuate, by the permission or disposal of Providence, from special or social views . . . [t]hus we behold Kentucky, lately an howling wilderness, a habitation of savages and wild beasts. (p. 49)

Increasingly Boone absorbs the wily ways of the wilderness, becoming a fearsome initiate of its bloody mysteries. Constantly pursued and attacked by Indians, he alone or with companions "defend[ed] ourselves and repulse[ed] the enemy," with the result that eventually the Indians "learned the superiority of the Long Knife, as they call the Virginians, by experience" (pp. 59, 62). While on one "roving excursion," Boone reports that he is "often exploited to danger, and death," but is "happy in the midst of dangers and inconveniences. . . . No populous city, with all the varieties of commerce and stately structures, could afford so much pleasure to my mind, as the beauties of nature I found here" (pp. 55–56). Now the "man in the middle," Boone absorbs what he perceives to be the tempers of nature, the behaviors of natives, and comes to show considerable understanding and respect for the Indians. Captured, he finds that

> the generous usage the Indians had promised before in my capitulation, was afterwards fully complied with. . . . During our travels, the Indians entertained me well; and their affections for me was so great that they utterly refused to leave me there with the others. . . . I spent my time as comfortably as I could expect; was adopted, according to their custom, into a family where I became a son, and had a great share in the affection of my new parents, brothers, sisters, and friends. . . . The Shawanese [Shawnee] king took great notice of me, and treated me with profound respect, and entire friendship, often entrusting me to hunt at my liberty. (pp. 63, 64–65, 66)

Escaping, then using his knowledge to help fortify settlements and mount counterattacks, Boone discovers his own savage potential: "We continue our pursuit through five towns on the Miami rivers . . . burnt them all to ashes, entirely destroying their corn, and other fruits, and every where spread a scene of desolation in the country. In the expedition we took seven prisoners and five scalps" (p. 78). Insofar as the "Adventures" approach any solution for Indian grievances, there is none really, only ultimate confirmation of the superiority of civilization: "I now live in peace and safety, enjoying the sweets of liberty and the bounties of Providence . . . which I have seen purchased with a vast expense of blood and treasure" (p. 81).

Probably because Filsen was not being consciously literary, he introduces in "Adventures" another then-unique trait that since has become a hallmark of westerns—the brisk, to-the-point style of narration. From earliest colonial times, writing was dominated by doctrinal rhetoric and pulpit eloquence, well suited for polemic commentary on the political and religious issues of the day. Literary narrative tended to be loose, disjointed, often containing ethical reflections and philosophical excursions propounded in a pontifical style by everyone including Indians. For example, Pontiac in Rogers's *Ponteach* and Shalum in Freneau's *The Indian Student* habitually speak in stately English blank verse. Hugh Henry Brackenridge in his *Modern Chivalry*, published in three volumes from 1792 to 1815, interrupts his narrative to discuss his career, even discussing reviews of the first two volumes in the third. History and travel books like those by Robert Beverley, Cadwallader Colden, Jonathan Carver, and John Bartram frequently digress with learned descriptions of wild animals, detailed descriptions of rivers, meadows, and odoriferous woods, and disquisitions on Indian life, garb, and customs.

To some extent, Filsen honored this tradition by composing *The Discovery, Settlement and Present State of Kentucke* in a commercially romantic style designed to entice potential emigrants from Europe. "The beautiful river . . . Ohio receives a number of large and small rivers, which pay tribute to its glory . . . The first rate land is too rich for wheat till it has been reduced by four or five years of cultivation . . . A medicinal spring is found near the Big-bone Lick, which has perfectly cured the itch by once bathing" (pp. 21, 25, 33). Then, as is evident in the quotations from "Adventures" cited earlier, Filsen shifted from promoting Kentucky to reporting Boone's supposed autobiography in Boone's own simple language, but essentially it is Filsen's "voice" that is recorded in the "Adventures" and develops Boone as a character. The result is an inauthentic yet relatively straight-forward action story told in narrative language that is clean, rugged, mostly unadorned, and usually unmetaphorical.

Filsen's book and particularly his appendix became extremely popular here and abroad, and were published in various editions. Daniel Boone became the quintessential American whose behavior and beliefs exemplify the national character, attitudes, and socially approved customs. As such, Boone is "not a portrait of an individual hero," as Northrop Frye says of Achilles, "but a great smouldering force of human desire and frustration and discontent, something we all have in us too, part of mankind as a whole" (p. 65). Serving symbolically, as an abstraction, Boone constitutes the first mythic hero for the frontier, the archetype of the idealized half-white, half-Indian protector of the weak and avenger of injustice. Accordingly, the title of this chapter is "Trailblazin'," referring to the path forged by Filsen's Daniel Boone, and followed by countless imitations in literature and the popular arts.

For example, Daniel Boone reappears in James Hall's *Letters from the West* (1828) as a loner of "hardy frame and versatile spirit" who, like

Filsen's Boone, does not fully belong to either the white or Indian worlds. Hall's Boone and his company have "boldly cut the tie which bound them to society" to "pursue yet deeper danger" in "the unsettled state of the country, [with] its reputed unhealthiness and the vicinity of Indian tribes" that is "too remote, too insulated, too barbarous" for the general populace (pp. 246, 252, 250, 251). James Hall, in other words, was among those who perceived the frontier not as a bountiful garden but as an implacable wilderness needing to be tamed by Americans of a "national character" personified by Daniel Boone: "All of us in the United States are the same—as the children of one family, when they separate from the world still preserve the impress of those principles which they imbibed from a common source" (p. 236).

An even harsher view is given by Robert Montgomery Bird in *Nick of the Woods; or, The Jibbenainosay* (1837). Here, Boone becomes the fictional Nathan Slaughter, also known as "the Jibbenainosay," an Indian-hater at the end of the Revolutionary War who devotes considerable time and energy to cleaning the frontier of savages, the utter incarnation of evil. Bird's murderous distortion of the Boone character proved quite popular, as did similar caricatures set at the extreme of the wilderness versus garden duality, such as Hugh Bradley in James McHenry's *Spectre of the Forest* (1823), Timothy Weasel in James Kirk Paulding's *Dutchman's Fireside* (1831), Hanson in Samuel Young's *Tom Hanson, the Avenger* (1847), and James Quinlan's homicidally obsessed Quick in *Tom Quick, the Indian Slayer* (1851)—of whom Quinlan confesses, "the writer cannot attempt to pallate and excuse Quick's conduct . . . in any other way than by supposing that . . . the refined and humane sentiments which are promoted by civilization and Christianity, were obliterated by the dark and unfeeling dogmas which obtain a lodgement in the human mind during perilous and bloody times" (p. 101).

During that first half of the nineteenth century, however, readers tended to prefer a more tempered depiction of Boone and his environs. Granted, the frontier had not proven to be the Edenic paradise once envisioned, but it still provided vast, golden opportunities that stirred the romantic and patriotic public imagination. Thomas Jefferson's controversial Louisiana Purchase in 1803 unleashed a period of unprecedented westward expansion and exploitation, providing a flow of published journals and accounts, from the Lewis and Clark expedition to Zebulon

Pike's survey of the Red River and Arkansas River regions, to the Frémont explorations of Oregon and California beginning in 1841. Increasingly, Indians were considered to be the lost Noble Savages, having all but disappeared from the East, scattered as the integrity of their cultures was broken, or forcibly removed by Secretary of War Calhoun's 1824 plan to resettle them at remote locations. The vision of the Noble Savage, moreover, was enhanced by more thorough and generally sympathetic studies of their fading cultures, particularly those by Indian agent Henry Rowe Schoolcraft; Superintendent of Indian Affairs Thomas McKenney and his collaborator James Hall; and Moravian missionary John Heckewelder, whose *Account of the History, Manners, and Customs, of the Indian Nations, Who Once Inhabited Pennsylvania and Neighboring States* (1818) served as a major source for James Fenimore Cooper. Considering these trends, it is not surprising that, as Larzer Ziff notes in *Writing in the New Nation*, "the great majority of those who wrote about Indians—from Jefferson well on into the nineteenth century, including, preeminently, James Fenimore Cooper—treat[ed] living Indians as sources for a literary construction of a vanished way of life rather than as members of a vital continuing culture" (p. 172).

One of the more intriguing juxtapositions of a moderate Boone hero and the Noble Savage is in William Gilmore Simms's short story "The Two Camps" (1845). Simms is best remembered for rather unremarkable poems and fictions about doomed Noble Savages who, like Iwatee in *The Cassique of Kiawah* (1859), are "savage rather in [their] simplicity than in [their] corruptions," unable to accept civilization or survive in the face of it (p. 15). But in "The Two Camps," the protagonist is Indian-hater Daniel Nelson, whose notion of Indians is that of painted devils intent on "sculping" every white within reach of a tomahawk. Nonetheless Daniel Nelson rescues a prominent young native, Lenatewa, who in turn saves Nelson and eventually establishes peace between local whites and Indians, thereby altering Nelson's opinion to one of qualified admiration and pity.

Simms's Daniel Nelson does not shift as far as the position taken by a reincarnated Daniel Boone in Timothy Flint's 1833 *Biographical Memoire of Daniel Boone*. As James K. Folsom contends in the introduction to his edition of *Memoire*, Flint portrays Boone as the preordained scout for advancing civilization—a "sphere which Providence called him to fulfill"

—who reads "the sign manual of nature" to trailblaze through a benevolent wilderness (p. 23). Three years before *Memoire*, Flint created a similarly nurturing frontier in *The Shoshonee Valley*, which relates the destruction of the Noble Shoshones and their bucolic valley by not only evil whites, but unwittingly by decent fur-trappers who in the style of Boone have become "imbued with an instinctive fondness for the reckless savage life . . . occupied in hunting, fighting, feasting, intriguing, and amours, interdicted by no laws, or difficult morals, or any restraints, but the invisible ones of Indian habit and opinion" (pp. 21–22).

Daniel Boone as the man in the middle even became the woman in the middle as Hope Leslie in Catharine Maria Sedgwick's *Hope Leslie; or, Early Times in Massachusetts* (1827). Heroine Hope, believing that natives are noble children of darkness requiring enlightenment instead of destruction, resists the constraints of her Puritan world and forms a close friendship with the female Indian Magawisca, who is similarly torn between loyalty to her people and to white civilization. While helping Magawisca escape prison, Hope declares, "We are commanded to do good for all" (p. 312), but she cannot prevent the inevitable; Magawisca returns to her doomed people, stating the theme that author Sedgwick weaves throughout the story: "The Indian and the white man can no more mingle, and become one, than day and night" (p. 330). Ironically, although Hope winds up, in traditional romance fashion, married to heroic colonist Everell Fletcher, her sister Faith defies even the story's theme by insisting on marrying Oneco, the Indian chief's son, in one of the rare instances of explicit rather than implicit miscegenation in early western fiction.

Of all the early Boone characterizations, the most dramatic and fully realized is the invincible pathfinder Natty Bumppo, who appears in James Fenimore Cooper's *Leatherstocking Tales*. As I have said, in creating Bumppo and the Leatherstocking series Cooper is commonly, if erroneously, credited with originating the western's characteristic protagonists, settings, and themes—which is not to detract from the many firsts that Cooper can rightfully claim. He was the first American novelist to support himself by his writings, shared with Washington Irving the first international reputation as a major author, and was first "to demonstrate in the novel that native materials could inspire significant imaginative writing" (Long, p. 13). Folsom remarks that Cooper's works "have at last been given the sober critical attention which they unquestionably deserve" (p. 36), resulting in a growing consensus that Cooper, as Jeffrey Rubin-Dorsky asserts in *The Columbia History of the American Novel,* was "in all probability America's first significant novelist" (p. 23). His reputation rests largely on his frontier stories, in which the "images of pioneers and Indians he created, above all in *The Leatherstocking Tales,* entered not only American but world popular mythography, [with] a power of social criticism that took them far beyond legend" (Ruland and Bradbury, p. 97). Certainly Cooper's lasting popularity was achieved by his Leatherstocking novels, which, despite suffering from frequent improbabilities, stilted dialogue, and blatant sentimentality, are still remarkably persuasive as action is piled on action, suspense accumulates, and encroaching civilization is countered by Indians whose menace arises from the primal depths of nature itself. Fittingly, Natty Bumppo is Cooper's greatest imaginative conception—a frontiersman who is "in many ways emblematic of the white hunter that Filsen, Hall, and Flint elaborated in Boone's name," as Mary Lawlor states, and "[a]s Lucy Lockwood Hazard [in *The Frontier in American Literature* (1961)], Henry Nash Smith [in *Virgin Land: The American West as Symbol and Myth* (1950)], Richard Slotkin [in *Regeneration Through Violence* (1973)], and Stephen Railton [in *Fenimore Cooper: A Study of His Life and Imagination* (1978)], and many others have noted" (p. 39).

Bumppo's initial appearance was not auspicious. In *The Pioneers* (1823), the first in the series, Bumppo is a minor, elderly character, disheartened and somewhat isolated, the story revolving less around him than—as the title suggests—around the intrusions, corrupt customs, environmental spoilage, and other conflicts that attend settlement. Bumppo assumes a central role in the second book, *The Last of the Mohicans* (1826), which is set at an earlier time when Bumppo is in his prime, fighting Indian-style to make the world safe for civilization, even while realizing that, like the Indians, he cannot be part of the richer, complex life that is advancing. Again older in *The Prairie* (1827), Bumppo moves ever farther west, carrying with him the very civilization he seeks to escape, until he dies on the distant frontier. After *The Prairie* Cooper took a thirteen-year hiatus from the Leatherstocking saga, returning to it eventually with *The Pathfinder* (1840), in which Bumppo is about the same age and up to the same fighting as he is in *Mohicans,* only this time he dabbles with society and domesticity until he recognizes that his destiny forbids such and he draws away in self-chosen obscurity. The last novel, *The Deerslayer* (1841), is the first if the series is read in the order of Bumppo's life, for here he is quite young, quite untested, and a bit naïve, rejecting the love of a civilized woman without fully comprehending that it is civilization—*her* civilization—that is beginning to erode the philosophical and moral import of everything he is coming to believe and represent. Overall, then, the Leatherstocking series "gave America the romantic narrative romance it lacked . . . a form permitting an epic enterprise, allowing a vigorous portrayal of American settings, and enabling the creation of an active and ingenious American hero" (Ruland and Bradbury, pp. 96, 102). Nonetheless, in tracing the progress of civilization, Cooper's tone throughout the *Tales* is that of tragedy, for "despite professions of faith in the future of American civilization, a poignant air of transience hovers over all the works of his pioneers" (Dekker, p. 109).

This tragic quality arises from Cooper's departure from Filsen's concept of Daniel Boone. Granted, Bumppo is a descendant of Boone, a participant in both civilized and savage worlds who embodies elements of each without belonging entirely to either. Yet Boone and others in the Boone tradition finish their adventures by returning to civilization, where their wilder methods and loyalties are muted for the sake of so-called civilized values. Bumppo, though, inhabits the middle ground between civilization and the wild, is always moving ahead of civilization, and by doing so remains a metaphor for the confrontation of American expansion with native environs. "In inventing Natty, Cooper had found a prime subject, that of the alternative possibility secreted *within* the wilderness, an ideal of life beyond legal and social conventions governed by moral ones in their Romantic essence" (Ruland and Bradbury, p. 98). Bumppo's hut in *The Pioneers*, for instance, stands apart from the settlement, so blending with nature as to become one with it, and is ultimately burned down by Bumppo rather than allow it to be searched by lawmen whose response to nature has been plunder and rapacity. Nor is this a unique circumstance; throughout the Leatherstocking series Bumppo champions natural over civil law—"When the Colony's laws, or even the king's laws, run ag'n the laws of God," he insists in *The Deerslayer*, "they get to be unlawful, and ought not to be obeyed" (p. 16)—which raises nature to an importance as great as the characters, becoming "a vision of perfection, not very different from the visions of men three thousand years before. Here, heroes enforced the highest and purest standards of manliness and morality" (Nash, p. 206).

In portraying nature-oriented heroes of manliness and morality, Cooper created not only Natty Bumppo but Bumppo's friend and ally Chingachgook, so noble a Noble Savage that their relationship is one of equals, rather than one of sidekick to leader in the manner of Tonto and the Lone Ranger. Loyal, courageous, stoic, ruthless when necessary, Chingachgook is the expression of the dying wilderness around him. Like Bumppo's, Chingachgook's introduction in *The Pioneers* is as a man in his seventies who dotes too much on memories and liquor, but he then appears in *The Last of the Mohicans* as a chief exhibiting the qualities of a warrior and a zeal for scalping—"a signal virtue in an Indian," Bumppo declares in *The Deerslayer* (p. 16). Indeed, although the first part of *Mohicans* centers around the dangerous journey by Major Heyward, Cora and Alice Monro, and their companions to besieged Fort William Henry in northern New York, the core of the story is made up by the adventures of Bumppo and the ethnic conflict between Chingachgook's "good" Mohicans and the "bad" Iroquois—the major emphasis lying with the Indians, as the title indicates.

Chingachgook and his son Uncas continue to play crucial roles in other books in the Leatherstocking series, always embodying the idealized virtues and distinctive aboriginal traits that Cooper, having little first-hand knowledge, derived from the benevolent John Heckewelder's *Account*. Chingachgook and Uncas display an innate courtesy and a chivalric attitude toward women, for example, and Chingachgook is ever the affectionate father while Uncas shows the deference and filial affection befitting the Indian code. When at the end of *Mohicans* Uncas dies, Bumppo laments, "before the night had come, have I lived to see the last warrior of the wise race of the Mohicans" (p. 178)—which is a tad melodramatic, inasmuch as Uncas is survived by many Mohicans, including Chingachgook, and, historically, by Chief Uhm-Pa-Tuh of the Lutheran Stockbridge Indians, who as late as 1932 could claim to be the last. But Cooper was following the Noble Savage predilection for heroes who are the end of their line, and besides, the vision of his Leatherstocking novels requires the sort of moral heroism reflected by indomitable bravery in the face of extinction. Other Indians are similarly valiant and befriending of whites, thereby earning Bumppo's admiration and respect as possible comrades. When in *The Prairie* Bumppo is asked, "Is that an Indian you see?" he replies, "Redskin or Whiteskin, it is much the same friendship and use can tie men as strongly together in the woods as in the towns—aye, and for that matter stronger" (p. 111).

If Cooper characterizes Indians at their best, he also characterizes them at their worst—cruel, cold-blooded, devious, and diabolical. In *Mohicans* he offers the vilest of the Leatherstocking villains, Magua, who is ruled by scheming vindictiveness, his countenance "so fiercely malignant, that it was impossible not to apprehend it proceeded from some passion even more sinister than avarice" (p. 48). The novels also are stocked with Sioux, Hurons, and particularily Mingoes, scoundrel fiends who become maniacal on liquor and indulge in crazed orgies. Yet beneath their evil they possess the bravery, dignity, and other redeeming merits that Cooper associates with Indians, their lapses into depravity due not to inherited barbarity but to contamination by civilization. In *The Deerslayer*, for instance, Bumppo slays a treacherous Indian in a scene suggesting their brotherhood, Bumppo's first victim dying in his arms "with the high, innate courage that so often distinguishes the Indian warrior, before he becomes corrupted by too much intercourse with the worst class of the white men" (p. 46). In his plots as well as descriptions, Cooper, despite his many pronouncements about the moral superiority of the white and the benevolent influence of Christian society, consistently portrays civilization as exploiting nature and eradicating Indian culture, creating entangling alliances that pit whites against Indians and Indians against themselves. As is observed in *The Deerslayer*, "It is true that white cunning has managed to throw the tribes into great confusion, as respects friends and enemies . . . thus throwing everything into disorder, and destroying all the harmony of warfare" (p. 96).

In exposing the greed, racism, hypocrisy, and vengefulness that can come with settlement, Cooper presents a rogues' gallery of white villains as well. Ishmael Bush, fleeing into the wilderness to avoid arrest, is instinctively predatory and cunning, taking captives like the Sioux and continually shifting his alliances with and against the Sioux. Ex-pirate Tom Hutter is a racist without conscience, who with his brutal partner Hurry Harry March—who admits that he "account[s] game, a redskin, and a Frenchman as pretty much the same" (p. 14)—murders Indians for the government bounty on Indian scalps; early in *The Deerslayer*, they raid an Indian camp when they figure only women will be there, and during the night a horrifying shriek of agony, apparently of a young girl, is heard. Whites also prey on other whites who are weaker and more vulnerable. In *The Pioneers*, Jotham Riddle, a lazy schemer, and Squire Doolittle, whose gaunt face expresses "formal propriety, mingled with low cunning" (p. 45) instigate confusion and direct the forces that cause Bumppo to leave the settlement. Throughout the Leatherstocking series, Cooper consistently casts his white villains and lowlifes as migrating from a decadent eastern seaboard or New England, bringing polluted values and pretensions to a western frontier where nobody needs "swallow-tail coats or white gloves to wear at Pawnee receptions . . . nor anything else necessary to make life calm and peaceful." Even reasonably decent whites are portrayed as killers oblivious to nature, as in *The Pioneers* when settlers fire a cannon in the air in a senseless slaughter of pigeons and use nets to catch fish by the thousands, though only a few are needed for food. So eager to kill are such civilized folk that nature is merely an impediment in their hunting of one another, as shown in the opening passage of *Mohicans:*

> It was a feature peculiar to the colonial wars of North America, that the toils and dangers of the wilderness were to be encountered before the adverse hosts could meet. A wide and apparently an impervious boundary of forests severed the possessions of the hostile provinces of France and England. The hardy colonist, and the trained European who fought at his side, frequently expended months in struggling against the rapids of the streams, or in effecting the rugged passes of the mountains, in quest of an opportunity to exhibit their courage in a more martial conflict. (p. 1)

In effect, whereas from Filsen to Cooper the agenda of Manifest Destiny is lauded, with frontier heroes symbolizing the influence of national values on nature and the replacement of natural with civil law, Cooper reverses the characterization and puts Bumppo on a frontier that America has defiled, in a nature that civilization has lost and despoiled even while conquering. As Bumppo says in *The Deerslayer* of his beloved Lake Glimmerglass, it has no "pale-face name, for their christenings foretell a waste and destruction" (p. 14). Closely associated with the Indians and the wilderness, yet providing no threat to white culture, Bumppo is simultaneously identified with both perspectives and opposing sets of values, and thus is in an unusually powerful position to be a mediator between the two worlds. That is, Bumppo *could* be a mediator, but as a number of critics have noticed, Cooper does not allow his hero to reconcile any deeply conflicting forces or to establish one set of values in full authority over the other. Literary historian Robert Shiller, for instance, points out that Bumppo "fails to reconcile the virtues of primitive nature, the morals of conventional Christianity, and the amenities of imported European civilization" (p. 148). Instead, Cooper tends to suggest the conflict and to leave the oppositions juxtaposed, combined but unresolved. Throughout the series, Bumppo insists that there can be no regeneration through violence, yet he consistently accepts the brutalities of both his white and Indian allies, adapting to circumstances against his own moral principles. He often, as in *The Prairie*, "gaze[s] at the desolation of the scene around him" and decries the white man's "pride, waste, and sinfulness" (p. 36), but he does nothing ultimately to prevent such decimation. Even when he perceives that America is squandering the best of the native "red gifts," he does no more than lament: "Ah's me! Your Delaware were the red-skins of which America might boast; but few and scattered is that mighty people, now" (p. 165). Bumppo wavers in his naïve courtship of Mabel Dunham in *The Pathfinder*, and vacillates between desire and reluctance when pursued by the sensuous and tormented coquette Judith Hutter in *The Deerslayer*. As Gaile McGregor comments in *The Noble Savage in the New World Garden*, "Unfortunately, as an essentially social being, the only *kind* of hero that Cooper can imagine is first and foremost a social hero, defined in terms of social values. Thus Natty cannot be a viable model unless he is symbolically socialized. On the other hand, the more socialized he becomes . . . the more he loses the character that made him a meaningful symbol for Cooper in the first place" (p. 145).

If in love there is no resolution, neither is there in religion. The Leatherstocking series, rife with religious overtones, presents Bumppo as always on trial, always earning his salvation, his Christian faith compromised by his living in pagan nature in the company of Chingachgook—a savage who when dying no longer pretends to be Christianized but addresses his own gods in his native tongue. God or Manitou, Deity or Great Spirit, the name "matters not" (p. 87), Bumppo tells Judith in *The Deerslayer,* and later adds, "Forts and churches almost always go together, and yet they're downright contradictions, churches being for peace and forts for war. No, no—give me the strong places of the wilderness, which is the trees, and the churches, too, which are arbours raised by the hand of natur'" (p. 103). Even in his own death there is no resolution for Bumppo. When he expires in *The Prairie* he is still in the middle, supported by the white man Middleton on one side and by the Pawnee Hard-Heart on the other, each "involuntarily extend[ing] a hand to support the form of the old man" (p. 172)—a dying hero in a dying West who, in words reminiscent of his eulogy for Uncas, declares that "when I am gone, there will be an end of my race" (p. 171). McGregor argues, I believe convincingly, that it was to Cooper's advantage

> to subsume widely diverse statements of belief or value *without* imposing any definitive conclusions about relative worth or forcing a narrow and unnatural synthesis of polarities. . . . It is in fact not so much his subject matter nor even his treatment of this subject matter that makes him so representative as the unique ability of his novels to *encapsulate untransformed* the full gamut of social and psychological facts that comprised his particular cultural ambience. . . . Indeed, without more than token attempts at reconciliation or interpretation Cooper, perhaps more than any other writer of his day, succeeded in documenting the full complexity of American consciousness in the first half of the nineteenth century. (p. 124)

Albeit ambiguous in its resolutions, the *Leatherstocking Tales* do chronicle Cooper's concern with the struggle of the Indians and the whites who live on the frontier against the incursions of a dynamic civilization. Thus, the stories lay the foundations of the American allegorical romance in the nineteenth century and link Cooper to other major American writers such as Nathaniel Hawthorne, Walt Whitman, and Henry James. Flawed though they may be, the novels are fully capable of evoking more than they say, of projecting persuasive symbols, and of suggesting a metaphysic of which the stories themselves are allegories. Thus Cooper demonstrated that westerns are capable of being literature.

Brush Bustin'

In summing up the legacy of James Fenimore Cooper, Richard Ruland and Malcolm Bradbury note that "by the end of his life he stood at the center of a large, multidirectional flow of American writing" (p. 102). Certainly in one direction flowed the romance novel, a serious literary form with great strength and complexity of narrative design, which anticipated what Richard Chase calls the more profound psychological romances of Hawthorne, Melville, and Poe (p. 19). In another direction poured inexpensive popular fiction in various formats, such as short-story tabloids and paper-bound pamphlets, which have become grouped collectively under the generic term "dime novel." One of the first mass media, the dime novel, in particular the dime western, was a commodity that responded to contemporary perceptions of American society and history, its sales dependent on altering plots and characters as swiftly as changing events and market conditions required. This chapter explores the dime western as an embodiment of the cultural and political consciousness of its readership during the latter half of the nineteenth century, and discusses how as a result the dime western contributed to the development of western fiction.

Initially, dime westerns neither cost a dime nor were set in the West, but were hard-bound novels costing a dollar or so and replicating the Leatherstocking stories—set in the Eastern woodlands during colonial or Revolutionary times, starring the stock Cooper characters of plucky heroines, mendacious villains, and stalwart heroes who were, like Bumppo, celibate older hunters with no fixed abode and of unequaled prowess in scouting, fighting, and marksmanship. By the end of the 1840s, however, stories were being set with increasing frequency in the contemporaneous Far West, an expansion that was reflective of changing national interests. Although historically venerated, the era of the Revolution was fading in memory and becoming overtaken by newer developments, such as the startling rise of the Rocky Mountain fur trade. During the 1830s and 1840s, the trappers and hunters of the Far West came to be known as "mountain men," in contrast to the Boone/Bumppo "backwoodsmen" of the Northeast forests, although they ranged the inhospitable trans-Mississippian wilderness in much the same manner that Bumppo had done, avoiding civilization and adopting Indian ways.

Popular writers and their publishers soon saw that "the successor of Boone and Leatherstocking in the role of typical Wild Western hero was certain to be a mountain man. Cooper had acknowledged this fact in *The Prairie* by transporting Leatherstocking beyond the Mississippi and trying halfheartedly to make him over into a trapper" (Smith, *Virgin Land*, p. 81). Whether these works concerned mountain men or backwoodsmen, sales of these rather simplistic frontier adventures were quite remarkable, considering the period and state of publishing. Hardbound books were relatively costly to produce, and distribution was restricted by a rudimentary transportation system, yet Emerson Bennett's *The Prairie Flower* (1849) and *Leni-Leoti* (1849) each sold an estimated hundred thousand copies, and his rivals were almost as successful (Jones, p. 3).

Such sales volumes, though, were mere trickles compared to the impending flood of derivative frontier fiction that "largely began the commercial life of American fiction" (Ruland and Bradbury, p. 101). That veritable tidal wave occurred with the technological revolution in printing, the rapid spread of newspapers, and the standardization of mass publishing and marketing. In printing, the introduction of stereotyping and the development of the rotary steam press allowed for much faster production runs on much cheaper "pulp" paper similar to the newsprint paper of today. This lowered the price of hardcover books, of course, but, more importantly, it cut the printing costs and raised the circulation of newspapers while displacing many compositors and pressmen whose skills had become obsolete or superfluous. Some of the surplus journeymen, seeking a livelihood, headed West to set up print shops in little towns and remote settlements. "Thousands of newspapers were started between 1846 and 1890," reports Barbara Cloud (p. 130), and she quotes Richard Hudson as saying that they were "so thoroughly read as to be completely deprived of all signs of printing-ink" (p. 3). Moreover, people could read; the 1840 Census claimed that 97 percent of white adults in the Northeast and 91 percent in the Northwest were literate (Denning, p. 31), and by 1880 only 9.4 percent of the population was reported as illiterate (Cloud, p. 12).

The link between mid-nineteenth century newspapers and fiction publication is twofold. The first connection lies in the content of the papers. Until the post–Civil War push to run railroad and telegraph lines westward, communication on the frontier was slow and mainly word-of-mouth, so that newsworthy events tended to be reported long after the fact, and these reports depended on local witnesses and hearsayers whose accounts were often embellished beyond credence. Stan Steiner relates what an "old-timer" answered when asked why he told whoppers: "'Cows are pretty boring,' he said, 'if you don't exaggerate its tits a little bit'" (p. 31). Many newspapermen were of the same creative pioneering stock as their readers; storytellers rather than scholarly historians, they were not above improving on reality or adding a dash of bombast and sensationalism to enliven circulation. The West quickly became the Wild West, "newspapers of the time contribut[ing] to this myth of law-lessness, concentrating, as the media will, on minor actions involving warring gangs at Tombstone's O. K. Corral and illegal ambushes by sworn officers of small-time criminals like Billy the Kid in New Mexico and a series of garish but quite lawful hangings by Judge Isaac Parker at Fort Smith, Arkansas" (Estleman, pp. 18–19).

The second connection is with the displaced printers who did not head West, but remained in the Eastern cities. These printers, according to Sean Wilentz in his examination of the contemporary printing trade, frequently became artisan entrepreneurs, struggling alone or banding to-gether with friends to operate small, marginal shops (p. 131). Hustling to stay solvent, they were quick to see that an avid readership weaned on dramatic if sometimes dubious newspaper stories might prove to be a profitable market for "newspapers" devoted to short stories and chapters from serial novels. These fictional papers started in 1839 with the weekly *Brother Jonathan*, which was soon joined by competitors such as *The Flag of Our Union*, *The New York Ledger*, and *The Youth's Companion*. The next step was the publishing of serial novelettes in tabloid size, such as *The Weekly Novelette* and *Gleason's Literary Companion*, which sold for fifteen to twenty cents through the 1840s and 1850s.

As an outgrowth of newspapers, and catering to similar audiences, the fictional papers gained their readership by publishing stories that were more fanciful and romantic than newspaper accounts, yet written in the same odd mix of pithy and florid styles that passed for popular journalism. This trend culminated with the appearance of dime novels. These were the inspiration of Erastus and Irwin Beadle, who had been sufficiently heartened by the success of their pamphlet *The Dime Song Book* to take a chance on engaging a business associate named Robert Adams and together publishing a complete novel for a dime. In June

1860 the house of Beadle and Adams released *Malaeska: The Indian Wife of the White Hunter*, a tale of white hunters and noble savages by Ann S. Stephens. The book was about seven inches high and five inches wide, 128 pages long, printed on cheap pulp paper, and covered in equally cheap saffron-colored paper. Within a few months *Malaeska* sold 65,000 copies (Jones, p. 6). Encouraged, Beadle and Adams began a weekly series of "yellow-backed Beadles"—a somewhat derogatory moniker that despite the real color of their covers stuck to the novels—an expansion that required the hiring of more writers, who produced so many novels that by April 1, 1864, "an aggregate of five millions of Beadle's Dimes Books had been put into circulation" (Everett, p. 303). As direct descendants of fictional papers, "dime novels are best considered as an essentially anonymous, 'unauthored' discourse, not unlike journalism. Indeed, dime novels and newspapers are linked by more than the coincidence of new technologies and new reading publics. Many dime novelists were newspaper reporters and editors . . . [and] plots were often constructed out of the events reported in the daily and weekly newspapers of cities around the country" (Denning, p. 24).

Soon challenging Beadle were a host of publications such as *Dewitt's Ten Cent Romances, Richmond's Romances*, and Beadle's most formidable rival, *Monro's Ten Cent Novels*. Like Beadle, they issued yarns about pirates, detectives, and soldiers involved in adventure, war, or romance, although all other subjects combined did not equal the popularity of western frontier stories, which comprised "approximately three-fourths of the dime novels [of which] more than half are concerned with life in the trans-Mississippi West" (Durham, p. ix). At their height, Beadle and its competitors published concurrently as many as a hundred different series, with some series running to more than a thousand titles. Novels with an initial printing of sixty thousand to seventy thousand copies often went through ten or twelve editions annually. Their formats varied little; as Pearson notes in *Dime Novel*, the competitors "decide[d] to give Beadle and Adams their sincerest flattery"—to the extent that Dewitt's covers had the same saffron color, and Monro's first publication was named *New Dime Novels* with Irwin Beadle's name on the cover (pp. 83–85). Until their demise in the 1920s, dime novels were usually twenty-five to fifty thousand words long; covered in colored or hand-tinted paper and illustrated with sensationalized woodcuts; double-titled with semi-colon and comma, starting with Beadle No. 5, *The Golden Belt; or, The Carib's Pledge* (1860); issued weekly or semimonthly in sizes ranging from pocket pamphlets to tabloid magazines; and sold for a dime, although starting in the late 1860s some shorter editions sold for a nickel, and in the mid-1880s came lengthier stories selling as "twenty cent novels."

Their fundamental similarity was not accidental. It was through the dime novel that the concept of standardization in publishing and marketing was introduced and implemented. Providing lines of readily identifiable commodities that were frequently restocked allowed for profitable distribution nationwide. Indeed, whereas distribution before the Civil War was through many small firms often limited to a single city or county, distribution after 1864 to 1904 was controlled by one national giant, the American News Company, which held a virtual monopoly over the distribution of dime novels and similar cheap publications to outlets like newsstands and mercantiles (see Denning, p. 19; Schick, p. 103; and Stern, pp. 303–305). "What Beadle contributed was persistence, a more systematic devotion to the basic principles of business," Henry Nash Smith observes in *Virgin Land*. "The customer must be able to recognize the manufacturer's product by its uniform packaging— hence the various series with their characteristic formats. But a standard label is not enough; the product itself must be uniform and dependable" (p. 91).

The product was also uniformly mediocre. Churned out at thousands of handwritten words an hour, westerns were "written by authors whose nearest acquaintance with the great plains was in White Plains, New York" (Pearson, p. 105), authors who used innumerable pseudonyms like "Buckskin Sam" (Major Sam S. Hall), "Ned Buntline" (E. Z. G. Judson), and "Wyoming Bill" (Gilbert Patten, who had passed through Wyoming once on a train). Virtually all the accounts by and about dime novel writers emphasize their marathon sessions and volume of work: Albert Aiken "used to grind out dime novels day after day with the steadiness of a machine" (Jenks, p. 113); Mrs. Alex McVeigh Miller produced "thirty pages of longhand writing on foolscap paper" a week (Lewis, p. 3); and William Wallace Cook claims to have "written two thirty-thousand word stories a week for months at a time" (Lewis, p. 54).

Such grueling speed resulted in stories of conventional predictability that lacked in irony, metaphor, symbolism, or any figurative language that might extend or contradict the literal meaning of the words. Action began early in chapter one, when the courageous hero was introduced and instantly thrust into marrow-freezing danger. From there on, a series of perils in a chase-capture-escape (and sometimes further pursuit) pattern formed the basic plot structure, the action spiraling until the climactic and invariably happy ending. Writers propelled plots through miraculous coincidences, daredevil skirmishes, witless decisions by the characters, and wondrous powers of the protagonists—for example, readers swallowed with relish Old Grizzly of *Old Grizzly, the Bear-Tamer* (1876) taming and riding grizzly bears, unable to stop reading for the same reason that audiences cannot stop watching the magician sawing the lady in half. There has always been fascination with the fantastic. These farfetched adventures were third-person narratives, in highly descriptive and melodramatic prose no better and often worse than the yellow journalism and fictional papers that had sired the dime novel. The "Buckskin Sam" novel *Giant George, The Ang'l of the Range. A Tale of Sardine-Box, Arizona* illustrates dime novel writing done in little time and with little talent, as a buckskin-clad, rifle-toting mountain man, Giant George, drags his burro Don Diablo into a saloon while ranting:

> "Hoop-la! Set 'em up! Sling out yer p'ison before I stampede through yer hull business. I'm ther Bald-headed Eagle o' ther Rockies, an' are a-huntin' sum galoot what's got ther sand ter stomp on my tailfeathers. Shove out a bar'l o' bug-juice afore I bu'st up yer shebang; fer my feed-trough are chuck full o' cobwebs, an' as as dusty as Chalk Canyon. Hoop-la! Don't be bashful, Don Diablo! Don't you go fer ter go back on yer raisin'. An' yer needn't try ter shake up vim enuff ter stampede outen this, for yer hain't got ther muscle arter our long trail ter kick over a cotton-tail'd rabbit. Glid this-a-ways, an' we'll pour down a small decoction o' chain-lightnin' what'll make us feel kinder nat'ral-like." (Pearson, pp. 108–109)

Wretched writing from the overheated imaginations of second-rate hacks is no doubt the reason, at least in part, why critics have tended to dismiss dime novels and their role in western fiction. Some early reviewers, such as the one in the January 1845 issue of *Ladies' Repository*, rejected cheap fiction for being "prostituted to the gratification of the grossest sensuality," its object "the murder of time, the dissipation of the intellectual energies, and the corruption of the heart; whose tendency is to habituate the mind to a morbid excitement which totally unfits it for healthy and rational action" (Baym, pp. 59–60). More commonly reviewers deplored public taste, which itself was something new, for in prior ages taste had been the prerogative of the elite. In the *New York Review* (October 1837), a reviewer warned that Catharine Sedgewick's *Live and Let Live* "is precisely the book we should wish to keep out of the hands of a numerous class of servants" (Baym, p. 47). But the mid-nineteenth century was the era of Jacksonian America, with its belief in the resourcefulness and natural wisdom of the common man (and woman) who "need not defer to an elite corps of the educated" (Steffens, p. 18). Dime novels and other popular literature, catering solely to public taste, were expressions of this democratizing spirit. Besides, as Pearson quips, "Popular literature, and its enjoyment, is seldom the concern of the scholarly critic, until three or four centuries have passed. It is a social phenomenon rather than a matter of artistic achievement" (p. 17).

Around the turn of the century there was a brief flurry of interest in dime novels, mainly in articles like George C. Jenks's "Dime Novel Makers" (*The Bookman*, October 1904) and Charles M. Harvey's "The Dime Novel in American Life" (*Atlantic Monthly*, July 1907). In 1929 appeared Edmund Pearson's *Dime Novels; or, Following An Old Trail in Popular Literature*, a chatty, affectionate reminiscence about dime novels—the fairly typical treatment accorded dime novels until after World War II. An exception is "Dime Novels and the American Tradition" (*Yale Review*, Summer 1937), in which author Merle Curti argues in the Marxist tradition that dime novels are "true 'proletarian' literature" illustrative of class cleavages (p. 778). Merle's essay prompted more Marxist analyses of genre fiction, one of the most recent being Michael Denning's provocative *Mechanic Accents: Dime Novels and Working-Class Culture in America* (1987), a thoroughly researched albeit ideological study of "the ways classes are represented and the ways classes represent their world to themselves" through popular stories that "are best seen as a contested terrain, a field of cultural conflict" (p. 3).

A more balanced look at the dime western in historical context is Daryl Jones's *The Dime Novel Western* (1973), a complex and detailed survey whose major theme is that the dime western is "an important medium" because "in the setting, characters, and plots" its readers found "reassurance that the ideal world was still a golden possibility" (pp. 165–166). On occasion *The Dime Novel Western* seems to make rather grand, unsubstantiated claims, such as that "the hero's quest to reorder reality in terms of a personal vision of an ideal world becomes the axis of the Western's moral structure" (p. 138). Still, *The Dime Novel Western* has proven an invaluable source for this chapter, and I suspect that no subsequent study of the dime western can be entirely independent of it. A shorter if similar study of dime novels in terms of historical and cultural events is Philip Durham's "Dime Novels: An American Heritage" (*The Western Humanities Review*, Winter 1954–55). More indispensable for sheer information is Durham's listing of Beadle and Adams novels by subject matter, "A General Classification of 1,531 Dime Novels" (*Huntington Library Quarterly*, May 1954), as well as Albert Johannsen's three-volume history and bibliography of the Beadle and Adams operation, *The House of Beadle and Adams* (1950, 1962), and University Microfilm International's *Dime Novels: Popular American Escape Fiction of the Nineteenth Century* (1984), the first major microfilm collection of dime novels.

On the whole, however, recent discussions of dime westerns have tended to be buried within the context of other topics, often to the detriment of the dimes. For example, Douglas Branch's *The Cowboy and his Interpreters* (1926), Philip Durham and Everett L. Jones's *The Adventures of the Negro Cowboys* (1966), William A. Settle's *Jesse James Was His Name* (1966), and Kent Ladd Steckmesser's *The Western Hero in History and Legend* (1965) present the historically ascertainable facts about cowboys, outlaws like Billy the Kid, gunfighters like Wild Bill Hickok, and mountain men like Kit Carson, and then give accounts of the mythologizing that separates the legends from the historical reality. Dime westerns, Branch asserts, simply "glorified the exploits . . . and used the background of these gun-toting warriors" (p. 182), and according to Settle, most dime westerns "are works of fiction that merely took their cue from real persons and events" (p. 190). Richard Slotkin as well looks at historical figures such as Kit Carson and Jesse James in dime novels, concluding that "conflict and conquest, not patient labor and steady rise in status, are the dream story of success purveyed in the dime novel" (*Fatal Environment*, p. 206), which is in keeping with his thesis that American history is a singular one of regeneration through violence—a half-truth, particularly in case of dime westerns. For example, Slotkin claims that the hero of post–Civil War dime westerns "is no longer the vindicator of the 'genteel' values of order and respectability . . . [but] stands in actual opposition to the moral values embodied in the Cooperian mythology" (*Gunfighter Nation*, p. 127). To the contrary; although some heroes are unethical, the vast majority fight in defense of personal integrity and moral standards against lawless violence, corrupt law enforcement, and other shortcomings of their contemporary society. Even as a bandit operating outside the law, "the hero's rigorous observance of social proprieties affirmed the values of society" (Jones, p. 75). John Cawelti virtually ignores dime westerns in *Six-Gun Mystique* (1971), and devotes a mere four pages to them in *Adventure, Mystery, and Romance* (1976) as he traces the western from Cooper through Zane Grey to John Ford and the film industry. Other acclaimed critics, such as John R. Milton in *The Novel of the American West* (1980) and Henry Nash Smith in *Virgin Land: The American West as Symbol and Myth* (1950), contrast the dime western with their main subject, novels set in the West and Southwest that tend to be termed "regional" or "realistic" or "serious," but surely not western. "I find it necessary to criticize the lack of literary quality in the standard western," Milton states, "in order to draw distinctions between this one kind of novel of the West and another kind which is a much higher form of art" (p. viii).

In dismissing dime westerns, and in ignoring their influence on western fiction and even on American literature, the critics sound strikingly similar. Cawelti: "During the heyday of the dime novel the western developed primarily as a form of adolescent escapism . . . and became primarily a fictional embodiment of fantasies of transcendent heroism overcoming evil figures of authority" (pp. 213, 215). Branch: "The West of the dime novels became a lurid background across which flamboyant caricatures stalked to shoot and be shot. . . . Facile stuff, perhaps, naive hero worship for bookkeepers and small boys" (pp. 182, 188). Milton: "[T]he purpose of the dime novel was not to portray the West or its people accurately and honestly but to provide the exaggeration and sensationalism which would appeal to the emotions and the sense of adventure of the mass audience," although Milton grudgingly allows that "the impact upon the nation's readers . . . was greater than we now care to admit as we attempt to find some redeeming grace in the modern western" (pp. 11, 10). Smith: "The unabashed and systematic use of formulas strips from [dime novel] writing every vestige of the interest usually sought in works of the imagination; it is entirely subliterary. . . . The Western story lost whatever chance it might once have had to develop social significance" (pp. 91, 119).

As simple and melodramatic as the dime western most certainly was, sales volume alone refutes the suggestion that its audience was confined to juveniles or juvenile adults of the ilk described by Don Marquis when he advised, "write the sort of thing that's read by persons who move their lips when they're reading to themselves" (Winokur, p. 14). The more comprehensive histories of the dime western, such as those by Pearson and Jones, relate at length how, "though dime novelists aimed their stories at the predominantly working-class audience, the appeal of the genre in fact pervaded the entire culture. Dime novels provided a source of entertainment and diversion for any individual of any social class who sought relief from the anxieties of the age" (Jones, p. 14). I would amend this slightly to say that along with relaxation and diversion, the draw of the dimes lay in tension—that men and women leading lives of quiet desperation turned to stories that told them about fictional characters leading lives of noisy desperation. My contention is that dime novelists, sensitive to the needs of a mass audience, intended not to write accurate representations of their readers' lives, but rather to address the concerns and aspirations of the day by reflecting their readers' images of reality—including the images of the creatures their readers wished they could have been—and that in the process, gradually over sixty years, they formulated many of the elements most characteristic of westerns. Thus the early dime westerns addressed the exploration of nature and the tensions inherent in the duality of wilderness versus civilization. During the last quarter of the nineteenth century, the wilderness and the threats of Indians and outlaws had lessened to the point where American attitudes toward the frontier underwent significant change. Consequently, there emerged in dime westerns different heroes—miners, railroaders, gunfighters, cowboys—confronting social issues and the tensions inherent in the duality of community versus the individual. In effect the dime western's transformation of characters and conflicts that continue to dominate westerns to this day reflects America's process of redefining values and pondering fresh interpretations of the past, a debate that has not diminished for more than a century.

That dime novelists were quick to reflect shifting social attitudes is evident in the way they early on resolved the duality of wilderness and civilization. The first dime novelist, Ann S. Stephens, composed *Malaeska* firmly in the manner of Cooper, drawing not only a Natty Bumppo protagonist, but also evoking the Leatherstocking vision of a sublime nature in which one communed with God and dealt with Noble Indians. "The traveller who has stopped at Catskill, on his way up the Hudson, will remember that a creek of no insignificance washes one side of the village" (p. 1) is her lyric opening, and not until page 10 is peace shattered: "Touch but a hair of her head, and by the Lord that made me, I will bespatter that tree with your brains!" Suggesting a mythology of exploration in an unsullied wilderness, such a view was powerful and appealing.

However, Stevens's glorification of the wilderness came at the very time when this landscape was rapidly being destroyed by the expanding ruralization of the East and increasing migration to the West. Within the same year appeared Edward S. Ellis's *Seth Jones; or, the Captives of the Frontier*, No. 8 in the original series—coming only seven novels after *Malaeska*—which better captured the current spirit of Jacksonian America by presenting nature as a reluctant contributor to civilization, a physical and moral challenge to be cultivated and utilized by the common man and woman. Ellis set his story back in Revolutionary times, where despite a remote location in western New York, "the rich virgin soil had been broken, and was giving signs of the exhaustless wealth it retained in its bosom, waiting only for the hand of man to bring it forth" (p. 6). As Daryl Jones points out, Ellis's attitude toward the wilderness causes the heroic acts in the book to become "an integral part of a grand historical process in which mankind is moving irrepressibly westward, conquering the wilderness and raising in its place a thriving civilization" (p. 19). Striking a responsive chord in the public far more than had *Malaeska*, *Seth Jones* sold out its initial printing of sixty thousand copies almost immediately, was translated into six languages, and ultimately sold over 600,000 copies (Harvey, p. 40).

Over the next five years, the resolution expressed in *Seth Jones* shifted profoundly. Instead of nature's being a resource for civilization, now nature is hell. The wilderness is "marred by the presence of savages; and blood stains the face of nature!" exclaims Quindaro in *Quindaro; or, the Heroine of Fort Laramie* (1865). "It appears as if the dark demon, which reigns within man's heart, must manifest itself everywhere—everywhere!" (Jones, p. 22). *Quindaro* is typical of the dime westerns issued during the next decade. Of course, dime novelists continued writing plenty of westerns in which nature is portrayed as benevolent or beneficial or even utopian, such as Rose Kennedy's *Myrtle, the Child of the Prairie* (1860); but the dominant theme was that of the extermination of wild Nature and its denizens, a reversion to the Puritan view of the wilderness as God's test to prepare Christians spiritually for salvation. It was the dime novelists' response to the prevalent belief of the day that the wilderness indeed was hell on earth.

This thematic story continued beyond the Civil War and the first wave of dime westerns, and for good reason: by 1865, most of the blank spaces on maps of America had been filled in, particularly along both coasts, and the only remaining region that could qualify as wilderness was the Great Plains, whose limitless prairies and hostile deserts stretched vast, flat, and arid to the horizon, beggaring the eighteenth- and nineteenth-century imaginations. Many prominent citizens and officials voiced the conviction that the plains were uninhabitable by civilized folk—for example, John Charles Frémont, writing in the *Southern Quarterly Review* in 1849, claims that the plains could be home only for trappers, miners, and "those whom misanthropy or outlawry might lead into the remote desert" (p. 84); and Lieutenant Gouverneur Kemble Warren declared in the late 1850s that "the people now on the extreme frontiers of Nebraska . . . are, as it were, upon the shore of a sea, up to which population and agriculture may advance, and no further" (Smith, p. 178). Elmer Kelton reports, "Old maps usually show the high plains only as 'desert.' One I have seen in archives has a single word inscribed across the top of the entire region: 'Comanches'" (p. 7). It is to be expected, then, that fictional depictions mirrored the public's perception of the plains. For example, "As desolate a scene as could well be imagined in that lonely region, the prairies of the Far West," runs a description in *Sib Cone, The Mountain Trapper* (1870). "As far as the eye could reach, nothing was to be seen but a dry and barren plain. . . . Silence and desolation seemed there to reign together" (Jones, p. 128).

The plains were made a hell not only by the terrain, but also by the natives. Immigrants crossing the prairie and settlers inhabiting the more fertile borderlands were encountering the Plains Indians, who were far more nomadic and brutal to captives than the Eastern woodland tribes. In a century of conquest before 1850, the Cheyenne, Blackfeet, and other Algonquian-speaking tribes had pushed westward and southward until they claimed a territory twice the size of New England, extending from the North Saskatchewan River southward to present Yellowstone Park, and from the Rockies eastward over the plains to the mouth of Milk River, Montana. Neighboring Indians fiercely resisted the Algonquian invasion of their hunting grounds; in particular, the Sioux not only repelled the invaders but also kept advancing westward, northward, and southward until they had taken over practically all the northern Plains. Similarly, in the Southwest the Apache and the Navajo were feared and hated by other desert tribes, whom they routinely attacked (see Divine, pp. 285–290; Kelley, pp. 393–396; and Paul 128–138, among others).

Consequently, the westerners of the 1860s and 1870s found themselves confronting seasoned mounted warriors, whose ability to live off that parched country was matched by their military tactics of stealth and surprise and their effective use of the harsh natural environment. "They made devastating raids on way stations, isolated farms, and unwary travelers, and usually their murder and pillage were completed and the perpetrators gone before the nearest contingent of troops could be sent on a futile chase after them" (Paul, p. 48). Even then the Sioux continued expanding their hunting grounds at the expense of the Crow, Pawnee, and other tribes—which is why Indians from these tribes helped the American troops in their battles with the Sioux—and "modern anthropologists have concluded that in all probability whites killed fewer Indians than were killed by other Indians in intertribal war" (Paul, p. 129). A saving grace for those Americans, in fact, was that the Indians were so busy fighting one another that they never put up a coordinated, sustained campaign against the whites.

It stands to reason that those losing family and friends to Indian attacks were scarcely ready to defend the image of the Noble Savage, and that under the circumstances the national mood turned by and large anti-Indian. "The people of the Western border, the plains and the Pacific Coast," *Oregonian* editor Harvey W. Scott wrote in 1867, "have learned something of the inborn perfidity and fiendish . . . villainy perpetrated by redskins incapable of good faith and knowing no law but that of fear and savage hate" (pp. 102, 119). Scott also quotes a Colorado militia major's testimony before an investigating commission: "I think and earnestly believe the Indians to be an obstacle to civilization, and should be exterminated" (Appendix, p. 70). Accordingly, as accurate reflections of the flavor, attitudes, and passions of the times, the dime-western portrayal of Indians shifted to that of vicious, superstitious, and innately wicked primitives not much past the hunter-gatherer stage of existence. In *Quindaro*, for example, chief villain Wontum sports "brows black as midnight," "snake-like eyes," and the nickname "The Evil One," and is pursued by Quindaro, who admits he will not "cease my work until the accursed race has been blotted from existence" (Jones, pp. 140, 31). Appealing to the prevailing climate were typical titles such as Thomas Harbough's *Kiowa Charley, the White Mustanger; or, Rocky Mountain Kit's Last Scalp Hunt* (1879) and Lewis W. Carson's [Albert Aiken's] *White Slayer, the Avenger; or, The Doomed Red-skins* (1870)—in which the protagonist has "abandoned all else for the destruction of the red man" (Jones, p. 31). Indian warfare was the customary conflict, depicted as grouped assaults on unsuspecting wayfarers or vulnerable encampments of one sort or another, or as skirmishes at box canyons or water holes or similar isolated, somewhat enclosed spots on the otherwise open prairie. Especially favored were ambushes: in an unnamed dime novel quoted at length by Pearson, its star "Deadly-Eye, the Unknown Scout,"

> was seen to suddenly raise his repeating rifle; a quick aim, a shout, and a painted warrior fell from his horse, and a yell of exultation from the emigrants was answered by a series of wild war-whoops from the infuriated Indians.
> "Now, Major Conrad, you see that I know yonder renegade guide [Red Dog] well, for he is doubtless the leader of the approaching band of red-skins, and was guiding you into a trap." (pp. 119–120)

A consequence of tarring Indians with one big brush and crowding them into action-oriented stories as so much gun-fodder was to make them appear vague and generalized rather than detailed and personal—to diminish them from individuals to token presences. The fictional Indian, as Gaile McGregor points out, came to be presented "with neither the profound simplicity of myth nor the subtle complexity of symbolic resonance to intimate that anything at all existed beneath the surface of his stereotyped role. In popular fiction as in the field of serious literature, the Indian as a locus of real emotion to all intents and purposes finally disappeared" (p. 210).

Reducing characterization to the lowest common stereotype was not confined solely to the Indian. Every character in the dime novel is "clothes upon sticks" moving unswervingly through the action on predictable courses, with only minor variations of a few recurring traits. Thus with the villainous Indians run villainous half-breeds and white renegades who combine, in the words of one dime novelist, "the worst passions of both races, without the slightest of their virtues" (Jones, p. 142). Allied with them are uncouth scoundrels of every ilk—thieves, arsonists, swindlers, bushwhackers—who strive for power and wealth through dirty practices like murder, kidnapping, and spreading malicious gossip, and who mistreat women and kill their husbands, making them widows and their children orphans, and who lust wantonly after innocent maidens—as can be expected from pockmarked, knife-scarred ruffians whose "beards and hair were long, scraggy and greasy. Their raiment was worn and filthy, and their language vile and profane" (Thomas D. Clark, p. 12). Villains are invariably called "beasts" by the heroines, these "paragons of beauty and virtue" with names like Isabelle Fearnaught and Edith Van Payne, who do not "wear cosmetics and endeavor to bolster flattened figures with false stuffing" (Thomas D. Clark, p. 12). Their fastidious charms incite nary a twinge of lechery in the heroes—now known as "plainsmen"—whose sensory abilities like those of backwoodsmen and mountain men are otherwise acute: "His hearing was superb, he could smell to perfection, sense his way in the dark . . . knew geographical situations by instinct, could see the north star while lying flat on his back in a tangled canebreak, use a knife with dexterity and swim the Mississippi River with as much facility as the average heavy-footed settler could jump a spring branch" (Thomas D. Clark,

p. 13). But all heroes suffer from terminal cases of pedestalism. Able to vanquish any man alive, they show inordinate deference to all women, even fallen women, and become sodden at the sight of heroines:

> If a form to which nothing could be added or aught taken away without marring its perfection, if a face whose complexion was so transparent, so blended with the lily and the rose, that even the envious man could not tarnish its loveliness—if eyes darkly, beautifully blue and liquid as a violet's in the dewy-morn—if hair like sunbeams twisted into waving golden curls, could constitute beauty, then was Migionette very beautiful. (*Red Ralph, the Ranger; or, The Brother's Revenge,* quoted in Pearson, pp. 115–116)

The notorious virtue of heroes leads to fisticuffs at the drop of a leer, and to Herculean efforts to rescue heroines from fates worse than death. This was the one area where "the Indians were, all of them, gentlemen. A thousand paleface damsels were captured by red-skinned warriors, during the progress of the dime novel, and some of them may have suffered death or grievous torment. But not one of them, Heaven be praised, ever came through the experience otherwise than as *virgo intacta*" (Pearson, p. 37).

In addition to heroes, heroines, and villains, other characters would include "chums" of the heroes, "cronies" of the villains, assorted bystanders as needed to move the plot along, and the scorned butt of dime novel humor, the Eastern Dude. "In far western regions, men are said to have become almost speechless with rage at the creatures . . . mutter[ing] threats to shoot these vermin on sight" (Pearson, p. 135). A variation of the Dude appeared soon after the plains began to be used for story settings: the inexperienced young tenderfoot, whom the older and wiser hero would befriend and wean from Eastern decadence to the healthier natural values of the West. A typical story is *Irona; or, Life on the Old South-West Border* (1861), in which handsome, genteel Ross Wellend first loses the heroine Irona Seraville to kidnapping Comanches, then loses his way on the plains, only to show up at the climax to get what he deserves: the heroine. Rescuing Irona are Ned Nuggens and John Smith, both irascible, dialect-speaking plainsmen who are venerable enough, and thus skilled enough, to carry the action of capture and pursuit.

However, heroes like Nuggens and Smith are too old to carry the love interest in an era of virginal heroines. Indeed, the reclusive nature of fictional backwoodsmen, mountain men, and plainsmen dooms them to bachelorhood, which forced dime writers to incorporate romance either through secondary heroes like Ross Wellend or through disguise and sudden character reversal—convoluted maneuvers at best. Moreover, civilization was fast encroaching on the last pockets of wilderness, making the Leatherstocking hunter-scout an increasingly endangered species. The obvious answer was to merge the experience and resourcefulness of the elder plainsman with the respectability and eligibility of the younger dude, a natural unification that happened only after external, cultural dynamics influenced the direction of the dime western.

As before with fur trapping, the initial change occurred in the Far West. This time mining created a national stir close to a frenzy, as prospectors were drawn in a gold rush first to California, then eastward and northward as gold and silver were discovered in what are now Nevada, Colorado, Idaho, and Montana, regions formerly inhabited only by Indians and fur traders. "Colorado and Nevada, for example, had no significant white population before 1859, yet even the census of 1860 and 1870, which caught only a fraction of this mobile and impermanent crowd, credited Colorado with more than 34,000 in 1860 and nearly 40,000 in 1870, while Nevada had nearly 7,000 at the former date and 42,500 at the latter. Idaho and Montana, with virtually no white populations in 1860, had 15,000 and 20,500, respectively, in 1870" (Paul, p. 46).

Dime westerns capitalized with yarns involving fabulous strikes, boom conditions, and bizarre characters, as in *Dandy Rock, The Man From Texas; or, A Wild Romance of the Land of Gold* (1874). Unlike their predecessors, the dime westerns about mining are usually set in the vicinity of mines, boomtowns, and similar frontier settlements. For example, all thirty-three of Edward L. Wheeler's Deadwood Dick series take place in and around mining camps or hastily erected hamlets. Indeed, it was awkward—and hence to be avoided—to write mining stories without a community setting, because mining was the most specialized of frontiers and consequently the least self-sufficient. The mines required not only professional miners but also surface workers, mechanics, ironmongers, and bookkeepers, who in turn attracted proprietors of stores, boardinghouses, restaurants, saloons, and livery stables, all of whom were dependent on freight outfits to deliver food, clothing, tools, machinery, and such necessities as cigars and smoked oysters. Moreover, in spite of, or perhaps because of, the tendency of boomtowns to become ghost towns as strikes petered out, the residents seemed to want community—community, that is, not as a specific place but as a concept, a spirit forged by trust among people. "They were known to collect town libraries of fiction, poetry, science, and reference works. They quickly organized chapters of their old fraternal lodges—notably Masons, Odd Fellows, and the Knights of Pythias—institutions that carried from home the echoes of a summer ball game and a band on the Fourth of July" (Hine, p. 80). Such community cannot be built by people trying to make up their minds whether to belong or to keep their bags packed and ready. Community demands commitment, a willingness to stick together and work on problems when they arise. Accordingly, the tensions and conflicts that occur between an individual and the community are social, virtually opposite from the struggles of an individual challenging the wilderness. In response, writers of mining stories began replacing plots about survival in nature with plots about survival in society, shifting from the duality of civilization and the wilderness to the duality of community and the individual.

For instance, the most pressing problem in mining communities was probably that of law and order, especially in its pragmatic if not always legalistic application. "The social contract was pared to the bare bones. Nuances and complexities that dwell in custom, like the 'frills' of due process and procedures of appeal in the law, were swept aside to grapple with the needs of the cabins and hills. In the bitter barrenness of the Yukon, for example, the theft of food brought automatic banishment into the deadly cold" (Hine, p. 80). Perhaps more refractive than reflective of reality, Deadwood Dick wreaks revenge on the swindlers Alexander and Clarence Filmore in *Deadwood Dick, Prince of the Road; or, The Black Rider of the Black Hills* (1877); establishes law and justice in the boomtown of Eureka in *The Phantom Miner; or, Deadwood Dick's Bonanza* (1878); rids the mining camp of Whoop-Up of crooked speculators and politicians in *Deadwood Dick on Deck; or, Calamity Jane, the Heroine of Whoop-Up* (1878); thwarts the corrupt scheme of a "purse-proud aristocrat" in *Deadwood Dick of Deadwood; or, The Picked Party* (1878); and perhaps in the most socially oriented of the series, *The Black Hills Jezebel; or Deadwood Dick's Ward* (1880), Deadwood gets entangled with pretty Kate Girard and her jealousy-crazed hunchback father as they seek her mother, so-called "Madam Cheviot," before the evil woman can remarry illegally for a second time.

Non-dime novelists like Bret Harte were also recording the West as a place of settlement rather than a wild frontier. The loyalty necessary to maintain community is magnified in Harte's ironic short story "Tennessee's Partner" (1875), in which Tennessee's mining partner is so faithful that he forgives Tennessee for absconding with his wife, attempts to bribe a judge when Tennessee is apprehended for banditry, and finally pines to death after Tennessee is hanged. Another problem common to mining communities was balancing less desirable elements such as gambling and prostitution with the concerted efforts of many citizens to ensure stable community development. Thus in Harte's "The Outcasts of Poker Flats" (1868), a gambler exiled from town vainly sacrifices his life for fellow outcasts, and a virgin clasps a dying whore in a cleansing snowfall. Similarly, in "The Luck of Roaring Camp" (1868), Harte tells of miners rearing the orphan child of Cherokee Sal, a camp follower who dies in childbirth, the miners' communal decision resulting in enormous prosperity until the child drowns in a winter flood. As tragic and bordering on bathos as "Luck" may be, it illustrates how Harte became one of the most popular American writers for a few years, providing just what his readers wanted by implying "that goodness is inherent and that it can be revived (when necessary) or regenerated by a life in the West, that is to say a life away from the stifling influences of the city and the artificialities of a highly organized society" (Milton, p. 13). In fact, the rousing acceptance of Harte's stories is an early indication that the public perception of nature as a desert was beginning to become tempered by a renewed vision of nature as a garden. Moreover, his view that the West could purify humanity and cure inclinations toward evil is certainly reminiscent of John Filsen's and James Fenimore Cooper's pastoral images, and predictive of the romantic approaches to nature taken by later dime novels and the westerns of Owen Wister and Zane Grey.

From mining operations arose a second factor contributing to the alteration of western themes. Because the major supply bases for miners were far west in California or farther east on the Missouri River, the successive booms and busts during the 1860s and early 1870s caused a massive growth in freight haulage, which created more friction between the Indians and the white intruders, which led to an increase in military and other government freight traffic. "With a veritable army of professional freighters plodding across the plains in the 1860s, with amateur trains of would-be settlers or miners marching beside them, and with road ranches and Army posts at intervals, the once empty expanses of the interior were well into a change of far-reaching importance" (Paul, p. 55). The importance of this lay in the inevitable pressures toward expansion brought on by the systematic penetration by overland trade and efforts to inhabit the plains.

The settlers were mostly homesteading farmers who perceived the prairie less as an infernal desert than as a potential garden. They were a different breed from the miners, for while they felt a strong communal bond, it was one in which individualism was allowed but nonconformity was ostracized, providing a peculiar common tie which historian Carl Becker terms the "individualism of conformity" (p. 9). Cultivating the plains required cooperative ventures to complete large tasks such as clearing acreage, raising barns, and threshing before the rains, thus spawning a sense of community and egalitarianism. Families were more crucial for farming than they were for mining, and whereas in 1870 the farming population of Wyoming and other plains territories was 80 percent male, by 1880 the population was 30 to 40 percent female, which in turn made children less of a rarity (see Dinnerstein and Reimers; Luebke; and Wright). Although shared hardships, blurred class consciousness, and extended families provided community, apparently the isolation of the farms and holiday rivalries between the families fostered competition and individualism. "There is no paucity of evidence for individualism. When John McConnel, for example, distilled from his lifetime on the Illinois prairie a composite pioneer settler, his figure was not cooperative but proud and solitary. This farmer might welcome a stranger, but he would not want him to stay long. 'It was but little assistance that he ever required from his neighbors, though no man was ever more willing to render it to others in the hour of need'" (Hine, p. 119).

Keeping pace with changing public taste, dime writers in the mid-1870s began revising the increasingly anachronistic Leatherstocking persona into a more appealing, more civilized hero who is youthful, eligible, physically attractive, and naturally noble. A Westerner in heart if not by birth, he is a self-made man of inner resources and stubborn individualism who rejects the class strictures of the East in favor of the Jacksonian belief that perseverance and integrity produce success. "Consequently, the rise of the Western hero satisfied, if only in fantasy, the increasingly strident popular cry for a homogeneous social order in which the status of the individual depended not on artificial class distinctions but rather on the individual's innate worth as a human being" (Jones, p. 47). Now more educated, he speaks more politely, correctly, and succinctly, and behaves with reserve, both conventions helping to set the hero apart from other characters whose lack of restraint indicates weakness. "Talking too much or laughing too easily or expressing fear too readily are more than mere signs of bad form; they reveal a general inability to maintain composure under the pressure of vivid sensationalism" (Mitchell, p. 166). This charismatic dime western hero is the sire of Owen Wister's soft-spoken Virginian, of Gary Cooper's laconic Marshal Kane, and of just about every protagonist played by John Wayne; and almost always he fights for Carl Becker's "individualism of conformity" as depicted by Western communities.

In reality, of course, community exists as much in the East as in the West, as much in tenement neighborhoods as in prairie junctions. But starting with dime westerns, community in western fiction has been portrayed as limited in locale, vulnerably isolated in perilous surroundings —such as remote settlements, military outposts, or wagon trains of immigrants—and it has represented the traditional values of American society. Besieging community interests are savage forces from the wilderness, such as renegades and outlaws, or corrupt forces from the decadent East, such as bankers and lawyers. Towns may be taken over, Army forts may be burned down, or wagon trains may be massacred, but the spirit of community introduced in the dimes has continued to flourish to this day as the good for which the western hero battles.

Personifying the western hero's transformation are the fictional characterizations of Kit Carson and Davy Crockett. The reputation of Carson as a scout and Indian fighter was established long before the legendary Carson first appeared in a bit part in Emerson Bennett's *The Prairie Flower* (1849). He became a heroic protagonist later that year in

Charles A. Averill's *Kit Carson, The Prince of Gold Hunters*, but in contrast to the actual historical figure, Carson is depicted as a plainsman "half-Indian, half whiteman in appearance, with rifle, horse and dog for his sole companions" (pp. 57–58)—the Leatherstocking figure shorn of his gentility and philosophical qualities, not to mention Cooper's literary abilities. By the 1880s, though, Carson came to be portrayed as young and virile, as in *Kit Carson, the Border Boy* (n.d.) and *Kit Carson, The Young Hunter* (n.d.) by "C. Leon Meredith" (George Blackeless), and *The Fighting Trapper; or Kit Carson to the Rescue* (1879) by James F. C. Adams; and Carson even gets married in *Kit Carson's Bride; or, The White Flower of the Apaches* (n.d.) by George L. Aiken. Similarly, the fictional Davy Crockett begins as a bear-wrestling braggart in *Kill-bar, the Guide; or, The Long Trail* (1869), and continues as uncivilized as the prairie he roams in *The Texan Trailer; or, Davy Crockett's Last Bear Hunt* (1871). "I've been hugged before, and I've no doubt such a good-looking gal as you have been hugged, too," he leers at *Texan Trailer's* naïve heroine. "If I haven't a blue-eyed little wife, down in Tennessee, I'd be tempted to play the bear with you" (Jones, p. 44). In 1873, however, Crockett is portrayed as a polite and even religious young hero in *The Bear-Hunter; or Davy Crockett as a Spy*, and then as a gallant master tracker in *Daring Davy, the Young Bear Killer; or, The Trail of the Border Wolf* (1879), in which he weds Rosebud Thornton, one of two damsels who each swoon over Crockett as "my idol, my king" (Jones, p. 45).

The mid-1870s brought transformations in heroines as well. To be sure, the angelic heroine buffeted by cruel fate and crueler men continued to thrive in dime westerns, just as the gruff, dialect-drawling old plainsman persisted as a protagonist. But the rapidly swelling population of pioneer women, in particular the wives and mothers who were helping to settle the prairie, began to undermine the Victorian stereotype of feminine delicacy and frailty. After all, if frontier life required men to be tough and self-reliant, it required women who could match the men. For example, author Joan Didion's great-great-grandmother Elizabeth Anthony Reese headed west "on a wagon journey during which she buried one child, gave birth to another, twice contracted mountain fever, and took turns handling and driving a yoke of oxen, a span of mules, and twenty-two head of loose stock" (p. 10). Many of the oxen drivers on wagon trains were women, and Stan Steiner records that some of them later became freight teamsters and stagecoach drivers. One, an ex-slave named Mary Fields, became not only a teamster but a pony express rider in Montana in 1880 (p. 86). Another woman, Mrs. E. J. "Mountain Charley" Guerin, was a second lieutenant in the Civil War (pp. 85–86), then a fur trapper, a saloon owner, and a prospector with her children in California. "In Colorado, the old saying was that pioneer women guarded the homestead, raised the crops, managed the livestock, taught the children, fed the family and stood guard with their rifles, while the men were out on the range moving a fencepost from one place to another" (p. 87). In fact, so tough was the average frontier woman "that many men might have been intimidated by the boldness and prowess of [her] new style of femininity, which was as uniquely and distinctively Western as the men" (pp. 85–86).

Newspaper and weekly tabloid articles on and by pioneering women garnered a growing audience, and "the editorials and broadsides that urged and cajoled women to come West were aimed at down-to-earth women whose heroism was practical: Send us women who have the strength of Indian women and the skills of white women. *The Laramie Boomerang*, in Wyoming, described the kind of women the frontiersmen wished for: 'Wyoming wants women, and wants them bad. But there is no very clamourous demand for sentimental fossils" (Steiner, pp. 86–87). Pioneering women's published journals, diaries, and (auto)biographies gained ready acceptance, as did stories of notorious women like Calamity Jane, horse thief Belle Starr, and Confederate spy Belle Boyd, whose autobiography *Belle Boyd in Camp and Prison* (1865) is a vivid memoir of her Civil War years. An avid public also followed the careers of performers like Lone Star May and Annie Oakley, who could shoot glass balls as fast as they could be tossed in the air, and rodeo rider Lucille Mulhall, who could rope eight galloping horses with one throw of her lariat.

Naturally, dime novelists, acutely sensitive to the demands of readers, sought to fashion women characters whose traits would better suit the changing trends and perceptions. Duplicating their success with fictionalized versions of Boone, Carson, and Crockett, writers began creating westerns that headlined actual well-known women like Annie Oakley, Belle Starr, and Calamity Jane, the exploits attributed to them pure hokum but often sprinkled with just enough facts to lend them credibility. Women of sterling reputation like Annie Oakley were portrayed as the equal of men yet ever the lady in the thick of adventure, only the most dastardly of villains daring to patronize or belittle them. Those of poorer repute like Calamity Jane behaved more in the manner of backwoods braggarts like the Davy Crockett of *Kill-bar*. In *Deadwood Dick on Deck; or Calamity Jane, the Heroine of Whoop-up*, Calamity Jane gallops into Whoop-Up "lighting a cigar at full motion," while giving "a ringing whoop, which was creditable in imitation if not volume and force to that of a full-blown Comanche warrior," heedless of her open shirt that exposes "a breast of alabaster purity" (p. 4). Writers were also introducing totally fabricated heroines with names like Hurricane Nell and Klondike Kit, who match their fictionalized counterparts in daring and adventure, and range from virtuous (Annie Oakley) to rough-cut (Calamity Jane). Frequently they were cast in the role of rescuers of men, like the "character known as Mysterious Ike; a masked person, who afterwards turned out to be a woman in love with Jesse James; this masked person always turned up in the nick of time, to show Jesse and Frank a short cut through the woods, or an underground passage" (Pearson, p. 244). Such heroines understand the necessity at times for righteous violence to rescue the hero from unrighteous violence, like Mountain Kate in Joseph E. Badger's *Mountain Kate; or, Love in the Trappings Grounds* (1872), who protects the hero by shooting his treacherous companions, her aim unerring, her "stately thumb and forefinger work[ing] like magic" (p. 94), or like the spitfire Carmela in Badger's *Mustang Sam, the King of the Plains* (1874), who downs a backstabber, then stands before the hero, "her face aglow, a still smoking revolver clasped in her right hand. Her aim had saved the scout's life" (Pearson, p. 113).

The more virtuous heroines, aside from series characters such as Annie Oakley, usually wind up marrying the hero. Not that their central concern at the beginning is love, marriage, and family, but the issues of sexuality and passion in "decent" women are successfully disguised in dime westerns with the more respectable and mentionable values of loyalty and social order. Hence, a favorite form of rescue—one that has since become a cliched staple of westerns—involves the virtuous heroine nursing a wounded, injured, or sick hero back to health, which provides a providential way for their romance to bloom, especially if the disabled hero has been acting the proud stoic, undaunted by pleasure or pain. Their roles are reversed, in essence, for in order for the hero "to rediscover his humanity, the 'woman's man' must find out how it feels to be a woman" (Showalter, p. 152). In Philip S. Warne's *A Hard Crowd; or, Gentleman Sam's Sister* (1878), for instance, perky heroine Iola maternally tends the gunshot hero while he in the subordinate position learns to be tender and sensitive to her feelings, until love sets in: "Unconsciously she yielded to the persuasive clasp of his arms . . . let her arms glide about his neck, as was most natural that she should, and clasped him closer and closer until their lips met" (p. 16).

The wilder heroines rarely catch the hero. They yearn for him, of course, even flirt brazenly with him at times, but deep down they realize that their checkered pasts and presents have tarnished their futures. Calamity Jane in *Whoop-Up* is considered unmarriagable (p. 31), and she herself remarks about a local vamp, blithely oblivious to the irony of her comment, that "life here in the Hills has—well, has ruined her prospects, one might say, for she has grown reckless in act and rough in language" (p. 13). Indeed, sexually aggressive heroines tend to resemble the promiscuous villainesses who populate dime westerns. Their seductions are uniformly rejected by the hero, and though the loose heroine is apt to rescue the hero through some act of redemptive valor, while the villainess joins forces with the villain to plot vengeance against the hero, in the end they usually die by the villain's hand or their own, or else endure an existence of public scorn and repudiation. For example, in Joseph E. Badger's *The Forest Princess; or, the Kickapoo Captives, a Romance of the Illinois* (1871), Aneola is a white girl reared by the Indians and free in her ways, but after the hero refuses to marry her despite threats of death, she flings herself off a nearby cliff.

Toward the end of the 1870s, an intriguing blend of the loose heroine and the hardened villainess appeared in the guise of the female bandit. For example, in William H. Manning's *Lady Jaguar, The Robber Queen; or, A Romance of the Black Chaparral* (1882), wounded hero Don Edgar meets Lady Jaguar, who is "clad in a plain but becoming costume, while a mask of unusual size concealed her whole face except for the dark, handsome eyes, which he felt sure were in keeping with her whole face." Lady Jaguar is scarcely the nursing type; when Don Edgar rises gentlemanly, she snaps, "Retain your seat, Don Edgar. If you would speedily recover from your wound, you must be discreet" (Pearson, p. 125). Embittered, the victim of false arrest, she has been driven outside civil law but nonetheless respects and even champions the natural law of justice and virtue. When she cattily alludes to another lady and Don Edgar reproaches her, Lady Jaguar reacts to his umbrage with honest if overwrought contrition:

> The robber queen shrunk under his touch and before his passion like a dying woman. Her strength seemed all gone, her breath came gaspingly, her bosom heaved, and only for his frenzy, Edgar would have been alarmed.
>   As it was, her emotion seemed to him more like the alarm of guilt . . . (Pearson, p. 127)

Male as well as female bandit protagonists, starkly drawn in stories emphasizing the duality of civil law versus natural law, proved so instantaneously and extraordinarily popular that sales "stunned even the publishers" (Jones, p. 76). Their mass-market success can be tied to dime writers' once again responding, if only intuitively, to changing cultural conditions. The last quarter of the nineteenth century was a time of rapid transition, in which the West, like the nation as a whole, moved swiftly from the age of merchant capitalism into an era of industrial and finance capitalism and business specialization. In mining, the romantic prospector with his battered hat and sluicebox was being displaced by factorylike corporations managed by eastern-trained engineers. The pioneer farms on the plains were being absorbed into consolidated, absentee-owned grain and livestock operations. The haphazard network of freight outfits and stagecoach lines was falling prey not only to railroad expansion but also to assimilation by Wells Fargo into a single transportation giant. While the railroads were laying tracks, they were founding company-ruled towns, reaching out to the sides to seize coal and timber resources, and regulating rates and routes through distant, centralized bureaucracies. The economy was no longer composed of thousands of small producers who sold to local markets, but was becoming dominated by a small number of monopolistic organizations like United Fruit and United States Steel, and by vertically integrated trusts like Standard Oil, which owned or controlled every step from extracting raw materials to delivering finished products (see Davidson et al.; Divine et al.; Fradkin; Hine; Kelley; and Paul). The workforce suffered accordingly, experiencing insecurity, unemployment, poverty, and crowding in urban life.

Labor strife broke out, as did union militancy and antagonism against minorities and immigrants, and even the majority who abstained from violence questioned the idealistic rhetoric about progress and the good life in America. Frustrated, resentful, believing with reason that the political and legal systems favored the special interests, many dime-western readers took delight and comfort in adventures starring social rebels who could defy the law and control their own destinies. They also wanted cultural ideals and moral imperatives, so corrupted in reality, to be confirmed at story's end by right's triumphing over might. The result was American versions of Robin Hood: bandit protagonists of honor and nobility who are the victims of injustice, and who consequently must flee to the wilder parts of the frontier where simply to survive they are forced into outlawry. Although plot variations are numerous, invariably the bandits demand a personal justice that in the course of the stories is transmuted into a passion for social justice, and this merging of private and public feeling lends the dime bandit western a universality rarely achieved elsewhere.

These characteristics were first incorporated by writer Edward L. Wheeler, "who, employing the persecution and revenge motif in the saga of Deadwood Dick, set the precedent which other dime novelists would later emulate" (Jones, p. 82). Wheeler soon concocted similar wronged, vengeful, and righteously indignant outcasts, like Sam Hathaway in *Solid Sam, the Boy Road-Agent; or, the Branded Brows* (1880), Bill Blake in *Apollo Bill, the Trail Tornade; or, Rowdy Kate from Right-Bower* (1882), and disgraced detective Fred Brayton in *A No. 1, The Dashing Toll-Taker; or, The Schoolmarm o' Sassafras* (1883). Other writers churned out yarn after yarn using Wheeler's recipe, many of them fictionalizing the careers of actual desperadoes such as the James brothers, the Younger brothers, the Daltons, and Butch Cassidy and the Sundance Kid, and in the process raising many of them to the mythic prominence they still maintain. For example, California's vicious outlaw Joaquín Murrieta is transformed in all eight of his dime westerns into the honorable victim of oppression, treachery, and ignorant citizenry. The sensationalized exploits of Jesse and Frank James "endowed them with perennial youth, dash, and charisma, and actual incidents in their lives fortuitously corresponded to the conventional motif of persecution and revenge" (Jones, p. 95)—although dime novelists were prone to alter blatantly biographical facts that did not fit, a habit picked up later and refined by motion picture producers.

That bandit protagonists must have a proper rationale for turning against society is perhaps best illustrated by the failure of the fictionalized Billy the Kid to achieve public approval and sales comparable to other bandit heroes. Certainly on the surface "William H. Bonney symbolized the whole pastoral epoch doomed by the railroad, tractor, and homesteader" (Fishwick, p. 35). However, "nearly all dime novels that exploited the Kid's career neglected to explain his lawlessness according to the familiar convention. As a result, he remains a consummate villain . . . [and] never became a recognized hero in the dime novel" (Jones, pp. 97–98). Only years later, after imaginative biographers and film producers revised his squalid history, did the public accept Billy the Kid as an unfortunate and misunderstood social rebel. In fact, whether protagonists are bandits breaking the law, citizens bending the law, or hunter-scouts out where there is no law, much of their popularity depends on their striking a balance between acceptable and unacceptable behavior—between self-reliant individualism, which readers admire and wish for themselves, and responsible interaction with the community, which readers acknowledge as necessary for stable social order.

Of all the types of protagonists who "managed to reconcile the reader's desire for unlimited freedom with his desire for the advantages of life in society" (Jones, p. 75), the next to appear after the bandit would capture and hold the public imagination as the icon of the West: the cowboy. As folk-hero, the cowboy is mythic in proportions yet rooted in reality, an image in legend and life who epitomizes our cultural dreams of solitude and self-sufficiency and intimacy with nature. Long considered common ranch-hands since the *vaquero* days of the Spanish Southwest, cowboys began to come into their own with the "long drives" of cattle after the Civil War. For only thirty years at most, more than forty thousand cowboys trailherded to Sedalia, Missouri, then to little frontier railheads across Kansas, "a well-informed Federal official estimat[ing] that from 1866 through 1884, less than twenty years, more than 5.2 million cattle were driven north from Texas" (Paul, p. 195). In effect, cattle replaced the buffalo in about equal numbers, spreading across plains that could be grazed if not farmed, and providing the economic stimulus to settle the last wild portions of prairie. This required genuinely intrepid men willing to court death for a chance at making a stake, their gutsy "risk-with-profit" attitude having always held appeal for Americans.

Another powerful emotional draw has been in the wanderlust freedom associated with cowboy life. To store clerks, soldiers, miners who must tend their claims, and teamsters who must follow their schedules, the cowboy's apparent independence and ability to travel at will has seemed enviably romantic. Actually, "cattle raising as an occupation was as committed to cooperation as early farming on the plains. As with farmers, unwritten codes demanded immediate help with emergencies like fires. Roundup and driving were counterparts to threshing and harvesting, and the spirit spilled over into other life activities. . . . Only organization made an open-range cattle system function" (Paul, pp. 164–165). Fictionally, dime writers centered few stories around everyday communal cattle ranching, but preferred the wide variety of colorful settings and adventurous plots that could be employed by using the roaming cowpoke character. "In magazines and dime novels the bachelor cowboy, melancholy and singular, talked little of his past and often had no name, which is to say no family," Paul observes, pointing out that as an unintentional consequence, "the literary image of lonely independence infected the cowboy himself and may also have hindered family attachment" (pp. 168–169).

If cowboys had no family, they did possess horses and guns. They depended on horses for punching cattle and for survival out on the plains, where men set afoot were vulnerable to fatal threats like renegade Indians, predatory animals, and dehydration from the sheer distances between waterholes. Dime writers, not content to leave the horse as basic transportation for the mobile hero, quickly boosted the horse to the status of faithful pal and then to that of brainy peer with trick steeds like Buffalo Bill's Powder Face, Jesse James's Sirocco, and former Texas Ranger Moccasin Mat's Storm Cloud, which could come at a whistle, untie rope knots with nibbling teeth, and gallop riderless to fetch back rescuers. Because cowboys had to make their own law when out alone, and when around others moved among armed men, their survival also depended on their physical strength, personal bravery, and ability to use firearms if necessary. The average cowboy kept a pistol or carbine handy, but rarely spent costly bullets practicing to become a crack shot, so the image of a holstered revolver strapped forever to the thigh has more to do with fiction than reality, as does a hero's blazing speed and incredible feats of marksmanship.

Cowboys did enjoy wasting lead "shooting up" railhead towns at the end of their months of traildriving, which helped earn them a bad reputation. Theodore Roosevelt wrote in 1885 that cowboys were considered "lawless" due to their penchant for "cut[ting] queer antics when, after many months of lonely life, they come into a frontier town in which drinking and gambling are the only recognized forms of amusement, and where pleasure and vice are considered synonymous terms" (pp. 6–7). Further scandalizing the sober, spartan-living plains farmers was the appearance of the cowboys. When working, they were "rough men with shaggy hair and wild, staring eyes, in butternut trousers stuffed into great rough boots," according to Laura Johnson in an 1875 *Lippincott's* magazine article (p. 695). According to Charles M. Russell, though, "in all the camps you'd find a fashion leader. From a cowpuncher's idea, these fellers was sure good to look at. . . . Of course, a good many of these fancy men were more ornamental than useful" (p. 3). When given the opportunity, such as at play, they festooned themselves in fancy duds. In 1879, Henry King in *Scribner's* described "herdsmen" (cowboys) wearing "old Castilian sombreros, and open-legged trowsers with rows of buttons, and jackets gaudy with many-colored braid and Indian beads, and now and then a blood-red scarf like a matador's" (pp. 139–140).

Their picturesque garb was picked up immediately by dime writers, who clad their cowboy protagonists even more outrageously. For instance, Dandy Dan in *Dandy Dan of Deadwood and his Big Bonanza* (n.d.) wears "a suit of neat black velvet, with patent leather boots on his feet. He wore a white shirt, the front of which was spotless, and in the center of the bosom blazed a magnificent diamond," all while roped to a remote rock pillar out in the plains (Jones, pp. 109–110). Thus began the trend lasting well into the twentieth century of attiring cowboy heroes in the likes of ten-gallon white hats, embroidered shirts, silk neckerchiefs, hand-tooled boots, silvered spurs with giant spiked rowels, and twin ivory-handled pistols in initialed holsters. Invariably, their costumes are matched by courtly bearing "as a means of delineating character instantly—good men dressed well and behaved decorously, ruffians did not" (Jones, p. 73).

In time cowboys married farmers' daughters, settled down to prairie ranching, and proved that they were not as disreputable as was first thought. During the 1880s "cattle-raising on the plains . . . became a prominent feature" for wealthy Easterners, who found ranching profitable and romantic in "a land of vast silent spaces, of lonely rivers, and of plains where the wild game stared at the passing horsemen" (Roosevelt, pp. 9, 103). With cowboys gaining more favor in public opinion, hardcover cowboy novels started to be published such as the Thomas Pilgrim's juveniles *Live Boys; or, Charley and Nasho in Texas* (1879) and *Live Boys in the Black Hills* (1880), which in 1882 were followed by cowboy dime novels beginning with Frederick Whittaker's *Parson Jim, King of the Cowboys; or, The Gentle Shepherd's Big 'Clean Out'*.

Cowboy westerns did not catapult to national prominence, though, until "Buffalo Bill's Wild West Show" emerged as a major attraction playing to capacity crowds. William F. "Buffalo Bill" Cody organized his first road show in 1883, after serving the previous year as Grand Marshal at the North Platte, Nebraska, Fourth of July celebration, which had stressed such cattle-country contests as roping, riding, and shooting. His show incorporated the same rodeo format, featured hundreds of Indians, bison, and cowboy personalites like Buck Taylor, "Mustang Jack," "Squaw Man" Jack Belson, and Annie Oakley, and starred Cody himself as an epic hero of American progress and civilization. A shameless showman, Cody already had spent eleven years acting in his own melodramas like "Buffalo Bill, King of the Bordermen," and had been the protagonist of twenty dime novels by Edward Z. C. Judson writing under the pseudonym "Col. Ned Buntline." Judson had introduced Cody in his 1869 story *Buffalo Bill, the King of the Border Men* as a gruff, buckskinned, hunter-scout plainsman, an image that persisted until the early 1880s when Cody replaced Judson with a staff writer, Colonel Prentiss Ingraham. Ingraham, in some two hundred stories about or "by" Cody that appeared over the next twenty years, recast Cody as a handsome young stage driver, pony express rider, and detective as well as expert hunter and guide, and he reclad Cody in the sort of extravagance that Cody wore in his Wild West shows, such as in *Gold Plume, the Boy Bandit* (1881): "a red velvet jacket, white corduroy pants . . . a gray sombrero, encircled by a gold cord and looped up on the left side with a pin representing a spur . . . a black cravat, gauntlet gloves, and a sash of red silk, in which were stuck a pair of revolvers and a dirk-knife" (p. 3). Cody's dime stories advertised his Wild West shows and his Wild West shows publicized his dime novels, heightening sales in both and confusing all distinction between Cody the historical character and Cody the fictional character; and this blending of the dime novel business and the western road-show business became a major contributor, along with other components such as P. T. Barnum's circus, to the nascent mass culture industry.

This combined promotional punch allowed the prolific Ingraham not only to perpetrate the Buffalo Bill legend, but also to launch the first popular cowboy hero in *Buck Taylor, King of the Cowboys* (1887), which was the alleged biography of Wild West show star and actual cowboy Buck Taylor. Taylor became a series cowboy character who, like Cody, is innately noble and flamboyantly dressed, as in *Buck Taylor, the Saddle King; or, the Lasso Rangers' League* (1891), with "a watch and chain, diamond pin in his black scarf, representing a miniature spur, and upon the small finger of his right hand there was a ring, the design being a horseshoe of rubies. . . . About his broad-brimmed, dove-colored sombrero was coiled a miniature lariat [sic], so that the spur, horseshoe and lasso designated his calling" (p. 2).

His calling may be cowpunching, but Taylor spends precious little time at the job. Instead, he is a fiddle-footed adventurer prone to encountering and capable of handling every kind of perilous situation, a portrayal replicated in the legions of cowboy heroes who followed, such as Hustler Harry, Maverick Mat, Hurricane Hal, Silver Spur Steve, and deadly shots "Top Notch" Tom Field and Hank "The Nailer" Kimble. They all fight Indians, of course, but increasingly Indians got cast as renegade dupes of master villains like crooked bankers or corrupt reservation agents. After all, by this time the Plains tribes were no longer much of a threat, mostly confined to reservations and dependent on the products of white technology, so demoralized and defeated that once again Indians were becoming viewed as the Noble Savage to be pitied more than feared. "Sympathy for a so-called dying race made Sitting Bull popular enough to parade in Wild West Shows, a cross between a dignified warrior and a beloved freak. A few years later Geronimo, the last great Apache chieftain, surrendered to federal troops for the second time in 1886, and after taking up farming and Christianity, he became a

celebrity, a special added attraction at the Omaha and St. Louis Exposi-
tions and at Theodore Roosevelt's inaugural parade" (Kaufmann, p.
494). Instead, like their mining and bandit predecessors in dime westerns, cowboy protagonists tend to battle thieves, murderers, counterfeit-
ers, politicians, corporations, bankers, and similar dark agents of social
injustice on behalf of defenseless individuals like orphan girls, elderly
widows, and sick or insane old men. For example, "Top Notch" Tom and
Hank "The Nailer" champion the water rights of small ranchers against
the land-grabbing Glasgow Cattle Company in *Top Notch Tom, the Cowboy Outlaw; or, The Satanstown Election* (1884) and *The Marshal of
Satanstown; or, The League of the Cattle-Lifters* (1884). And, like the mining and bandit dime westerns, the message inherent in cowboy dime
westerns is that "the common man must stand up for his rights. He must
overcome his ignorance and apathy. And he must rally behind those
strong-willed individuals who refuse to be exploited, who will not surren-
der their rights or stand by idly while others are inveigled to do so" (Jones,
p. 155). Or, in the words of Silver Spur Steve in *Cowboy Steve, the Ranch
Mascot* (1891): "I am simply defying lawlessness" (Jones, p. 104).

The arrival of the cowboy hero coincided with the departure of the
cowboy lifestyle. By the turn of the century the westward-expanding
frontier had drowned in the Pacific Ocean, barbed-wire fencing had
come to enclose range, waterhole, and trail, and impersonal corporate
ranch operations had squelched the cowboy's celebrated mix of independent spirit and loyalty to a spread, turning the cowboy into a drifting
labor supply as vulnerable to dismissal as any factory worker. For example, at the Spring Ranch in Texas after 1885, 64 percent of the cowboys
stayed for only one season and only 3 percent lasted for five years (Rojas,
p. 194). Nonetheless, the fictional cowboy has continued to live and
thrive in a frontier of open range and savage wilderness, ever courageous
and honorable, an expert rider and shooter, and defender of decent men
and virtuous women. "Among all the frontier children of the Old West,
the cowboy proved the most irresistible, and it is this folk character that
fiction writers have enshrined in more pages of print than any other figure in the history of Anglo-American folk life on this side of the Atlantic" (Franz and Coathe, p. 70).

The cowboy persona surely stands out as the most conspicuous legacy of the dime western, as measured by frequency of appearance and

degree of popularity. Because such market appeal was a prime motivator for dime writers, in their relentless quest for sales they also introduced and popularized a succession of other western protagonists—prospectors, ranchers, lumberjacks, railroad surveyors, stage and wagon drivers, soldiers and Indians—which is why this chapter is called "Brush Bustin'." Cowpunchers busting cattle in brush country had to ride with open eyes and swift reflexes to dodge thorny scrub, often swinging from one side of a horse to the other or standing straight in the saddle to avoid being snagged or gouged. Dime writers had to be similarly agile in spotting trends, devising solutions, and avoiding pitfalls, knowing that to be out of step was to be out of work.

Indeed, so successful was the dime western at accommodating public taste that it proved instrumental in establishing the patterns westerns have developed up to the present day. Until the dime western, the general theme of frontier fiction was that of exploring nature, either to cultivate it as in the case of Filsen's Daniel Boone, or to commune with it as in the case of Cooper's Leatherstocking. This focus on the duality of civilization and wilderness became increasingly irrelevant for a nineteenth-century society preoccupied with issues of progress, industrialization, urbanization, and balancing individual and communal interests. The dime novel shifted accordingly, and though wilderness tales featuring the solitary hunter-scout were never discontinued, they were displaced increasingly by post–Civil War stories set among ranchers, farmers, sheepherders, townsfolk, lawmen, outlaws, gamblers, railroaders, gold-hearted whores, and of course cowboys.

These frontier characters and this era from 1865 to 1900, as developed by the dime western in conjunction with Wild West shows, have continued to provide the ingredients for the currently definitive legend of the West. To understand how the western has evolved since the dime, then, requires that the conventions inspired by the dime, the relation of the dime to the cultural issues of its day, and the position of the dime in the historical development of western fiction be taken together in a multidisciplinary approach. Such a broad perspective is what previous critics, even those as authoritative as Daryl Jones, have not developed thoroughly. To be sure, as discussed earlier in this chapter there have been insightful articles about the dime, such as those by George Jenks and Merle Conti; and books that have emphasized important aspects of the dime, such as those by Henry Nash Smith, Douglas Branch, and William Settle. Their points of view are valuable, as are authoritative histories by scholars such as Daryl Jones, informal chronicles by enthusiasts such as Edmund Pearson, and controversial theories by ideologues such as Richard Slotkin and Michael Denning. Still, to do justice to their subjects, they have had purposely to limit discussion about the dime western. For example, Jones's *The Dime Western Novel* covers the role of the dime, but not of subsequent western fiction. Settle's *Jesse James was his Name* and Steckmesser's *The Western Hero in History and Legend* recount the lives of famous Westerners and mention dime westerns only in terms of how they fictionalized real people. Slotkin's *Regeneration Through Violence*, *The Fatal Environment*, and *Gunfighter Nation* argue his thesis that America's history and mythology are viciously exploitative, at the expense of treating American literature, including dime novels, in a less than balanced manner. Other critics such as John Cawelti ignore the dime western, or, like John Milton and Henry Nash Smith, dismiss it as juvenile rubbish.

Unfortunately, neglecting the dime western has led some critics to misinterpret the contributions of Owen Wister, Zane Grey, and later writers, and to misconstrue the influences of historical and cultural events in the twentieth century on western fiction—topics that, along with the impact of film and other new media, are considered in the next chapters. Integral to these topics is the dime western, for despite the admittedly poor writing, it depicts the experiences of the final frontier and represents the values of the American Dream, and in the process discusses the factors of ideology and social, economic, and political conflict that still engross the nation.

Highballin' Camp

Legendary silent cowboy star William S. Hart's exclamation is from a prologue he filmed in 1939 as introduction to his reissued silent western *Tumbleweeds* (1923). Although Hart is referring to his relish for making westerns, he also is expressing the fervent enthusiasm for countless audiences for watching westerns, and for much the same reasons: "It is the breath of life to me. The rush of the wind as it cuts your face. The pounding hoofs of the pursuing posse. Out there in front—a fallen tree trunk that spans a yawning chasm, and an old animal under you that takes it in the same low, ground-eating gallop. The harmless shots of the baffled ones that remain behind and then . . . the clouds of dust through which comes the faint voice of the director: 'Okay, Bill, okay! Glad you made it. Great stuff, Bill, great stuff'" (Barbour, p. 363). If the excitement generated by galloping hoofs, pursuing posses, yawning chasms, and clouding dust sounds familiar, it should. When western films became the craze following Edwin S. Porter's *The Great Train Robbery* (1903), the frontier myth as popularized by dime westerns and Wild West shows passed into a new medium. One point of this chapter, then, is to demonstrate that during the first three decades of this century, westerns were characterized less by change than by continuity with dime western conventions. Not that western fiction remained static, of course. Another point of the chapter is to show how western writers, particularly Owen Wister and Zane Grey, altered the conventions to reflect personal themes, market requirements, and contemporary culture from the Progressive era to the Great Depression.

The Progressive era, dated by historians from 1901 to 1917 and the U. S. entry into World War I, was a reform movement aimed at correcting excesses which had accompanied the growth of big business in the post–Civil War period. Federal agencies were established to curb monopolies and trusts, laws were passed to protect consumers from abuses by meat packers and drug manufacturers, and regulations were instigated to prohibit child labor and improve working conditions in general. Naturally, such changes garnered wide popular support. Well into the 1920s the Progressive movement provided the average person with a sense of optimism and faith in the power of social science to cure civic ills—in contrast to a brewing disillusionment among intellectuals and "Lost Generation" belletrists following World War I (see Davidson et al.; Divine et al.; and Kelley). As well, the cumulative effect of rising prosperity, urbanization, and new employment opportunities created by technological advances contributed to growing leisure time and demand for entertainment. From 1890 to 1920, for example, the average manufacturing workweek fell from sixty to fifty-one hours while average annual income rose from $418 to $1342, certainly providing the time and money to read copious magazines and books; buy 100 million records by 1921; listen to 800 radio stations by 1925; and attend movies at the weekly rate of 10 million people in 1910, 40 million by 1922, and over 900 million by 1930 (Divine et al., pp. 379–380, 396, 424; Kazin, p. 106). Box-office preference was for films that stressed pathos and laughter, especially when combined in a palliative for those yearning for a simpler, bygone era that was less coercive and less dominated by urbanization and industrialization—even if such a West never existed other than as figments of imagination—but equally important, westerns found favor because their stories promoted the Progressive vision of social justice and the essential nobility of mankind (Davidson, pp. 825–826). Hence, "slick" magazines printed on shiny paper such as *Harper's, Atlantic,* and *The Century* greatly increased their circulation by carrying western fiction and nonfiction. The successor to the dime novel, the pulp magazine —so called because, like the dime novel, it was printed on cheap pulp paper—flourished in a market dominated by pulp westerns such as *Western Story Magazine, Ace-High,* and *Wild West,* which were devoted exclusively to a format of western short stories, serials, and novels. Moreover, because advertisers, publishers, and film and record producers were not ones to leave crossover or tie-in opportunities undeveloped, screen characters spawned pulp westerns such as *Movie Western* and *Cowboy Movie Thrillers;* short stories such as Johnson McCulley's serial "The Curse of Capistrano" in *All Story Weekly* (1919) inspired United Artists' *The Mark of Zorro* (1920) and numerous sequels; and cowboy movie star Tom Mix branched out into the *Tom Mix* radio show in 1933 and into *Tom Mix Comics* and *Tom Mix Commando Comics* in the early 1940s (see Barbour; Garvey; Goodstone; Goulart; Hitt; Horowitz; Hovland and Wilcox; Kazin; Presbrey; and Schudson). By necessity, mass production of mass entertainment tended to be high and hasty, an avalanche of westerns flowing from prolific yarnsters like Rex Beach, Dan Quin (A. H. Lewis), and Max Brand (Frederick Faust) and from low-budget movie studios like Mascot, Mutual, and First National—which is why the chapter is called "Highballin' Camp," meaning a busy cattle camp in which everyone works at top speed.

Ironically, the swift urbanization, industrialization, and other cultural changes that helped create the markets for westerns and the means of fulfilling them also led some Western historians at the time to lose themselves "in nostalgia as they invented a lost golden age, an earlier period in Western history which was the very antithesis of the rapidly changing West of their own day" (Nash, p. 208). Prompted by more than just a nostalgic mood, this pervasive view was clearly influenced by Frederick Jackson Turner. Reading his essay "The Significance of The Frontier in American History" to the 1893 annual conference of the American Historical Association, Turner defined the frontier as "the meeting point between savagery and civilization"; argued that "the existence of an area of free land, its continuous recession, and the advance of American settlement westward explain American development"; and concluded that as of 1890 "the frontier has gone, and with it has closed the first period in American history" (in Faragher, pp. 32, 31, 60). The validity of the "Turner thesis," as it is called, has since come under criticism for its vague and inconsistent use of terminology, its concept that democracy developed on the frontier when it actually had been brought by the settlers, and its argument that the frontier process was unique when in fact it resembled the development of other rural areas and was simply part of a larger movement from country to city, which continued long after the disappearance of the frontier. Still, the thesis spurred an immense amount of investigation and "has caused more reconsideration of American development than any other single suggestion" (Adams, p. 304), to the extent that "writing on the West since 1900 has been given over to the composition of obsequies on the frontier—to funereal laments . . . over the demise of the frontier" (McWilliams, p. 427). Indeed, eulogies poured forth from contemporaneous authors like Frank Norris—"lament it though we may, the Frontier is gone, an idiosyncrasy that has been with us for thousands of years, the one peculiar picturesqueness of our life is no more" (p. 1729)—and Hamlin Garland—"all these frontiers . . . are now gone, utterly gone. America no longer has a region of mystery, of untracked spaces, and something fine and strong and free is passing from our national life" (p. 286). All these dolorous refrains "contributed to the development of the West as myth in the early years of the century" (Nash, p. 221). Consequently, westerns of this period must surely "bewail the loss not only of the virgin land but of a primitive way of life that is extremely masculine in requiring strength, adaptability, resourcefulness, courage, and an almost stoic self-control . . . [and] present protagonists who revel in their freedoms, whose loss creates nostalgia for the way things were" (Wylder, p. 121).

To assert as a sweeping generalization that westerns after the turn of the century were perforce nostalgic is to risk oversimplifying western fiction and slighting the influences of the Progressive era. To be sure, innumerable westerns were produced, then and since, that are nostalgic in the sense that they are set in a mythic past when the West was wild, men were men, women were women, and everyone knew one's place in life. In fact, pulp westerns such as *Frontier Stories* and *North-West Romances* specialized in stories set on frontier wildernesses unpeopled by anyone but savages and backwoodsmen, mountain men, or plainsmen of the Natty Bumppo/Kit Carson type, the protagonists motivated by individualism free from domestic or community responsibilities. However, I venture that whereas turn-of-the-century historians, allied scholars, and authors writing as historians may well have known about rampant industrialization and the Turner thesis, the mass consumer of westerns was either unaware of or unconcerned about an academic closing of the frontier. Granted, a new way of life was emerging—urban, industrial, and commercial, largely founded on mass production of heavily advertised consumer goods—but the vast majority of goods were simply improvements, their basic functions or purposes already familiar to consumers. Electric motors did the same task as steam engines, only better; incandescent lights did the same task as kerosene lamps, only brighter; even automobiles did the same task as horses and wagons, and not always more effectively, either, considering the dearth of roads and highways. Major parts of America remained rural and agricultural, and many farming communities as well as most of the South remained poor. During the Depression and well into the 1940s, a great many people lived in small crossroads towns, rural labor still used horses and wagons, and railroads still handled most public and commercial transportation. Another cause for fundamental cultural changes passing almost unnoticed at the time was the sharp increase in immigration; from 1901 to 1920, 1.4 million immigrants entered the country (Divine et al., p. 398), "which helped to meet the demands of the rapidly expanding urban industries which accompanied the closing of the frontier" (Alexander, p. 14). Moreover, the frontier did not necessarily close. "Far more public land in the trans-Mississippi West was taken up in the years after 1890 than in the years before" (Faragher, p. 6), and "using Turner's own definition of 'unsettled,' there are in the late twentieth century 149 'frontier' counties in the West, and . . . many areas of the western Great Plains are steadily *losing* population. . . . Even now, in this last quarter of the twentieth century, the pastoral life thrives as well as it ever did. The techniques of range and herd management may have changed, but the basic ecological mode has remained intact" (Worster, pp. 28, 29). Besides, during the early decades, western fiction and film existed alongside the last of the real Old West. For example, Mark Twain appeared on screen in *A Curious Dream* (1907), and Emmett Dalton of the Dalton Brothers debuted in *Beyond the Law* (1915). Buffalo Bill Cody showed up five times: *The Life of Buffalo Bill* (1909), *Buffalo Bill's Far West and Pawnee Bill's Far East* (1910), *The Indian Wars* (1913) (whose cast included many of the troopers and Indians who had actually fought in the final Indian wars) *Sitting Bull—The Hostile Indian Chief* (1914), and *Patsy of the Circus* (1915).

From the perspective of everyday audiences of westerns, then, neither a national nostalgia nor Frederick Turner's watershed date of 1890 would have been as commanding as contemporary scholars believed. To the contrary: instead of pining for the good old days, "Americans were optimistic" about the Good New Days and "believed that technology and enterprise would shape a better life" (Divine et al., p. 394). Certainly the economy seemed to provide plenty of opportunity and to place prosperity within the grasp of anyone with gumption. It was the American Dream revitalized, except that now it was more apt to be a factory worker who was dreaming of becoming a millionaire. Pulp western publishers, loath to miss a sale, catered to the dreamer with stories that mixed past and present, the Old West and the day before yesterday —saddle horses and automobiles ("Wild Men of Wallowa"), sixguns and telephones ("Boothill Beller Box"), and cow herds and airplanes ("Satan Rides the Sky")—and movie producers were quick to cash in with "B" westerns like *King of the Arena* (1933), in which Ken Maynard gets the drop on Lucille Browne in a biplane. Clearly, the frontier did not vanish but adapted to the times, becoming a dynamically interacting boundary between technology and provincialism rather than between civilization and the wilderness. It did not seem to matter much to audiences that instead of free land there was now inventiveness and enterprise at the edge of settled life, to which the venturesome, the discontented, and the economically depressed might head to win their fortunes, or at least wrest a livelihood.

That western fiction could be contemporary fiction is perhaps exemplified best by Owen Wister's novel *The Virginian: A Horseman of the Plains* (1902). Set in the cattle country of Wyoming in the early 1890s, *The Virginian* tells of the rivalry between the eponymous hero and the villain Trampas in wooing the pretty Vermont schoolmarm Molly Wood. Wister considered his novel to be nostalgic, of "a vanishing world" where "no journeys, save those which memory can take, will bring you to it now" (p. ix), and his critics have generally agreed. Lee Clark Mitchell, for example, speaks of *The Virginian's* capacity to satisfy "the desire for nostalgic escapism" (p. 118), and Donald Worster argues that Wister "intended to recreate nostalgically a frontier world that was passing away" (p. 81). It is also true that Wister's frontier world is the Old West of nineteenth-century dime-novel conventions, which Erastus Beadle, Edward Wheeler, and Prentiss Ingraham would have recognized on the spot. For instance, Wister's nameless Virginian clearly displays the characteristics of the dime cowboy hero: a self-reliant loner, at least up until winning the heroine; either orphaned as a child or, as in the case of the Virginian, abandoning home as a youngster to head west; and now grown, "a slim young giant" with "splendor that radiated from his youth and strength" (Wister, p. 4), and a penchant for fancy duds.

> "I have made one discovery," [Molly] said. "You are fonder of good clothes than I am."
> He grinned. "I certainly like 'em. But don't tell my friends." (p. 500)

Moreover, in the style of dime western cowboys, the Virginian is superior in riding, roping, fighting, and shooting, the natural nobleman who is formed less by civilization than by the pastoral influence of the West. "It cannot be said that he is arrogant, for, simply and in all nonchalance, he is better, as some men are naturally better than others" (Klein, p. 76). Spending less time tending cattle than rescuing and romancing the heroine, he is the typically polite and genteel dime hero who, although in a western setting repeatedly described as silent, carries on elaborate conversations that "match her verbal sophistication and her early condescension to him as an untutored cowhand gives way before his rhetorical skill" (Mitchell, p. 98). Molly Stark Wood, too, is the traditional dime cowboy heroine: feisty, educated, proper, critical of the hero's demeanor at first, then warming to him while nursing him back to health, and finally becoming the domesticated wife and mother. "She shall teach school no more when she is mine" (Wister, p. 375). Their marriage "crystallizes a reconciliation of East and West" (Bold, p. 41), a symbolic unification that serves as a common structuring element in dime westerns. Another dime-western element is the contrast between the Virginian's articulate self-control and villain Trampas's uncouth imprudence, which initially is used to indicate the Virginian's superior nature, and eventually becomes the cause of the cumulative gunfight: "Now [Trampas's] own rash proclamation had trapped him. . . . He dared not leave town in the world's sight after all the world had heard him" (Wister, p. 481). And as for that final showdown in the street, despite critics such as Richard Maxwell Brown, who states that "the archetypal expression of the myth of the gunfighter was provided by Owen Wister" (p. 46), the walkdown gun duel actually derives from George Ward Nichols's 1867 article "Wild Bill" in *Harper's*, wherein Nichols describes a romanticized encounter between Wild Bill Hickok and Dave Tutt in the Springfield, Missouri, public square (pp. 273–285). Richard Maxwell Brown claims as well that *The Virginian*'s plot "became the model" for the western, yet its sequence of "hero meets heroine, villain threatens hero, hero kills villain, and hero weds heroine" (p. 48) was a standard storyline that predates dime westerns and James Fenimore Cooper. Not only Brown, then, but other critics such as James Folsom, Richard Etulain, Darwin Payne, Loren Estleman, Delbert Wylder, and Bernard DeVoto are simply incorrect when they suggest that *The Virginian* "sprang full-grown from the imagination of Owen Wister" (Estleman, p. 25) to be the model or "principal archetype" (Wylder, p. 125) that "created Western fiction—created the cowboy story, the horse-opera novel, the conventions, the clichés, the values, and the sun god" hero (DeVoto, p. 8).

It would be equally incorrect to conclude that, because Wister believed he had written a nostalgic "colonial romance" (p. ix) and relied on stereotypical dime plotting, setting, and characterization, *The Virginian* cannot be considered as contemporary fiction. Rather, on the simplest level, the novel is contemporary because it is the fictionalized account of a contemporary event—the 1892 Johnson County War in Wyoming, which, having occurred only ten years prior, was still fresh in the memories of readers. Essentially, the war had been a minor class conflict between corporate cattle ranchers who ran huge herds on unfenced public rangeland and the growing influx of small ranchers and farmers who homesteaded on it and occasionally rustled a corporate cow or two. The corporate ranchers imported gunmen as vigilantes to oust the homesteaders, the homesteaders took to guerrilla tactics, and the U.S. army got caught in between so badly that the secretary of war and the president were rousted out of bed to order a rescue (see Helena Huntington Smith's *The War on Powder River*). Well publicized by newspapers, the Johnson County War, along with similar clashes like the 1894 Pullman Strike, illustrated the economic and social disruption that gripped the nation and led by decade's end to the Progressive reform movement. Consequently, while in 1902 there may have been some corporate ranchers wishing for their unfenced fiefdoms back, not enough time had passed, nor was there any reason for the vast majority of *The Virginian's* readers to wax nostalgic over the Johnson County War, any more than today we pine for the Persian Gulf War.

Still, for Wister to have based his story on this contemporary event is crucial because, as Bernard DeVoto notes, "the themes of the book are from the Johnson County War" (p. 12), and through these themes Wister makes social commentary on contemporary America. The themes seem initially to be in line either with the Cooper dichotomy of wilderness versus civilization—a position favored by critics like Jim Hitt, who asserts that "the Virginian is a romantic primitive who rejects the traditional values of civilization in favor of a free life in the West" (p. 120)—or with the conventional duality of community versus individuality found in later dime westerns, a motif subscribed to by other critics like Cynthia Hamilton, who perceives the novel as an "initiation process" in which "the hero is 'civilized'" while "the heroine learns to accept Western ways" (p. 14). When Wister's treatment of the Johnson County War is examined carefully, however, the themes that emerge are not about nature and civilization but two theories or visions of civilization: the Turner thesis and reformist Social Darwinism.

In his introduction to *The Virginian*, Wister laments that the cowboy "will never come again. He rides into the historic yesterday" (p. x), which certainly echoes the part of the Turner thesis that claims that the frontier is extinct. But the development of American society by frontier conditions, Turner argued, does not grow out of the expansion of wilderness but from the encounter, the dynamic interaction, between wilderness and civilization. Although the physical frontier may be gone, the customs and character traits shaped by the frontier still remain important, as Turner declares in his later essay "Contributions of the West to American Democracy" (1903): "Long after the frontier period of a particular region of the United States has passed away, the conception of society, the ideals and aspirations which it produced, persist in the minds of the people" (Faragher, p. 96). For Turner, the "conception of society" was the conception of yeoman democracy advocated by Jefferson and Jackson: "The West has created a larger single body of intelligent plain people than can be found elsewhere in the world" who have "laid deep foundations for a Democratic State" with their "belief in liberty, freedom of opportunity, and a resistance to the domination of class" (pp. 96, 98). In turn, the "values and aspirations" produced by democracy for Turner's "common man" were the "love of freedom, the strength that came from hewing out a home, making a school and church, and creating a higher future for his family" (p. 99). Clearly, the frontier values Turner espouses are in keeping with the traditional middle-class virtues of piety, chastity, monogamy, family, and community. And because the frontier is gone, "it is to the realm of the spirit . . . that we must look for Western influence upon democracy in our own days" (p. 93). Rather than yearn for a return to bygone times, then, Turner is calling for a present and future revitalization of core middle-class values. Similarly, I believe, Wister is commending the maintenance of middle-class morality in his contemporary society.

Some critics, such as John Cawelti, argue to the contrary that for Wister, "the rise of the Virginian symbolizes the emergence of a new kind of elite" (*Adventure*, p. 227). This is because, as Richard Maxwell Brown asserts, "Owen Wister was an ultraconservative member of

America's elite of the elite" (pp. 46-47). According to Hamilton, Wister's "sympathies and attitudes are those of the upper-class Eastern establishment. He was born into an upper-class Pennsylvania family of distinguished history. His private schooling in Switzerland, England, and the United States, his Harvard degree, and his membership in the prestigious university clubs, the Dickey and the Porcelain, provided him with further credentials appropriate to his family's social sphere" (p. 17). But although Wister may have been an aristocrat at heart, what his critics seem to overlook is that Wister was a writer by trade. *The Virginian* is put together from seven short stories Wister published between 1893 and 1902 in *Harper's* and *The Saturday Evening Post*. These "slicks" were "caught up in the demands of the commercial world, most obviously by being in the van of large-scale magazine advertising," and as such "their pieces were decidedly middlebrow; they were not trying to appeal to an elite readership. In the late nineteenth century, *Harper's* magazine led the way in publicizing the West of the Indian, the cavalryman, and the cowboy to a vast, mainly Eastern audience" (Bold, pp. 38–39). It follows that whatever he felt personally, Wister had to appeal to the market and write stories extolling the middle-class values of middle-class readers if he was to sell successfully to *The Saturday Evening Post* and *Harper's*— "the great successful middle-class magazine" of the time (Mott, pp. 391).

For example, the majority of the action in *The Virginian* centers on the cattle kingdom of Judge Henry, whose spread is comparable to the corporate ranches in the Johnson County War. The environment and lifestyle are less civilized than in the effete East, and Wister graphically describes the differences, but the situations encountered are social, not solitary in nature, and scarcely tantamount to surviving in the wilderness. The Eastern tenderfoot who narrates roughly half of *The Virginian* initially finds not the West so much as its inhabitants inscrutable. Arriving in Medicine Bow, Wyoming, the narrator ignores the Western landscape when he overhears a cowboy talking "and had no desire but for more of this conversation. For it resembled none that I had heard in my life so far" (p. 4). Indeed, the opening line of the novel describes passengers on a steam train "starved for entertainment" as they pull into the bustling town: "Some notable sight was drawing the passengers, both men and women, to the window; and therefore I rose and crossed the car to see what it was" (p. 1). The sight was cowhands breaking horses in a corral, as much a social construct of blue-collar life as travel by passenger coach and the workaday world of rural towns—albeit told with the romantic spin of an Eastern writer creating a fictional West for an Eastern middlebrow audience. The narrator then undergoes adventures that constitute a journey in which he changes in mind and heart, growing from a wondering visitor to a friend of the Virginian acclimated to Western ways.

Molly Wood experiences a parallel transformation, evolving from a spunky if prim New England lass to a woman who perceives both the Virginian and his land with increasing clarity, tolerance, and appreciation. "Perhaps she never came wholly to understand him; but in her complete love for him she found enough. He loved her with his whole man's heart . . . At the last white-hot edge of ordeal, it was she who renounced, and he who had his way. Nevertheless she found much more than enough, in spite of the sigh that now and again breathed through her happiness when she would watch him with eyes fuller of love than understanding" (p. 499). That Molly Wood "renounced"—that is, went back on her word to leave the Virginian if he fought Trampas—and ends up as his domesticated housewife have led some critics like Mitchell to charge that she is simply "the traditional dependent woman" in a story that is "a defense of male hegemony" (p. 98). This may seem valid to current revisionist historians like Jane Tompkins, who claims that "the Western has nothing to do with the West . . . it is about men's fears of losing their mastery" (p. 45). But critics who argue that *The Virginian* and other westerns are about male supremacy tend to assume that western readers must be almost exclusively men, and relatively uneducated men to boot. John Cawelti, for one, asserts that westerns appeal to "lower and middle class working males" and "that a culture of working-class groups had traditionally placed a strong emphasis on masculine dominance, and it is not hard to see how the Western might fill an important psychological function for these groups" (*Six-Gun*, p. 42). However, as Hamilton notes, such critics "have ignored the actual readership . . . substituting their own preconceptions about appeal" (p. 55), and she points out that a number of leading women's magazines regularly serialized Zane Grey's westerns, and that the pulp *Western Story* had a faithful female following. Similarly, Wister crafted *The Virginian* out of stories sold to slicks whose readers were predominantly female, and by Mitchell's own admission,

"Wister could hardly have devised a more appealing plot, of spirited schoolmarm courted by a handsome cowboy in an exotic high plains locale" (p. 97), both plot and place staples of romance fiction. Moreover, portraying *The Virginian* as a romance, which Wister did in his introduction, would have been a strong selling point because historical romances, particularly those set in the West, were at their heyday and enthusiastically received by readers who, again, were predominantly female (see Beauman; Lears; Mann; and Radway). Consequently, whether or not Wister believed privately that men were superior and woman should be confined to the home is irrelevant—as well as questionable, inasmuch as he was married to the outspoken feminist Molly Wister—because his short stories and *The Virginian* reflect the values of the contemporary middlebrow women who were the bulk of his audience.

In 1902, the code of Victorian morality still set the tone, prescribing stern standards of dress, manners, and sexual behavior. It was both obeyed and disobeyed, and it reflected the tensions of a generation that was undergoing a major change in moral standards. One crucial change was the growing number of women asserting their humanness and seeking self-fulfillment. "In the old days," said a woman in 1907, "a married woman was supposed to be a frump and a bore and a physical wreck. Now you are supposed to keep up intellectually, to look young and well and be fresh and bright and entertaining" (Divine et al., p. 324). Accordingly, Molly Wood is quite the contemporary woman, "far too intelligent" to be "put off with mere platitudes and humdrum formulas" (Wister, p. 435), with a "very spritely countenance" (p. 91) and "a spirit craving the unknown" (p. 95), who "talked as the women he [the Virginian] had known did not talk . . . a free language, altogether new to him" (p. 63), and whose "character was the result of pride and family pluck battling with family hardship" (p. 92). Nonetheless, 1902 also fell during a period of strong pride in virtue and self-control. Patriotic and religious values were encouraged, with society's leaders emphasizing the value of homemaking, and the church as a center of community life setting the tenor for family and social relationships (see Davidson et al.; Divine et al.; and Kelley). Of course Molly gets married—she doesn't make love with the Virginian beforehand, either, else she would not have been respectable enough for marriage in the eyes of middle-class morality. Of course Molly Wood is expected to quit work after marriage—not because she becomes chattel condemned to domestic drudgery, but because homemaking was the preferred choice in an era of industrialization and urbanization when "working-class families, mothers, fathers, and children separated at dawn and returned, ready for sleep at dark" (Divine et al., p. 323). Wister's audience would not have had it otherwise.

For Molly to be a homemaker obliges the Virginian to earn more than he can make as a ranch hand. In a second story, told through an omniscient viewpoint, the Virginian rises from cowboy to foreman to partner in a cattle ranch, and in a merging more Eastern than Western, travels to the East for its technology and civilization and "is accepted by the Easterners as almost a model of the reinvigorated man" (Wylder, p. 125). Contemporaneously, Frederick Turner addressed this same relationship of the West to opportunity and success in "The Problem of the West" (1896): "The self-made man was the Western man's ideal, was the kind of man that all men might become. Out of his wilderness experience, out of the freedom of his opportunities, he fashioned a formula for social regeneration—the freedom of the individual to seek his own" (Faragher, p. 68). Largely by "goin' my own course" (Wister, p. 478), the Virginian becomes "an important man, with a strong grip on many various enterprises, and able to give his wife all and more than she asked or desired" (Wister, p. 506). His Horatio Alger–style success, along with his ambitious and industrious qualities necessary for the upward mobile businessman, held appeal for the middlebrow readers believing in the American Dream, not for rich aristocrats who had already made it to the top.

Like the wealthy, however, middlebrow readers understood the desire to protect private property. The turn of the century was the beginning of a consumer society fueled by rampant advertising, and as Thorstein Veblen and other economists have shown, societal success often was (and is) measured on a scale of conspicuous consumption. Besides, defending and retrieving one's property, whether stolen gold or rustled cows, had been standard plot devices since Cooper. Certainly a major convention of dime westerns was heroes righting wrongs by taking the law into their own hands, either because there was no law available or the legal system was corrupt. Hence, when the Virginian leads a vigilante crew in lynching his best friend Steve, who has become a rustler, he is following the long tradition of heroes who fight to protect the institution of private property and, more broadly, to defend the concept of justice in an unjust society. "But in Wyoming the law has been letting our cattle-thieves go for two years," Judge Henry tells Molly. "The courts, or rather the juries, into whose hands we have put the law, are not dealing the law . . . And so when your ordinary citizen sees this, and sees that he has placed justice in a dead hand, he must take justice back into his own hands where it was once at the beginning of all things . . . so far from being a *defiance* of the law, it is an *assertion* of it—the fundamental assertion of self-governing men, upon whom our whole social fabric is based" (pp. 438–439). Such a view met a sympathetic hearing during the Progressive reform era. Progressivism had begun as a "vote the rascals out" response to corruption between politics and business, with ministers, intellectuals, social workers, and lawyers joining in a movement that brought pressure on government agencies for tenement house laws, more stringent child labor laws, and more and better schools and community services. Working-class as well as college educated women were particularly active, especially in the political sphere. "Drawing attention to women's concern for social reform, Mrs. Sarah P. Decker, who became president of the [General Federation of Women's Clubs] in 1904, told the members of her organization, 'Dante is dead. . . . I think it is time that we dropped the study of his *Inferno* and turned our attention to our own'" (Divine et al., 370).

Surely, then, the theme of battling for justice which runs through this portion of *The Virginian* is more in keeping with the reformist attitude of the general public than with any defense of the status quo by the privileged elite. This argument, however, does not seem to tally with the Virginian working for Judge Henry. The dime novel convention of the hero siding the weak and vulnerable underdogs against the rich and powerful appears to be reversed, with the Virginian fighting and killing for an upperdog land baron who is akin to the corporate ranchers of the Johnson County War. Accordingly, critics such as Brown assert that "the hero, the Virginian, is in effect an incorporation gunfighter—a cowboy protagonist who represents the conservative social values so highly prized by Owen Wister" (p. 47). True enough, Wister visited the ranches of "Wyoming's cattle-holding elite" (Richard Maxwell Brown, p. 47), and no doubt he was comfortable with their sociopolitical outlook. However, although Wister drew from the events of the Johnson County War, this part of *The Virginian* is not a tale of cattle kings versus homesteaders but of ranchers versus rustlers. The Virginian's opponents are not hardscrabble nesters poaching cows in their struggle to eke out some measure of the American Dream. Rather, Wister depicts a more simplistic opposition of greedy, squandering outlaws—"a certain gang of horse and cattle thieves that stole in one Territory and sold in the next" (Wister, p. 382)—who possessed no redeeming merit and no intent to construct anything of value with their ill-gotten gains. As Wister pointedly remarks at the end, "the thieves prevailed at length . . . forcing cattle owners to leave the country. . . . Then, in 1892, came the Cattle War, when, after putting their men in office, and coming to some of the newspapers, the thieves brought ruin on themselves as well. For in a broken country there is nothing left to steal" (Wister, p. 506). By warning that failure to quash injustice will lead to ruin, Wister is confirming his call for individual morality and collective action, which were social values stressed by Progressives (Divine et al., p. 369), and can hardly be construed as conservative or elitist or, as DeVoto charges, as writing "in the interest of the master class" (p. 14).

Confusing who Wister was with what he wrote has induced a number of critics to reason that because he was an ultraconservative elitist, and because he portrayed the Virginian as rising to success out of natural superiority, therefore Wister patterned *The Virginian* after his belief in Social Darwinism—or more precisely, in a particular doctrine of Social Darwinism. The Social Darwinism cited by the critics is the original doctrine as proposed in the 1870s by English professor Herbert Spencer, who applied Darwin's evolutionary theories of natural selection to society, combining biology and sociology in a theory of "social selection" that explained human progress. "Like animals, society evolved; slowly, by adapting to the environment. The 'survival of the fittest'—a term Spencer, not Darwin, invented—preserved the strong and weeded out the weak" (Divine et al., p. 331; see also Bannister; Davidson et al.; Hofstadter; Goldman; Kelley; Shapin and Barnes; Wilson; and Wyllie). Thus, Mitchell states that the Virginian "can demonstrate his own inherent superiority and prove, that despite his immediate station, he is worthy of her [Molly's] affection. The narrator has long shared this creed and succinctly states it in social Darwinist terms: 'true democracy and true aristocracy are one and the same'" (p. 109). Cawelti agrees: "America, as Wister saw it, was as much a class society as any other country; the difference lay in the fact that the American elite was not determined by family status or traditional prerogative, but by inner worth tested in the competition between men" (*Adventure*, p. 227). Hamilton asserts that "the contempt Wister shows for the weak was enshrined in the social theories of his day, especially in social Darwinism. As popularized in the United States, this creed provided justification for the brutality of competitive individualism. . . . The success of the self-made man demonstrated the fairness of the contest, and served to highlight the more positive aspects of social mobility by espousing 'self-improvement'" (pp. 18, 19). Hamilton goes on to declare that for the western genre overall, "projecting the brutality of current social conditions backwards onto a frontier setting demonstrated the universality of social Darwinism" (p. 19). Similarly, in discussing Wister as well as Bret Harte and Hamlin Garland, Richard Slotkin alleges in *Gunfighter Nation* that their works "developed at length the central ideas and historiographic scenarios of such ideological systems as Social Darwinism" (p. 160), which in *Fatal Environment* he defines as "'survival of the fittest' used as a rationale for social order," one of "the building blocks of our dominant ideology along with 'laws' of capitalist competition, of supply and demand . . . and of 'Manifest Destiny'" (p. 34).

The flaw in all this is that the Social Darwinism of the 1870s was not the Social Darwinism of the Progressive era. Indeed, "debates over the social meaning of Darwinism constituted a major motif in social thought from the 1870s through the 1910s," and by the 1880s the slogans of Social Darwinism "were catchwords used by those who opposed unrestricted competition and the cult of individual success" (Bannister, p. 11). In the 1890s, a "corrected" reading of evolution postulated that big was better and, because competition was jungle anarchy, corporate empires and industrial trusts were necessary for social law and order. As Samuel Dodd, the legal framer of the Standard Oil Trust proclaimed, competition "carried to the furthest extreme without cooperation or compromise . . . would be a fit mode for savages, not for civilized men" (p. 14). Therefore, as Andrew Carnegie wrote, "the concentration of business . . . in the hands of a few; and the law of competition between these [is] not only beneficial, but essential to the future progress of the race" (p. 16). This convenient rationale for the powerful to stay in control and stave off reform collapsed in the face of the labor violence, agrarian protest, and urban poverty that by century's end triggered the Progressive movement.

In demanding increased governmental regulation of industry and legislation to address poverty and other ills of industrial society, reformers stressed the need to intervene against the brutal laws of Social Darwinism for group welfare and individual well-being. For example, in *Foundation of Sociology* (1905), Edward Ross asks, "Does not *society* impose decisive conditions as well as *nature?*" (Bannister, p. 278). To which Ross answered yes, and because not only nature but also society is a jungle, more systematic controls are required to protect the social fabric. Another popular and influential sociologist at the time was Benjamin Kidd, who in *Social Evolution* (1894) argues for "equality of opportunity," not in the original Social Darwinist terms of "survival of the fittest" and "natural selection," but rather in the Progressive spirit of providing means and opportunity for everyone. Pointing to "the increasing tendency to raise the position of the lower classes at the expense of the wealthier classes," Kidd insists that "all future progressive legislation must apparently have this tendency . . . the general tendency must be expected to be towards state interference and state control on a greatly extended scale" (pp. 233, 237).

By turning Social Darwinism to their own advantage, Progressive reformers reversed the Social Darwinist thesis and created Reform Darwinism, as Eric Goldman termed it in *Rendezvous with Destiny* (1952). Reform Darwinism became "an important ingredient in the progressive era quest for stability through the substitution of artificial controls (whether government or private) for natural ones" (Bannister, p. xxv), and although it is important to add the caveat that Reform Darwinists cannot be treated as a class but "came in all stripes" (p. xxii), certainly the general arguments advanced by Reform Darwinists to support Progressivism were in vogue at the time Wister was working on *The Virginian.* When considered within the context of Reform Darwinism, the underlying ethos of the Virginian as well as of Wister himself reflects the tenor of his times. There is a rejection of original Social Darwinism, with its "survival of the fittest" doctrine and resultant laissez-faire policies: "There is a levity abroad in our land which I must deplore. No matter how leniently you may try to put it, in the end we have a spectacle of a struggle between men where lying decides the survival of the fittest. . . . I can think of no threat more evil for our democracy, for it is a fine thing diseased and perverted—namely, independence gone drunk" (Wister, pp. 229, 268). There is an equal rejection of the Social Darwinism used as an apologia by industrialists and the privileged elite. In his preface to the 1911 edition of *The Virginian,* Wister strikes a Progressive note by declaring, "after nigh half-a-century of shirking and evasion, Americans are beginning to look at themselves and their institutions straight. . . . Our Democracy has many enemies, both in Wall Street and in the Labor Unions; but as those in Wall Street have by their excesses created those in the Unions, they are the worst" (p. vii). Wister had held this position for some time. In the preface to his 1896 collection of western tales, *Red Men and White,* he laments, "It is sorrowful to see our fatal complacence, or as yet undisciplined folly, in sending to our State Legislatures and to that general business office of ours in Washington a herd of mismanagers that seems each year to grow more inefficient and contemptible" (Bold, p. 41). Perhaps his sharpest condemnation came in the preface to his 1911 collection of stories, *Members of the Family:* "The citizens are awakening to the fact that our first century of 'self' government merely substituted the divine right of corporations for the divine right of Kings" (Klein, p. 115).

Hence, the philosophy of America "divided into two classes— the quality and the equality" (Wister, p. 147), espoused in *The Virginian,* is readily understandable in terms of Reform Darwinism. "We have seen little men artificially held up in high places, and great men artificially held down in low places, and our own justice-loving hearts abhorred this violence to human nature. Therefore, we decreed that every man should henceforth have equal liberty to find his own level" (p. 147). The result is to "see folks movin' up or movin' down, winners or losers everywhere" (p. 144). The Virginian does not suffer losers gladly, seeing them as weak: "Poor stupid Shorty's honesty had not been proof against frontier temptations, and he had fallen away from the company of his old friends" (p. 382); or plain bad to the bone: "Trampas had enticed Shorty away from good, and trained him in evil" (p. 390). He finds that they blame everything save themselves for losing: "Call your failure luck, or call it laziness, wander around the woods, prospect all yu' mind to, and yu'll come out the same old trail of inequality" (p. 144), when actually their inability to measure up is due to a lack of moral fiber: "One day you find him putting his iron on another man's calf. You tell him fair and square those ways have never been your ways and ain't going to be your ways. Well, that does not change him any, for it seems he's disturbed over getting rich quick and being a big man in the Territory" (p. 399). Thus the proclamation "Let the best man win, whoever he is!" (p. 147) refers to a man of innate integrity and courage operating within a society that encourages and rewards such qualities, rather than "best" as one who has adapted to existing conditions no matter how debased from some moral perspective. Honor, then, is to be prized. "What men say about my nature is not just merely an outside thing. For the fact that I let em' keep on sayin' it is a proof I don't value my nature enough to shield it from slander and give them their punishment. And that's being a poor sort of jay" (p. 478). The Reform Darwinist argument for providing equal opportunity without guaranteeing equal outcome was, to Wister, "true democracy. And true democracy and true aristocracy are one and the same thing. If anyone cannot see this, so much the worse for his hindsight" (p. 147).

Clearly, the contemporary populace saw eye to eye with Wister. *The Virginian* sold over a million copies by 1920 and almost two million by 1968, was adapted for the stage and as a musical, was made into movies four times, and formed the basis of a 1960s television series (Klein, p. 76; Hart, p. 219). Unfortunately for Wister, despite the enthusiasm spawned by his novel, he was never able to replicate its success in subsequent books; indeed, "all his other Western fictions prepare for, or decline from, this novel" (Bold, p. 68). *The Virginian* stands as a singular accomplishment, emphasizing the continuity of American values by effecting the fusion of the old era to the new era and a reconciliation of East and West. Certainly *The Virginian* has its limitations; the language in which it is couched seems still and stilted by today's standards, and "the marriage of East and West is not convincing at any but the plot level, for the validity of the cowboy's adaptation to the East, the modern West, and marriage is undercut by the network of inappropriate imagery and ambiguous statements on which it rests" (Bold, pp. 44–45). Nevertheless, in comparison to dime westerns and most hardcover competitors of the day, *The Virginian* is a serious and respectable work that, as Frank Gruber has said, took the western out of the woodshed and into the parlor.

Unlike Owen Wister, Zane Grey was a prolific writer who produced more than seventy novels, as well as innumerable serialized magazine stories that later became novels or were anthologized—many after his death in 1939. (The dates of the cited texts are those of their first publication as novels, irrespective of when they were composed or serialized.) Grey even wrote screenplays for his own film company, although most of the 105 movie adaptations of his work were done by other writers for other studios. Considering the output over his writing lifetime—1904 to 1937—it is not surprising that Grey is rather inconsistent in his treatment of plot, character, and theme; indeed, critics can and have asserted diametrically opposite claims about Grey, with each side well argued and supported by relevant quotations. For example, Gary Topping proposes that Grey's heroes "represent an entire system of values that contradicts, point by point, the values of modern capitalism" (p. 62), whereas Cynthia Hamilton postulates that the values found in Gray's stories are "central to the ideological tradition of the United States; to that body of ideas which form the basis for its political, economic and social system" (p. 9). As Christine Bold states, "Grey's most interesting novels demonstrate the author's contradictory impulses" (p. 79). Consequently, assessing Grey to any depth beyond shallow generalizations—for instance, that Grey produced westerns about brave heroes defeating wicked villains while rescuing spunky heroines—requires restraint, caution, and the caveat that exceptions surely exist.

The key to understanding the bulk of Grey's work, I believe, lies in two quotations. The first is from Grey's 1924 autobiographical article "Breaking Through: The Story of My Own Life," in which he recalls as a student being "friendless" and "out of my element" (p. 9), and then relates how, like so many adolescents who feel excluded, he escaped by daydreaming and reading adventure stories. The second quote is from a letter to him by his fiancée Lina Elise Rother, dated September 14, 1905, in which she discusses the partial manuscript of The Last Trail (1906) and makes suggestions for the unwritten balance: "I am very anxious to read the course of Miss Helen's love making. I suppose like the proverbial course of true love it is far from smooth. Make it as rough and exciting as possible for that stimulates interest and makes people so much more when they do get each other" (Gruber, p. 54).

Taking his fiancée's advice to heart, Grey became a writer of romances in which love plays a major role, providing motives and complications and rewards. More dominant than romance in the sense of love stories, however, is romance in the sense of escapist entertainment. Reflecting his formative years as a loner doting on adventure fiction, Grey preferred for most of his career to concoct tales that relied on invention or fancy rather than on reason or the imitation of reality, thereby following the literary tradition of Robert Louis Stevenson, Washington Irving, and Sir Walter Scott, who wrote in 1827 that "we now use the term *romance* as synonymous with fictious composition" (in Williams, p. 314). In doing so Grey distanced his fiction both from historical actuality and from contemporary reality which proved so troublesome for Wister, in effect preserving an embalmed West within a mythological context— myth, that is, as "a form of imaginative thinking, [whose] direct descendant in culture is literature, more particularly fiction" (Frye, p. 72). The construction of Grey's stories, then, follows a quasi-mythical pattern that relies on the principle of repetition and recurrence, which is what fosters the rhythm in music, the design in painting, and in Grey's work the replication of character, setting, and plot. "By stressing echoes from classical mythology, he emphasized that his world of adventure was cut off from its historical background and he underlined this impression by gesturing toward the limitations of his setting and characters" (Bold, p. 87).

Fundamentally, mythic romances are journeys or odysseys. Heroes leave their familiar, ordinary surroundings to venture into strange, dangerous worlds, which become arenas for conflict with antagonistic, challenging forces. The plots, despite their surface differences, consist of the archetypal separation-initiation-return cycle, which is exemplified by captive narratives and medieval passion plays, and which was mutated by dime westerns into the interminable chase-capture-rescue cycle. To the mythic romance Grey adds his love romance, usually a feisty heroine who is chronically threatened by diabolical schemes, devious secrets, and rapacious abductions by outlaws, Mexicans, Mormons, or other allegedly evil sorts. Typical is *Riders of the Purple Sage* (1912), possibly his best and probably his best-known novel. The protagonist Lassiter, searching for his abducted sister Mille, enters the strange world of Mormons in Utah. Finding that Mille has died in despair, he starts hunting her ruiner—the Bishop Dyer, as he eventually learns—and in the process helps heroine Jane Withersteen resist Elder Tull, who craves her for one of his wives. To force Jane's consent, Tull and his Mormon henchmen resort to rustling, murder, and the kidnapping of her adopted daughter Fay, only to be thwarted in a series of chases, captures, and rescues. Also borrowed from dime westerns is the use of wonder horses (Night, Black Star, and Wrangle) and the inclusion of a masked bandit who turns out to be a young woman (Bess, the captive daughter of Mille and her ravisher). Finally Lassiter kills Dyer, the Mormons give chase, and the classic climax ends the cycle with two returns: Bess and her beau Venters escape across the desert to the ordinary civilized world; and Lassiter, Jane, and Fay return to a conventional domestic life by sealing themselves off and settling down in impenetrable Surprise Valley. Not only in *Riders* but in novels like *Desert Gold* (1913) and *The Light of Western Stars* (1914), the return is not strictly physical but is symbolized by marriage and the restoration of traditional family values. In other novels the return is quite literal, to the extent that in *Heritage of the Desert* (1910) hero John Hare winds up back at the oasis where he started, thinking, "I've travelled in a circle!" (p. 230).

Also related to myth, and to be expected from a male writer weaned on adolescent adventure fiction, Grey's heroes are of epic stature continually enmeshed in fast, furious, and perilous action. In *Riders,* Lassiter is "like a man in a dream" (p. 16) and Venters is "tall and straight, his wide shoulders flung back, with the muscles of his bound arms rippling and a blue flame of defiance in [his] gaze" (p. 5). As Arthur Kimball observes, "Piercing eyes, gentle disposition, disposed to helping people in trouble, a fighter when need be. . . . Give or take a detail or two and any number of Grey cowboy heroes fit this stereotype; faced with descriptions taken out of context, one would be hard put to distinguish Pecos Mith, Brazos Keene, Panhandle Smith, and Arizona Ames" (pp. 100, 101). Lassiter at the end is exhausted and bleeding profusely from five bullet wounds, yet he boosts Jane and carries Fay up the sheer side of Surprise Valley and then shoves a massive boulder over the cliff to block pursuit. A similar superhuman quality infests almost all Grey's action sequences, and his descriptions of fighting and killing seem particularly prone to melodramatic gusto. In *Code of the West* (1934), some half-dozen pages are devoted to depicting "disfigured" Cal Enoch after a brawl, beginning with a face "scarcely human, beaten and swollen out of shape, purple in spots, raw like beef in others" (p. 283). Grey is therefore open to the same criticism leveled at so many writers, that of larding stories with excessive and gratuitous violence. Cawelti, for example, condemns Grey for "orgies of violence . . . carried out with a kind of transcendent religious passion" (*Adventure*, pp. 237–238). Topping counters that most of the "carnage" is necessary and well integrated, and that much of it "takes place off stage, as does the massacre of the wagon train early in *The U. P. Trail*" (p. 44); and though Kimball disagrees, arguing that some violence is offstage but "a lot of it is not" (p. 175), he proposes an astute explanation that ties the graphic action common to mythic romances with the emotional motivations common to love romances: "In short, a sizable number of Grey's narratives suggest that the real rationale for violence is desire . . . good when chastely united in a true love match, bad when obsessively linked with seduction and stolen cattle, but the prime mover in either case" (p. 178).

Another aspect of myth incorporated by Grey is that the journeys undertaken by his protagonists often stand for inward journeys of the mind, the heart, the spirit. Secondary characters too are capable of learning, growing, and changing from, say, folly to wisdom, lawlessness to lawfulness, or youth to maturity over the course of adventures that serve metaphorically as rites of passage. Venters, for instance, has "gone away a boy—he had returned as a man" (p. 164) who tells Bess that he is "a man you've made" (p. 185). Of course, in order to change, the characters must be flawed to begin with. Consequently, many of Gray's characters are variations of the dime western's outcast, well intentioned and innately honorable, who for one reason or another has strayed and is in need of reform. A favorite of Grey's is the gunslinger as portrayed by Lassiter, and in greater detail by Buck Duane in *The Lone Star Ranger* (1915). Initially a fugitive who is offered a pardon in return for catching the outlaw Cheseldine, Duane has "a driving intensity to kill" with a gun that is "a living part of him" (pp. 3, 41). He enters the strange world of outlawry, where he falls in love with Ray Lonstreth and discovers that her father Granger is in fact Cheseldine—but instead of capturing the outlaw, Duane defends him to Ray: "I once heard a well-known rancher say that all rich cattlemen had done a little stealing. Your father drifted out here, and like a good many others, he succeeded. It's perhaps just as well not to split hairs, to judge him by the law and morality of a civilized country" (pp. 285–286). Duane's belief that Cheseldine can change is paralleled by his realization that he, too, must transform himself: "At last he shuddered under the driving, ruthless, inhuman blood-lust of the gunman . . . And those passions were so violent, so raw, so base, so much lower than what ought to have existed in a thinking man" (pp. 294–295). At the end there are two reforms coupled with two returns: Cheseldine quits his outlawry and returns to Louisiana, while Duane marries Ray and also departs for Louisiana to regain a peaceful, ordinary life.

By contrast, Grey's villains cannot change other than to die. Indeed, being unregenerate is the mark of their evil nature, and thus a difference is drawn between characters who are not so bad as to be intolerable—and who are potentially redeemable—and criminals whose incorrigibility makes them pariahs. This distinction is overt when portraying archvillains, but even is implied when differentiating minor scoundrels, as when Duane remarks: "That Blandy. His faro game's crooked. . . . Not that we don't have lots of crooked faro dealers. A fellow can stand for them. But Blandy's mean, back-handed, never looks you in the eyes" (p. 215). Because they lack the ability to change, to display human frailties or anxieties, the villains tend to resemble dime-western stereotypes in their speech and behavior. For example, villains who operated where there is no law act in the manner of gang leader Hays in *Robber's Roost* (1932) who, when a robbery victim declares, "If there is law in this—country—you'll pay for this," sneeringly retorts with a cliché, "Haw! Haw! You ain't lookin' for law, air you granpaw? . . . Wal, the only law is what you see here in my hand—and I don't mean your money" (p. 6). Grey's other type of stock villain is the conspirator who operates where the law is corrupt or inept, akin to Jack Harriman in *Valley of Wild Horses* (1947), who shows up with the hackneyed "claims, papers, witnesses, and law back of him. He claimed to have gotten possession of the homestead from the original owner. It was all a lie. But they put us off" (p. 65).

Villains cause change through such standard plot devices as perpetrating injustices, murdering innocents, and terrorizing settlements, thereby galvanizing heroes and heroines into action which in turn effects change within themselves. Buck Duane is led in part to reform by becoming increasingly outraged at conscienceless bandits marauding with impunity, until he finally decides that "a cold, secret, murderous hold on a little struggling community was something too strange, too terrible for me to stand long" (pp. 219–220), and ultimately concludes that he as a gunslinger is no better than they. "He realized it now, bitterly, hopelessly. The thing he had the intelligence enough to hate he had become. . . . He reasoned that only intelligence could save him—only a thoughtful understanding of his danger and a hold upon some ideal" (pp. 294, 104). Duane is also helped to convert through the catalyst of love, as is the fate of virtually all heroes in romances who are "made to be reformed by the right woman" (Fiedler, p. 270).

But no less than his heroes, Grey's heroines experience rites of passage. They are nonconformists who carry guns, wear pants, own property and businesses, and demand equality and sexual independence. Underneath, and sometimes in spite of rapes and shady pasts, they remain maidens chaste to an incredible degree, which creates incredible that must be taken, like so much in myth, with a severe suspension of disbelief. Bandit queen Bev in *Riders*, for example, is

> a girl dressed as a man. She had been made to ride at the head of infamous forays and drives. She had been imprisoned for many months of her life in an obscure cabin. At times the most vicious of men had been her companions; and the vilest of women, if they had been permitted to approach had, at least, cast their shadows over her. But—but in spite of all this—there thundered at Venters some truth that lifted its voice higher than the clamoring facts of dishonor, some truth that was the very life of her beautiful eyes; and it was innocence (109).

"Nothing shows more clearly how far away Mr. Grey's world is from actuality," notes critic T. K. Whipple, referring to Grey's treatment of sex, and then cites instances of his heroes and heroines together in the wilderness in perfect innocence (Topping, p. 41). As with the heroes, love is a major catalyst by which heroines change, transforming them through the symbolic loss of innocence from girls into women. Granted, there are evil females who, like the villains, refuse to quit their wicked ways and suffer a bad end. But many heroines endure a physical and emotional rite of passage, maturing like Bev from a "stripling" to an adult who "no longer resembled a boy. No eye could have failed to mark the rounded contours of a woman" (p. 142); and thus awakened to their sexuality, they become like the Biblical Eve after eating the fruit of wisdom with Adam: "And the eyes of them both were opened, and they knew that they were naked" (Gen. 3:7). Older heroines like Jane Withersteen have matured already, but like the younger heroines they must change from prizing their independence to desiring marriage and a family with the hero. Their passage, like all rites of passage, is scary and largely compulsive. Finding herself contemplating marriage, Helen Rayner in *The Man of the Forest* (1920) "did not analyze that strange thought. She was afraid of it as she was of the stir in her blood when she visualized Dale" (pp. 222–223). Once they determine what—or rather, who—they want, they pursue their quarry using sexuality as bait without compunction, as Jane does when she plies her "grace and beauty and wiles" to domesticate Lassiter (p. 62), proposing that he "take me" in trade for hanging up his guns (p. 226). Naturally, heroines employ their sexuality for other causes; as Kimball observes, "Grey's heroines are never really helpless, for they embody the erotic power which vanquishes hero and villain alike. Hands tied and locked in as she is, Mescal [in *Heritage of the Desert*] in a very real sense 'triggers' the self-destructive violence between Snap Naab and Holderness and the beginning of the gang's disintegration. . . . Invariably, in this way, the abducted heroine initiates the undoing of the gang from within, though the hero and his pards come in and mop up" (p. 178).

The betrothal of hero and heroine is certainly in keeping with mythic romances, let alone love romances. But in the plotting of their troubled journeys to the altar, Grey seems, wittingly or not, to mirror his contemporary culture, specifically its ambivalent views about feminism and feminist concerns. In most of his stories he acknowledges the movement toward candid sexuality and experimentation with gender roles, and allows that women do not and should not want to thoroughly housebreak their men. When Lassiter finally capitulates to Jane's demands, she realizes that he is a "smaller man" for it and insists he put his guns back on (p. 215); and Madeline Hammond in *The Light of Western Stars* rejects her genteel Eastern lovers for cowboy Gene Stewart because they "were without the only great essential [natural nobility] that a hard life had given Stewart" (p. 161). On balance, though, Grey favors traditional values and roles, and regrets that "modern woman" is not more like the "schoolgirls of long ago when something of America still survived in our girls" (Karr, p. 171). The only proper solution for him remains conventional marriage, because this provides the morally and socially acceptable haven for all that stormy sexuality and hence contains inducements for taming wild men (and increasingly wild women) into family folk. "How full and perfect her trust, her happiness," Helen Rayner muses at the conclusion, "in the realization that her love and her future, her children, and perhaps grandchildren, would come under the guidance of such a man!" (p. 382).

Probably the catalyst most associated with Grey is nature—specifically the nature of the West. Inspired by the Western panorama from his first trip in 1907, Grey incorporated nature as more than simply background for his stories, but as an active and often major player influencing the characters and sequence of events. Indeed, as Carlton Jackson points out, "in so many of his novels, Grey makes setting and description more important than characterization" (p. 44). Whether Grey portrays nature as malevolent or benevolent is determined to a large degree by the needs of his romance and adventure plots, but in either case the Western landscape can be viewed both as the strange world that mythic heroes enter and as a force that they encounter during their rites of passage. In *Thunder Mountain* (1915), the mountain is the object of attack by prospectors gripped by gold fever, the draw for protagonist Lee "Kalispel" Emerson and dance-hall girl (later wife) Nugget, the provocation for a long journey through lengthily described nature, and the instructor that teaches Emerson and Nugget to reject corruptive greed—whereupon Thunder Mountain buries the villains in a massive slide: "As if in mockery of the littleness of man, Nature pealed out the doom which the wise old beaver and the savage chief had foreseen—For ages its foundations had groaned warnings. And now the hour of descent had come" (p. 382). Similarly, "the desert brought out primitive instincts of man that could be used for purposes of good or evil" (Jackson, p. 22). The Indian Nophaie in *The Vanishing American* (1925) observes that "over all the immensity of ghastly desert brooded a spirit of desolation and death and decay" (p. 218), and, prophetically, his tribal brethren are killed by murderous whites and the influenza plague, until finally the survivors disappear into a dying sunset. In the symbolically titled *Stairs of Sand* (1943), the perilously shifting desert is "a Collosus [sic] of natural elements in process of decay, dying through the ages, destructive, terrible, dominated by the spirit of the sun" (p. 99), which nonetheless for Ruth Virey "had given her many of its attributes—its changeableness, its fiery depth, its mystery and moods and passion, and its beauty" (p. 253) and so becomes the catalyst by which she develops from a bratty girl into a self-reliant woman.

In the stories depicting nature as malevolent, the struggle to survive provides much of the action and motivation, so some critics have concluded that Grey, like Wister, was propounding the Darwinist doctrine of "survival of the fittest." Hamilton, citing *Wanderer of the Wasteland* (1923), declares that "in Grey's work one plainly hears the echo of Darwin rather than Jefferson: 'Here at last was revealed the deepest secret of the desert, the eternal law men read in its lonely, naked face—self-preservation and reproduction. The individual lived and fought and perished but the species survived'" (p. 19). Similarly, Topping argues that "Grey's Darwinism owed more to Darwin himself than to Spencer and the other Social Darwinists, in spite of the fact that Grey also used Darwinism as a basis for social theory. Contact with raw nature was the vital factor in Grey's West, not the strife of man versus man emphasized by Spencerians" (p. 43). Topping then quotes from *The Man of the Forest*: "If you're quick to see, you'll learn that the nature here in the wilds is the same as that of men—trees fight to live—birds fight—animals fight— men fight. They all live off one another. An' it's this fightin' that brings them all closer an' closer to bein' perfect" (p. 126). Jackson also quotes the same dialogue when asserting that "the novel is replete with passages about the evolution of man from a state of barbarism to that of civilization. Such statements indicate that man is but part of a grand, inscrutable design in which the trials of life . . . are necessary to all living things. Thoughts of 'natural selection' or 'survival of the fittest,' underlie these passages" (p. 42).

However, as with Wister, the critics have misconstrued Darwinian theory and as a result have misinterpreted Grey's concept of nature. Darwinian theory does not insist that natural selection is predicated upon constant fighting and preying on one another. It was Thomas Malthus in his *Essay on the Principles of Population* (1788) who postulated this image of struggle in nature, "defin[ing] struggle as the battle of an individual or group against the environment" (Bannister, p. 24). Rather, Darwin held in *The Origin of Species* (1862) that although brute force may be one factor in evolution, equally so may be harmony among species and their environment, a "dependence of one being on another," and that the struggle for survival should be taken less literally than "in a large and metaphorical sense" (p. 62). Nor in Darwinian theory is there "a grand, inscrutable design." There is design in the long discredited notions of Chevalier de Lamarck, who in his *Histoire Naturelle des Animaux Sans Vertebres* (1815–1822) proposes that nature seeks perfection through "progressive differentiation," meaning that biological changes occur in species when they alter habits or have "new Wants," and that these acquired characteristics are transmitted to offspring—for example, generations of giraffes stretching to eat treetop leaves resulted in their growing long necks. Along with Lamarck's idea of material causation was the spiritual causation of the Cosmic Theists, led by Asa Gray, who argued that species were preconceived products of the deity (see Dupree); therefore, evolution was "materialistic" and "contradict[ing] the whole idea of a personal Divine interference in the affairs of the world." Darwin skirted the issue of spiritual causation, in part to avoid unnecessary controversy, and even Asa Gray admitted "that Darwin left readers in the dark concerning his views of 'philosophy and theology'" (Bannister, p. 19). But it can be inferred that he would have rejected Lamarck's idea of an inherently progressive design in nature; he believed that "the laws of nature were statistical rather than mechanical, that is were approximations concerning probabilities rather than fixed rules from which one could deduce certain consequences" (Bannister, p. 18). For Darwin, then, evolution is a predilection toward a cumulative but not necessarily progressive development, whose natural selection derives neither from random accident nor from immutable procedures (see Bannister; Darwin; Dupree; Gillespie; Green; and Schwartz).

Hence, quotes from Grey's work cited as evidence of his Darwinism suggest instead that it is *not* Darwinian. Indeed, when placed back in context, some quotes seem to question or even contradict the whole "survival of the fittest" philosophy. For instance, following the "fighting brings them all closer an' closer to bein' perfect" quote from *The Man of the Forest*, Topping cites more of the exchange between Milt Dale and Helen Rayner: "When she asks, 'what of the mental and spiritual development of man and woman,' Dale replies brutally, 'Both are direct obstacles to the design of Nature.'" (p. 43). But as Kimball points out, Topping "does not mention the oddity of Dale's argument—worth at least a chuckle—about a natural evolutionary 'mission' somehow divorced from or hindered by anything mental . . . nor does Topping note that Helen's sister Bo falls off the log laughing at the arguments of the two lovers" (p. 174). Moreover, the mislabeled Darwinism of the critics can be interpreted as simply illustrative of mythic rites of passage, either describing the deadly trials encountered in nature, or expressing the philosophies of those enduring these trials. Despite his so-called Darwinism, Dale implies that he and Helen are engaged in rites of passage when he says, "There must be a great change in either you or me, accordin' to the other's influence. An' can't you see that change must come in you, not because of anythin' superior in me—I'm really inferior to you—but because of our environment!" (pp. 158–159). The symbolism is transparent in *Captives of the Desert* (1952) when hero John Curry remarks to the Hopi Magdalene, "Going through life is something like riding a deep canyon where the light seldom shines. . . . Don't you want to struggle on a little longer, Magdalene? I'm boxed in at the present myself, in a canyon dark as hell, but I'm feeling around for the way out" (p. 197). During an even more grueling and metaphysical journey in *Wanderer of the Wasteland,* hero Adam Larey ponders how

> a man of evil nature survivin' in the desert becomes more terrible than a beast. . . . On the other hand there are men whom the desert makes like it. . . . I've met such men, an' if it's possible for the divinity of God to walk abroad on earth in the shape of mankind, it was invested in them. The reason must be that in the development of the desert, in [the] case of these few men who did not retrograde, the spiritual kept pace with the physical. (p. 64)

The test of spirit as well as body is another indication that Grey did not write as a so-called Darwinian. Topping himself concedes that after Dale's debate with Helen, Dale "cannot account for such things as pain and suffering. Also, he cannot account for the seeming meaninglessness of a cosmos that has no end but the perpetuation and perfection of itself. These two problems can only be solved by religion or some other philosophy, as Helen had pointed out to him" (p. 43). Here Helen appears to be speaking for Grey, who, as Hamilton notes, "welcomed the excitement which nature 'red in tooth and claw' could produce, but was troubled by the spiritual vacuum at its centre. Social Darwinism could provide no aura of heroism, nor could it support the old morality of small-town America" (p. 42).

Although an aura of heroism can be attributed to the mythic elements in Grey's fiction, his support of conventional morality can be found in his stories' religious connotations, such as in the Larey quote just cited and in descriptions in *The Rainbow Trail* (1915) of heights with "cathedral spires" and rivers with "the soul of the devil" (pp. 18, 238). However, orthodox Christianity is not as celebrated as a strand of unchurched, or popular, religious thought that developed during the nineteenth century. As the wilderness shrank and Americans grew increasingly confident that its dangers were only possibilities rather than probabilities, they tended to extol the virtues of nature—much in the same manner that after the threat of Indians had passed, Americans came to perceive them as Noble Savages. This somewhat nostalgic view of nature as sublime was rooted in the initial colonial vision of the New World as a Garden of Eden, and consequently "the sublime in nature became evidence of God's power and moved humanity to stand in awe of His Work" (Hyde, p. 18). The powerful influences of transcendentalism soon made the pristine wilderness the equivalent of God, as is evident in the writings of corn-flake inventor John Harvey Kellogg: "God is *in* nature. . . . God actually entered into the product of his creative skill, so that it might not only outwardly reflect the divine conception, but that it might think divinely and act divinely" (p. 40). From Kellogg's suggestion that matter and spirit are dimensions of a single reality, it was only a short extension to the concept of nature as a cosmic source of healing power which can provide individuals, as William James wrote in 1902, "serenity, moral poise, and happiness, and prevents certain forms of disease as well as science does, or even better" (p. 110). From there it was but a step to asserting that contemporary American life was so unnatural that it caused disease or "dis-ease" in people. According to medical historian Robert Fuller, "Urbanization, industrialization, immigration, and the splintering of any theological consensus around which national life might revolve all jarred the American psyche loose from traditional sources of stability. Whether psychosomatic illness actually increased around the turn of the century is difficult to ascertain. It is, however, safe to assume that Americans' awareness of the mental/cultural origin of many of their ailments increased dramatically" (p. 63).

The rapid industrialization and attendant corruption, Topping points out, "forced in Grey's mind the idea that the open West had indeed served as the source for much that was virtuous and creative in American history. With the end of that source, it seemed to many that America was truly becoming indistinguishable from the Old World in its increasing weakness of moral fiber. This explains much of the longing for a lost world that characterizes Grey's fiction" (p. 40). Combining the vision of metaphysical healing with the mythical rite of passage, Grey wrote of the transforming potential of western life, in which typically his characters arrive from the artificiality and oppressiveness of the East to gain spiritual composure, physical health, economic well-being, and appropriate social roles. One of his oft-repeated plot lines, for instance, is "An Easterner—that is, an innocent—arrives in the West. He, or she, has been a failure in the past and seems unprepared to meet the challenges ahead," explains Ann Ronald. "Gradually, however, the neophyte becomes a man. Rather than be beaten by the environment, he learns to conquer the elements, and in doing so he acquires a deep appreciation for the land. . . . The West, seeming almost a Garden of Eden, becomes a proving ground for man. Here he loses his innocence and gains knowledge" (*Zane Grey*, p. 13). The portrayal of nature as healer and teacher is particularly clear in the stories wherein nature is benevolent—such stories providing, by the way, a telling argument against Grey's being a Darwinist, because nature as nurturer is antithetical to a doctrine of constant fighting for survival of the fittest. In *Rainbow Trail*, hero Shefford is a lapsed minister from the East seeking to find Fay Larkin—and himself. Early on in the desert, Shefford, "divining whence his help was to come, embraced all that wild and speaking nature around and above him and surrendered himself utterly" (p. 39), and toward the end he senses in "a spirit in the canyon . . . the life of the present, or the death of the ages, or the nature so magnificently manifested in these silent, dreaming, waiting walls—the truth for Shefford was that this spirit was God" (p. 226). Likewise, Nophaie in *The Vanishing American* discovers "the immanence of God" during his mythic quest to "find his soul" (p. 7): "The great breathing spirit of nature all around him was as true to him as any spirit the

Indians might have worshipped. It was there—the mysterious power—the eternal thing—the infinite" (p. 115).

For nature to be redemptive requires that, at least initially, people must be in need of redemption. "Human nature is imperfect," Nophaie observes. Eastern dandies, such as Boyd Harvey in *The Light of Western Stars,* are unworthy of reproduction; if Harvey "ever had any sons they would be like him, only a generation more toward the inevitable extinction of his race" (p. 256). And Eastern coquettes are "idle, luxurious, selfish, pleasure-craving, lazy, useless, work and children shirking, absolutely no good" (*The Call of the Canyon,* p. 229). Of course, Grey's nature is akin to karma, in that those who do not seek to better themselves will inevitably get what they deserve—or as Dismukes says in *Wanderer of the Wasteland* (1923), "Let every man save his own life—find his own soul. That's the unwritten law of the wastelands of the world" (p. 63). Thus the bandit Gulden in *The Border Legion* (1916) is someone "beneath morals," who at first "can have more power" because "on the border" he can flout civil law (p. 116), but who cannot avoid the natural law of consequences and is eventually done in by Kells, his conscience-stricken boss. For Grey, then, nature is inexorable and his West is neither "lawless" nor in need of "the restraints of civilization," as Hamilton asserts. In *The Deer Stalker* (1949), the balance of nature is first broken when the bounty-killing of cougars creates an overpopulation of deer, and then again when the government's solution is to promote open slaughter of the deer herds. "The whole gory situation illustrates to Grey the baneful effects of man's meddling with nature" (Jackson, p. 43). Arguably the government had good intentions, but the result is the unleashing of mercenary hunters—which is in keeping with Grey's primary motivation for his villains, that of greed.

The greed in Grey's fiction is that of exploitation, of "capitalism gone haywire in the form of villains who exploit weakness and vulnerability by unfair means" (Kimball, p. 227). Often such selfish interests are tied to industrial and corporate giants in the East, and when the predators are vanquished, the conquering heroes are rewarded with a stake in the American Dream—for example, Dale in *The Man of the Forest* locates gold, Warren Neale in *The U. P. Trail* earns the top chief engineer position, and Gene Steward in *The Light of Western Stars* marries into wealth. The stories, then, cannot be read as condemnations of the capitalist system in general, but rather of the violence and excesses that can occur when the system is abused. They are not veiled rationales for "the warfare between man and nature, between race and race, exalted as a kind of heroic ideal," as Slotkin, among others, likes to portray westerns (*Regeneration*, p. 5); rather, they extol the principles that so often propelled dime-western plots, of independent individuals overcoming criminal combines to achieve personal, social, and financial success. "These are stock American values, stock American dreams, and . . . [by] placing such heroes and plot patterns in the wild and woolly West, Grey emphasises the continuity of key American values" (Hamilton, p. 91).

Support of the American Dream was not the only comment Grey made about his contemporary society. Several stories written from 1918 to 1925 center on historical events as Grey perceived them, as when in *The U. P. Trail* incorporates the political corruption and machinations of the Crédit Mobilier in the construction of the transcontinental railroad. *Western Union* (1939) depicts the despoiling of Indian culture and wilderness in general in the stringing of a telegraph line from Omaha and Salt Lake City. In *The Vanishing American, The Desert of Wheat* (1919), *The Call of the Canyon* (1924), *The Shepherd of Guadaloupe* (1930), *30,000 on the Hoof* (1940), and *Rogue River Feud* (1948), Grey addresses the wretched plight of the returning World War I veteran and the rejuvenating effects of the West in a modern postwar society. Perhaps his strongest social commentary was his support for equal and humanitarian treatment of minorities, particularly Indians, long before the position was fashionable. "Why, if there is a god," Magdalene asks in *Captives of the Desert*, "did He make races, one to conquer the other, one to be superior to the other, one to break the hearts of the other?" (p. 90). At least in one case—*The Vanishing American*—Grey's commentary conflicted with his formulaic writing for the market. *Vanishing* tells of the Eastern-raised and -educated Nophaie who, upon returning to his tribe, cannot accept either the white or the Indian ways of behavior and belief. Worse yet, he wishes to marry a white woman, Marion, who follows him West. Initially the story ended with Nophaie and Marion married. But before it first appeared as a serial in the April 1923 issue of *Ladies' Home Journal*, the editors forced Grey to revise its ending into a Noble Savage death scenario, Nophaie gasping, "I had to die as a white man. . . . White woman, savior of Nophaie, go back to your people" (p. 235). When *The*

Vanishing American came out as a novel in 1925, Grey avoided miscegenation again by having Marion eulogize not only the dead Nophaie but also his decimated tribe: "They are vanishing—vanishing! Oh! Nophahs! Only a question of swiftly flying time! My Nophaie—the warrior—gone before them!" (p. 308). When the original manuscript version was published posthumously by Grey's son Loren in Zane Grey's *Indian Tales* (1977), Marion's eulogy was revealed to have been a rewrite of a lament delivered by her live groom, Nophaie: "They are vanishing—vanishing! My Nophahs! . . . Only a question of swiftly flying time! And I too— Nophaie, the warrior! In the end I shall be absorbed by you [Marion]— by your love—by our children!" (pp. 123–124).

His social commentary limited, even muted, by the constraints of the marketplace, Grey nonetheless achieved a modicum of influence, especially on the views of politically conservative readers. After all, Grey was fundamentally conservative, extolling the manly virtues and moral imperatives of earlier, simpler times. "He was baffled and repelled by many aspects of twentieth-century America. His unease with the current direction of American social and economic trends was also typical, as was his faith in the essential goodness of the American way of life and his optimistic view of the future" (Hamilton, pp. 24, 25). Unfortunately, the division between current directions and his conservative values widened to the point that, by the late twenties, his optimism had turned to pessimism, and in 1930 Grey left Arizona after publicly declaring that "commercial interests were taking over, and spoiling, Arizona's forests and desert resources. Thereafter he would only deal with the 'real' Arizona—the one he had come to some twenty years before, and only as part of the mythic West of his novels" (Kimball, pp. 200–201). Grey had never confined his settings to Arizona, of course, and after moving he wrote novels set outside the West, such as Oregon in *Rogue River Feud*, California in *Boulder Dam* (1963), and even Australia in *Wilderness Trek* (1949). His subsequent stories tend to suffer from his melancholy, lacking the colorful spirit and/or social commentary of his earlier works. For example, *Wildfire* (1917) revels in the hunting of wild horses and the heroic martyrdom of the red stallion Wildfire, whereas *Horse Heaven Hill* (1959) is a morose tale of now-anachronistic wild horses doomed for slaughter as chicken feed.

If we judge his total output as a whole, Zane Grey can be seen to be more akin to James Fenimore Cooper than to Owen Wister. Granted, both Grey and Wister present the conventional western recipe of adventures set on frontiers about personal character striving to overcome perilous circumstances, and their heroes are typical of dime westerns— tough, resourceful, combative individualists who uphold decency and ethics in the face of non-existent, ineffective, or corrupt legal institutions. However, like Cooper's Natty Bumppo, Grey's heroes operate on a largely preindustrial frontier where civilization is an encroachment; indeed, the more developed Eastern society becomes, the more it corrupts the healthy vistas of the open West. And, as with Bumppo, the characteristics needed to survive in the West often make Grey's heroes unable to accept, or be accepted by, civilization. In contrast, Wister's Virginian is a lineal descendent of John Filsen's Daniel Boone, living on a relatively socialized frontier and fighting its savage elements for the sake of settlement and civilization. These two views of the West, then, are modifications of the original opposing visions of the New World as a Hell on Earth or a Garden of Eden, only altered by Grey and Wister to reflect their contemporary cultural and market conditions.

The bulk of this chapter is devoted to Wister and Grey because they were the most prominent and critically acclaimed practitioners of the western during the first three decades of this century. It would be a mistake to leave the impression, though, that there were no other popular and successful western writers during this period. Probably most notable is O. Henry (William Sidney Porter), who in his short story "The Caballero's Way" (1907) created the Cisco Kid, that charming rogue who prefers to outwit rather than outfight his enemies. The Cisco Kid has appeared in numerous films and television adaptations, including the first all-talking western movie In Old Arizona (1929), and started a trend for Hispanic heroes in south-of-the-border westerns. The north country was a favorite setting for prolific writers such as Rex Beach in The Spoilers (1905), William Macleod Raine in The Yukon Trail (1917), Jackson Gregory in Wolf Breed (1917), and James Oliver Curwood in Back to God's Country (1911) and The Alaskan (1923). Although their stories sold well at the time, they are badly dated by heavy sentimentality and, in the case of Curwood, by blatant racism. Also flawed by sentimentality and cardboard characterization is the work of Peter B. Kyne, who nonetheless became a celebrity when his mediocre *Saturday Evening Post* story "Bronco Billy and the Baby" (1910) formed the basis for movie star G. M. Anderson's "Bronco Billy" character; Kyne subsequently expanded his short story into the equally poor novel *Three Godfathers* (1917), and if it weren't for "Bronco Billy" and later films based on *Three Godfathers*, Kyne would have long ago slipped into well-deserved obscurity. Other writers provided vivid descriptions but implausible plots, such as Dan Quin (Alfred Henry Lewis) who wrote the *Wolfville* series from 1897 to 1913; Steward Emerson White, whose mining camp story *The Westerners* (1901) became the first big-budget western film in 1919; and Emerson Hough, whose novels *The Covered Wagon* (1922) and *North of 36* (1923) were made into highly popular films and helped establish wagon train and trail-drive stories as staples of the genre. The livelier, crisper writing of Frank Spearman ages better, and his *Whispering Smith* (1906) is still reprinted on occasion, as are the poetically intense "Pasó Por Aqui" by Eugene Manlove Rhodes and *Wolf Song* (1927) by Harvey Fergusson, who blends realism, romanticism, and a love of nature into one of the finest novels about mountain men.

Still, in tracing the trends and cultural connections of the western, it is clear at this juncture that, through the patterns popularized by dime novelists and applied by Owen Wister and Zane Grey, the frontier myth initially embodied in Filsen continues to this day to provide the underlying metaphors and imagery for most traditional western fiction. Imitating Wister's and Grey's work, the majority of Grey's contemporaries and the writers who followed have been lesser talents dependent on formulaic models, often removing the political, philosophical, or social commentary needed to understand the "why" of the action, sometimes even eschewing the specifics of region or local color needed to indicate the "when" and "where" of the action, and concentrating instead on concocting some distinctive style or peculiar twist to set their stock westerns apart from others. Consequently, while there have been some writers, like Walter D. Edmonds in *Drums Along the Mohawk* (1936) and Kenneth Roberts in *Northwest Passage* (1937), who have attempted to portray historical events accurately, for the most part writers have found it easier to dispense with any pretense of reality, lift original ideas of others, rely on the mythical structures used by Grey, and fabricate illusory Wests of adventure and romance.

For instance, William Colt MacDonald avoided Grey's moralizing on contemporary events, dropped any notion of historical accuracy, and swiped the Three Musketeers from Alexander Dumas to create Tucson Smith, Lullaby Joslin, and Stony Brooke as "The Three Mesquiteers" in *Law of the Forty-Fives* (1933). Similarly, Johnson McCulley rewrote Baroness Emma Orczy's protagonist Scarlet Pimpernel as Zorro in "The Curse of Capistrano" and its sequels. Legions of other writers wrote mythically in the sense that they churned out heroes superhuman in brawn if not brain. During the fifty years of W. C. Tuttle's pulp career, starting with *Reddy Brant, His Adventures* in 1920, Tuttle composed innumerable westerns starring wisecracking range detectives. Archie Joscelyn, whose fictional output under his own name and the pseudonym "Lynn Westland" is estimated to be around fifteen million words, produced yarns involving fur traders, railroaders, freighters, gamblers, rodeo performers, and women whose skin "was fair as new-fallen snow on an old fence post" (Westland, *Trail to Montana*, p. 25), set on riverboats, mountains, and prairies that spread "as flat and unending and monotonous as a yellow hound dog scratching its fleas" (Westland, *Shootin' Iron*, p. 42). Charles "Chuck" Martin invented series characters like Bible-thumping gunman "Gospel" Cummings, fiddle-footed range-hands Roaming Reynolds and Texas Joe, and aging Wells Fargo trouble-shooter Alamo Bowie—normally a two-fisted, two-gun man, but who in *Gun Law* carries his left arm "like the broken pinion on an eagle that has been wounded in battle" (p. 10). Characters like Border Buzzard, Ferg Slake, and Snag Roke populate locales like Snaketrail Gorge and the Plugged Peso Saloon in Walter "Tommy" Tomkins' stories, frequently up to their dirty necks in shoot-outs, knife fights, dynamite bombings, and quicksand traps. Tom Roan introduced characters like Anvil Lord, his son Devil Lord, stepson Brill Wilde, the one-eyed old horse thief Don Juan Leon de Casa Grande, and the cussed Old Bow and Arrow Hanks, who during brawls would yell "Eat 'em up alive, yuh punkin' heads! . . . Wrop their ankles 'round their jawbones! . . . Raised like goats, a' I believe the bellwether of the breed was a ram!" (*Gun Lord of Silver River*, pp. 249–250). Most of Roan's plots revolve around the mythic theme of a man undergoing violent trials and tribulations in a transforming rite of passage, as do the heroes in the stories by Frederick Faust, the prince of prolific pulpsters, who wrote well over three hundred book-length stories under the byline Max Brand and nineteen other pseudonyms. As a variation on Grey's mythically restorative West, Faust ignored the landscape and focused on seemingly inconsequential protagonists with hidden heroic stature, such as the cripple in *Larramee's Ranch* (1927) who cannot fire a gun, Faust often combining the hidden potential with a character flaw, such as the pairing of honesty and vanity in Harry Destry in *Destry Rides Again* (1930).

This formulaic version of the western, in which melodrama and mythology are dominant motifs, has flourished largely unaltered to present times. Its rather immutable persistence can be seen in the fact that writers like Martin, Tompkins, Tuttle, Roan, and Faust plied their craft successfully for upwards of fifty years, ceasing only when they retired or died. Simplistic western movies kept flowing from Hollywood studios, adding featured heroes like Gene Autry, Roy Rogers, Johnny Mack Brown, William Elliot, and Tex Ritter to the ranks of silent film stars who had made the transition to talkies, such as Tom Mix, Ken Maynard, Bob Steel, Buck Jones, and Hoot Gibson. And the plots remained pretty much the same, too, with little difference in how the action plays out in oaters like *The Big Trail* (1930), in which John Wayne is a wagon train scout; *Partners of the Plains* (1937), in which Hopalong Cassidy saves a young woman's ranch; *Black Market Rustlers* (1949), in which "Crash" Corrigan and the Range Busters bust rustlers; *Canyon River* (1956), in which George Montgomery heads a cattle drive; and *Ride the Whirlwind* (1956), in which not only Cameron Mitchell but also young Jack Nicholson and Harry Dean Stanton are cowboys wrongly pursued as outlaws.

Also continuing unabated were contemporaneous stories mixing the Old West with the present, even incorporating current issues like building Boulder Dam ("Ride 'Em Rocketpants") and foiling Nazi spies ("Bucky Swings the Whip"). Spies and saboteurs were favorite enemies of Tom Mix, who in *Tom Mix Comics* and *Tom Mix Commando Comics* fought "such menaces as an army of invisible invaders and a squadron of real flying dragons from Japan" (Harmon, p. 120). Episodes of the *Tom Mix* radio program frequently blended old and new. For example, Mix's sidekick Pecos once rode to the rescue with a replacement propeller for a downed airplane, and in another episode, the horse of an "invisible rider" responded to commands radioed by a walkie-talkie in his saddlebags. This approach was even more prevalent in western movies, such as the Tom Mix serial *The Miracle Rider* (1935) in which the tracks of a stolen herd are erased by a gas-powered wind machine, and *Raiders of the Range* (1942) which features saloons with Dixieland jazz bands and muddy streets with traffic-jamming Model-T Fords. The Gene Autry and Roy Rogers films were the best of this breed, with cowboys on horses chasing Mack trucks, Pierce Arrow phaetons, and machine-gun-firing aircraft. Occasionally the movies went beyond the here and now, perhaps the most prominent if not peculiar example being *The Phantom Empire* (serial, 1934; feature film, 1935) in which Autry in his first starring role defends his Radio Ranch from Murania, an underground extraterrestrial queendom replete with robots and ray-guns but with only horses and chariots for transportation. Later with the advent of television, Autry and Rogers both produced shows involving newfangled technology, such as the Jeep named "Nellybelle" that Rogers drove when he was not riding Trigger.

Television also broadcast other juvenile fodder like *Buffalo Bill Jr.* and *Annie Oakley,* and for more than a decade ruled prime time with series like *Gunsmoke, Bonanza,* and my personal favorite, *Maverick.* Cheap paperbacks, first introduced by Penguin in 1936, took up where pulp magazines left off and flooded newsstands, book shops, drugstores, and grocery stores with westerns. Many of their writers told conservative stories in the Wister-Gray tradition, such as Louis L'Amour, Philip Ketchum, Ray Hogan, and Frederick Glidden, who as Luke Short published formulaic westerns often involving heroes wishing to atone for their past, as in *Gunman's Chance* (1941), which became the western *film noir* classic *Blood on the Moon* (1948). Others followed the brazen excesses of a Tom Roan or a Frederick Faust, such as Walt Coburn, out of whose alcoholic hallucinations arose yarns like *Border Town* (1967), replete with a squalid cantina owned by Quo Wong, "a slant-eyed close-tongued half-caste" knife expert; Jon Sharpe, whose *Slaughter Express* (1986) has a cook named Upwind Muldoon because of the flatulent effects of his biscuits; Tabor Evans, whose *Lone Star Showdown* (1986) has an international crime cartel wiped out by a Chinese sect in a trap-doored pagoda temple high in the Sierras; and Wesley Ellis, whose *The Hardrock Payoff* (1983) has a mad scientists running a slave camp to mine "virilium" (uranium) in the remote Thundermug Mountains (see

Barbour; Goodstone; Goulart; Harmon; Horowitz; Knight; and Lackmann).

Since Wister and Grey, the vast majority of westerns have been simplistic entertainments, pruned by the market of their tragic endings, ambiguous characters, complex situations, and, up until the 1970s, of extraneous romance. However, to suggest that only the market has provided the form and content of western fiction would be misleading. Although it is true that all western writers live by the market, a number of them have resisted wholesale abdication to commercial values and have struggled to retain their autonomy and develop artistically. There were subtle but discernible signs of their presence in the 1920s and especially during the Depression, when for many the Good Life promised by industrialization collapsed, and they perceived, if only intuitively, that the frontier had indeed closed and that the West as myth was suspect, its traits of individualism and aggression seen as contributing factors to the economic crisis. So some western writers began to shift from escapist fare extolling a primitive and pristine West, profitable though it may have been, and tackled topics that emphasized the concerns of ordinary people in relatively realistic frontier settings. And because they, as well as writers in other fields, were confronted by a present and future that conjured diminished freedoms and opportunities—particularly the frontier dream of starting afresh in some unspoiled place—they began exploring the frontier of the self, adding a degree of psychological realism by stressing subjectivity through more meditative and philosophical characters, and injecting social commentary through plots that delved into authentic issues about democracy, decency, individualism, and community. This stage is the subject of the next chapter, with its history traced from gestation in the 1930s to birth at the eve of World War II and its continued evolution through the Vietnam War era to the present day, along with a discussion of the tensions that resulted from writers' attempting to be artists and social commentators within the generic parameters of the western.

Runaway Buckin' to Bitin' the Dust

CODE OF THE OLD WEST
A cowboy:
1. Never takes unfair advantage, even of an enemy.
2. Never betrays a trust.
3. Always tells the truth.
4. Is kind to small children, to old folks, and to animals.
5. Is free of racial and religious prejudice.
6. Is always helpful, and when anyone's in trouble, lends a helping hand.
7. Is a good worker.
8. Is clean about his person, and in thought, word, and deed.
9. Respects womanhood, his parents, and the laws of his country.
10. Is a patriot.
Gene Autry

As we have noted, through the first two decades of this century an increasing number of Americans came to realize that the old agrarian society was being replaced by a new industrial-urban order. That awareness was accentuated by the Great Depression of the 1930s, when, following the stock market crash in 1929, American industrial capitalism seemed to disintegrate into economic deprivation, massive unemployment, the loss of market values, and the marginalization of millions of individuals and families. During that time, writes literary historian David Minter, "The marriage rate fell sharply, the birthrate plunged to its lowest level in history, and the suicide rate rose. Soon ordinary people began to fear that the whole political economy might collapse" (p. 149). A public seeking some relief from a rapidly changing society and from the dolorous present turned to westerns more than ever. "On one hand," writes historian Gerald Nash, "the Depression did foster further disillusionment with contemporary society and a lack of confidence in existing institutions among historians and intellectuals. But on the other hand, on the level of popular culture, the [frontier] myth provided millions of Americans with an easy escape into a carefree world" (p. 222). Beyond simple escapism, the positive image of the western also served a vital role as an antidote to public pessimism, emphasizing such private values as courage, honor, and integrity, which foster personal independence and promote the belief that despite societal collapse, individuals can reinvent themselves and so become whatever they wished to be—the very essence of the American Dream since its inception. Again, the western reflected the contemporary culture, for although "radicals made a great deal of noise in the 1930s, relatively small numbers adhered to their causes . . . Americans still seemed to believe in the capacity of the American political system [and] expected to see arise, out of the inborn creativity and strengths of the American people themselves, a set of answers to this latest of the great challenges to face them" (Kelley, pp. 599, 600).

Measured by sales, ratings, and box-office receipts, the western gained popularity in hardcover books, pulp and slick magazines, radio network programs, and motion pictures, and significantly, it continued to increase its audience after the Depression until the late 1960s. From 1930 to 1955, 2,772 western commercial films were produced, an average of over 110 features per year (Adams and Rainey, p. 38). In the 1950s, at a time when dramatic radio shows were coming to an end, weekly westerns on radio attracted major stars like Raymond Burr as the star of *Fort Laramie,* James Stewart as the star of *The Six-Shooter,* and William Conrad as Matt Dillon on *Gunsmoke,* which remained in production for 419 episodes until June 1961 (MacDonald, pp. 54–55). Although the number of radio programs and movie features fell as television became the principal medium of entertainment—films, for example, tapered to 447 between 1956 and 1969 (Adams and Rainey, p. 38)—their decline was more than offset by television westerns, which dominated popular preferences. In 1956, *Variety* reported that the average rating for fifteen prime-time westerns was 25.4—23 percent higher than other evening shows, which averaged 20.7 (MacDonald, p. 55)—and by 1968 the typical week provided ten hours of prime-time western series such as *Gunsmoke, Bonanza,* and *The Virginian* (MacDonald, p. 58). According to John Reddy, television westerns in their heyday represented the film footage equivalent of four hundred movie features annually (p. 136).

The halcyon days began to wane at the end of the 1960s, as the Vietnam War, racial crises, ghetto turmoil, political assassination, and the Watergate scandal led to national anger and even despair. Traditional westerns no longer meshed with widely accepted social and political views of the time, and consequently withered in popularity. Other westerns, those reflecting the undercurrents of contradiction and cynicism in contemporary society, provided existentialist stories in which society was the enemy. Protagonists were questionably moral, flatly immoral, or psychopathically amoral, shorn of community ties and values, and operating in a world populated by misfits and dupes. Sardonic, violent, and spiritually void, these offerings attracted a diminishing audience. By July 1984, out of 1,693 television movies and miniseries broadcast over the previous twenty years, only ninety-two were westerns and all were "ratings disasters" (MacDonald, pp. 124–126). Book publishing and film production plummeted; in the last decade, an average of three western features have been released a year, and "the sixty-plus original paperbacks issued in 1991 were halved in number by 1996," with the trend continuing downward to where "western shelf space in even the big gym-sized book chains shrinks to a lower corner in the back wall" (House, pp. 3, 11). Currently, the western appears to be moribund, and in the view of critics such as J. Fred MacDonald, Joe Hyams, and Christopher Viviani, "the genre, such as it is, is dead" (Viviani, p. 17).

The rise and fall of the western from the Depression to now is the subject of this chapter and the reason it is called "Runaway Buckin' to Bitin' the Dust." A runaway bucker is a horse that, as soon as it is mounted, breaks into a gallop for fifty yards, leaps four or five feet high, and lands stiff-legged. The fast forward motion ceases so abruptly that many a rider has been jackknifed off, "biting the dust" spread-eagled and knocked out of breath. As well as being slang for spilling from a horse, "biting the dust" can also mean to be killed. Whether the western is dead or merely winded will be discussed in the final chapter.

To meet the avid interest in westerns, Depression publishers and producers churned out simple, formulaic stories emphasizing action that climaxed in Good's vanquishing Evil. Fortunately, by this time the competing diversions of popular culture were enhancing the prospects of serious writers. Mass entertainment, driven by sales and underwritten by advertisers, "attracted readers and helped train them . . . bath[ing] the minds of the nation's people in stories and serials that had discernible beginnings, middles, and endings and yet made wholesale use of jumps and shifts as well as blurred, coalescing images in order to tell stories" (Kazin, p. 106). As a result, "the fact that the West has been victimized by so many tawdry writers should not blind us to that literature of the west which is good nor to the fact that the Western does attract the occasional good writer" (Franz and Coathe, p. 9). The better western writers worked on improving the quality of their dialogue, their literate style, the drawing of characters, and the accuracy of their settings. As author Charlie Eckhardt points out, "The first duty of any writer is to tell a story that will keep the reader interested. There is a second duty that is as important as that first duty. It is to tell the story, whether fact or fiction, with historical accuracy" (p. 21). The closing of the external frontier was coming to mean the opening of an inner frontier, of inner complexities, and though plenty of action remained replete with saloon brawls and shoot-outs, the better writers strove to blend dramatic conflict with natural and psychological realism in a more mature story line.

Among the better writers who began during the Depression are Edna Ferber (*Cimarron*, 1930), Vardis Fisher (*The Dark Bridwell*, 1931; *In Tragic Life*, 1932), B. Traven (*The Treasure of the Sierra Madre*, 1935; film, 1948), Pulitzer-prize winner Conrad Richter (*The Sea of Grass*, 1937; film, 1947), Paul Hogan (*Far from Cibola*, 1938), and Paul

Wellman (*Bronco Apache*, 1936; film, *Apache*, 1954); *Jubal Troop*, 1939; film, *Jubal*, 1956). But perhaps the writer of this period who best exemplifies the move away from formulaic elements toward deeper themes and content is Ernest Haycox. "His preoccupation with history and extensive research distinguished him from the average writer of westerns, to say nothing of his literary skill," notes Stephen Tanner (p. 7), and John Milton cites *Bugles in the Afternoon* (1944; film, 1952) as indicative of how Haycox is "possibly the best in terms of craftsmanship and of at least a modicum of integrity that caused him to veer away from the cowboy formula in the 1930s and turn to the historical western which could be a gateway to the literary novel" (p. 36). More influential than his skill at portraying authentic settings and historically accurate events, however, was his ability to endow his characters with complex emotions and concern with moral dilemmas. In *Man in the Saddle* (1938; film, 1951), for instance, protagonist Owen Merritt "is complex and introspective," while antagonist Will Isham "is not so much villain as a man tragically flawed, possessed by envy, greed and power" (Hitt, p. 199).

Not only did Haycox provide much-imitated examples of psychologically impaired heroes and heroines, but he also profoundly affected the course of the genre with his short story "Stage to Lordsburg" (1937), which served as the basis of John Ford's evocative film *Stagecoach* (1939). Until "Stage," traditional westerns limited community to a setting, to some locale vulnerably isolated in perilous surroundings—such as a remote settlement, army outpost, or pioneer wagon train—that represents the civilized values and virtues for which the hero battles. Such an approach has consistently appealed to western fans disenchanted with their contemporary lives and yearning to return to fundamental ideals, but it also tends to confuse society with social order—or rather, community as a spirit with community as a place. Literarily speaking, by the eve of World War II there was no more advancing from East to West; long before, the frontier had drowned in the Pacific, and because everywhere Out West was now Back East, the perception arose that western towns and other communal settings suffered from the same corruption and cynicism as the Eastern "social order." So although Haycox set his story in a vulnerable, isolated stagecoach rolling from Tonto to Lordsburg, he, and later Ford to a much greater degree, reversed the convention by portraying the towns and their outwardly respectable citizens as hypocritical, perfidious, and sexually repressed. In neither version do the roguish hero and the fallen heroine show any desire or make any attempt to become integrated in the social orders of Tonto or Lordsburg. In "Stage," hero Malpais Bill and heroine Henriette simply unite; in *Stagecoach*, hero Ringo Kid is an escaped outlaw who refuses to flee the law with heroine Dallas and hide in the wilderness, to take, in effect, the side of savagery in their confrontation with civilization. Rather, they decide to leave for a mythical Mexican ranch where, it is implied, they will settle down, breed, and generally live by the basic norms of rural American society without, as Doc says sarcastically, "the blessings of civilization." The spirit of true community prevails.

Besides John Ford, Hollywood produced a generation of western director virtuosos such as Howard Hawks, Raoul Walsh, William Wellman, and Budd Boetticher, "but Ford was beyond any doubt the greatest of these tough primitives" (Workman, p. 38). His later westerns, shot like *Stagecoach* with astonishing and forceful imagery, continued his social criticism and support for traditional virtues. For instance, in *My Darling Clementine* (1946), Wyatt Earp is interested solely in his family and cattle business, and refuses the town's request to become its marshal until his brother is killed and his cattle rustled. Although becoming a lawman for personal reasons, he acquires a sense of trust and bonds with people outside his immediate clan, thereby confirming the human need for community and social values. Another implication established in *Stagecoach* and carried forward is the desirability and even necessity of cultural myths, even while characterizing the myths as fiction. In *Fort Apache* (1948), Major Owen Thursday is a glory-seeking, promotion-conscious martinet whose rash attack on the Apaches causes his and his men's deaths. In the last scene, his successor Captain Kirby York lies for the good of the command by praising "Thursday's charge" as heroic. "The film makes it apparent that history is frequently romanticized to sustain in the popular imagination 'heroes' who in actuality were anything but 'heroic'" (Emmert, p. 17). A similar stance is taken in *The Man Who Shot Liberty Valance* (1962), wherein the protagonist Ransom Stoddard does not kill Valance, but accepts the credit and heroic status for doing so, and reaps his reward in a successful political career. Ford's message, that many of America's cultural heroes are manufactured, is obvious early on when a reporter declares, "When the legend becomes fact, print the legend."

Along with exposing fabricated heroes, this period also saw the challenging of the entire concept of heroes. Granted, dating from the dime westerns there have been "good-bad" protagonists like Deadwood Dick and Lady Jaguar the Robber Queen, but they nonetheless fit the mold of "knight-errant of the plains" (French, p. 51) and "the instrument of a just retribution" (Calder, p. 110). As such, the formulaic western hero rarely ponders good and evil or questions a course of action—action through which the hero is portrayed, any private doubts or torments kept contained behind a self-assured demeanor. Lacking fullness of character, the formulaic western hero triumphs because of innate superiority, a position that grew increasingly difficult to justify once Haycox and other serious writers began exploring the ironies and conflicts and contradictions of the human condition. With increasing frequency, protagonists had to face personal crises before confronting the villain, their inner terrain the last frontier which is, according to historian James Folsom, "finally something more than an aspect of the American West," its topography coming "to resemble the landscape of the human mind" (p. 32). Some of the better writers even managed to exclude traditional villains altogether. In Frank Waters's *The Man Who Killed the Deer* (1942), the issue is wholeness, how to be at one with life, and the villain is alienation, the effect of division and separation. The protagonist Martiniano—part Pueblo, part Apache, educated in the white man's world—is at a personal frontier concerning his mixed heritage and the opposing forces of white and Indian, rational and instinctual, while his Pueblo tribe is at a similar crossroads concerning the preservation of their sacred Blue Lake and their spiritual way of life versus the granting of concessions to white civilization.

Other writers carried the troubled hero further and developed the nonhero, thereby countering the traditional western's overarching premises that progress is inevitable and that individuals succeed through character and endurance. The nonheroic vision intimates that change is inevitable, but not necessarily for the better, and that individuals can succumb to their weaknesses and fail miserably; at its bleakest, it echoes faintly the fatalism found in the literary naturalism of authors like Henry James, Edith Wharton, and Theodore Dreiser. Perhaps no western illustrates this dour dimension better than Walter Van Tilburg Clark's *The Ox-Bow Incident* (1940), which was made into a memorable film by William Wellman in 1942 and remade as an episode in *The Twentieth-Century Fox Hour* on television in 1955. *The Ox-Bow Incident* is a powerful sociopsychological study of the hysteria that leads to an unjust lynching and of its tragic consequences, "boldly defy[ing] the conventional patterns of the shoot-out and the clear-cut victory of good over evil" (Milton, p. 202). The tale provides no heroes or saviors or even, as Milton notes, "'superior' characters in this crowd . . . These are real people, exasperating in their plausibility" (p. 203).

The Ox-Bow Incident presents a political as well as social statement. Clark admitted in the afterword of the 1960 Signet Classics reprint that *Ox-Bow* is an antifascist work: "The book was written in 1937 and '38, when the whole world was getting increasingly worried about Hitler and the Nazis, and emotionally it stemmed from my part of this worrying . . . as something approaching an allegory of the unscrupulous and brutal Nazi methods, and as a warning against the dangers of temporizing and of hoping to oppose such a force with reason, argument, and the democratic approach" (pp. 223–224). *Stagecoach,* too, has a political element, about the need for individuals to stand against not only natural savagery but the decadent aspects of civilization. It is hardly surprising that in 1939, when savagery by a civilized nation was threatening Europe and America, Ford would be concerned with the relationship of wilderness and civilization and conventional American values. The outbreak of World War II caused a surge in westerns with political messages, many of them overtly propagandistic with the simple moral basis of the formula western, such as the patriotic derring-do of *Men of Texas* (1942), but the war also affected the more complex motivations and issues of the serious western. In particular, the campaign to unify the country, discredit the Nazi race theory, and celebrate democracy (see Davidson et al.; Divine et al.; and Kelley) combined with the depictions of flawed heroes and nonheroes—who were generally white males—to produce a better balance between white males and everyone else.

For example, stories sympathetic to Indians have been produced from colonial times through the Depression, including D. W. Griffith's *Massacre* (1912), James Cruzes's *Covered Wagon* (1923), and Zane Grey's *The Vanishing American* (1925). The interest in minorities and ethnic literature brought on by World War II, however, created a trend in portraying Indians as heroic and often as protagonists. Martiniano in *The Man Who Killed the Deer* is heroic. In *Fort Apache* the Indians assert themselves as the rightful owners of the land, and moreover they win while the racist Thursday loses. In Anthony Mann's *Devil's Doorway* (1950), a Shoshone brave returning from Civil War service finds himself an alien in his Wyoming home. In *Broken Arrow* (1950) Cochise is depicted as peace-loving while white civilization is garish. The Crow are featured with authenticity and understanding in Dorothy Johnson's "A Man Called Horse" (in *Indian Country*, 1953), and later changed by her to the Sioux in the film version (1969), "a task she felt equal to . . . because of her constant delving into materials which documented the lives of a number of tribes" (Hart, p. 22). Informed portraits of Indians appeared regularly after the war in such westerns as A. B. Guthrie's *The Way West* (1949; film, 1967); *Comanche Territory* (1950), *Cyclone Fury* (1951), *Apache* (1954), *Sitting Bull* (1954), *The Indian Fighter* (1955), *The White Feather* (1955); Mari Sandoz's masterful *Cheyenne Autumn* (1953; film, 1964); Thomas Berger's picaresque *Little Big Man* (1964; film, 1970); William Eastlake's trilogy *Go in Beauty* (1956), *The Bronc People* (1958), and *Portrait of an Artist with Twenty-Six Horses* (1963), which probe the conflicts between brothers, races, and cultures; and the overwrought *Run of the Arrow* (1957), in which Rod Steiger as a Confederate soldier joins the Sioux, whose chief (Charles Bronson) tells him, "We have the same god, only with a different name." Henry Clay Allen, who wrote under the names Clay Fisher and Will Henry, acknowledges that "all but a handful" of his fifty-three novels have Indians "close to center stage"—telling, for instance, of Heyets, Chief Joseph's pony boy, in *Where the Sun Now Stands* (as Will Henry, 1960), of the Sand Creek massacre in *The Last Warpath* (as Will Henry, 1966), and of Crazy Horse in *The Bear Paw Horses* (as Will Henry, 1973)—because "ninety-nine percent of those who have written to me through the years, Indian or white or any other color of skin, have been appreciative of the picture I have drawn of the horseback tribes of the West. There seems to be a reader hunger to know more of these famed old chiefs and warriors and warrior women" (Walker, p. 17).

Also increasing were sympathetic treatments of blacks, Hispanics, Asians, and half-breeds, due largely to the vast migration that took place during wartime, when an estimated 700,000 blacks and 350,000 Hispanics, among others, entered service or moved to urban centers for defense work, their intermingling helping to "transform relations from a regional issue into a national concern" (Kelley, p. 470). In Henry Allen's *Red Blizzard* (as Clay Fisher, 1951) the struggle by Pawnee Perez to be accepted as white is heartwrenching, the book a vivid condemnation of racism. Black cavalrymen are protagonists in Tom Lea's *The Wonderful Country* (1952; film, 1959) and John Ford's *Sergeant Rutledge* (1960), in which Woody Strode declares, "The Ninth Cavalry was my home, my freedom, and my self-respect." Depicted sympathetically are Filipinos in Carlos Bulosan's *America Is in the Heart* (1946), Japanese in John Okada's *No-No Boy* (1957), Mexicans in Harvey Fergusson's *The Conquest of Don Pedro* (1954), and Chicanos in Jose Antonio Villareal's *Pocho* (1959) and Floyd Salas's *Tattoo the Wicked Cross* (1967)—all to wide public and critical acclaim. White families stand together to protect an adopted Indian girl in Alan LeMay's *The Unforgiven* (1957; film, 1960) and a half-breed brother in Cliff Huffaker's *Flaming Lance* (1958; film, *Flaming Star,* 1960) from white prejudice or Indian reclamation. "Thematically they are declarations in favour of the American melting pot; dramatically they are a recognition of the profound difficulties and personal tragedies involved in the process of assimilation" (French, p. 85).

As well, a major beneficiary has been the female character. Changes in her portrayal were noted by a number of critics, including Frederick Elkin, who asserts that around 1950 a new type of western was emerging that "sets up a companioniate relationship . . . in which the man and woman participate in the same activities" (p. 72). Although Elkin is correct that the woman protagonist was involved in "companionate relationships [of] equality and identity with man" (p. 72), he overlooks the heritage of strong woman protagonists dating back to the earliest captive narratives and running steadily through Cooper's *Leatherstocking Tales* and the dime westerns to recent examples such as B. Capp's *A Woman of the People* (1966), which relates the experiences of Comanche-captured Cynthia Ann Parker in 1836. In these stories women are often depicted in companionate relationships—which places Elkin at least thirty-seven years ahead of revisionist historian Sandra Kay Schackel, who in 1987 claimed that contemporary society will create a new female western heroine: "Increased public awareness of women's rights as well as changes in scholarship have finally recognized the complexity of women's roles on the frontier. . . . And as the genre moves away from roles men thought women ought to play and toward roles they actually did play, Western films will more realistically reflect women's roles in the celluloid winning of the West" (p. 215). Just considering westerns written by women, those in which females play prominent roles have long proven popular, among the early works are the fictionalized historical accounts *Winding Waters* (1909) by Frances Parker, about the Nez Percé campaign of 1877–1878, and *When Geronimo Rode* (1927) by Forrestine Cooper Hooker. Other popular novels had half-breed heroines, as in Helen Hunt Jackson's *Ramona* (1884), Marah Ellis Ryan's *Squaw Elouise* (1892), and Ada Woodruff Anderson's *The Strain of White* (1909). Cherry Wilson wrote a number of novels and short stories with women protagonists, the most notable a 1929 "book-length" serial in *Western Story Magazine* wherein Cleo Craig is a professional rodeo rider "'bad' in that she hopes to steal a prized stallion and to seduce a hero type who loves someone else, 'good' in that she matures, gives the man and her rival her blessing" (Yates, p. 126).

Moreover, around the turn of the century, women writers developed a subgenre called the domestic western. Most notable are those by Bertha Muzzy Bower, whose sales of sixty-eight books and some 150 novelettes and short stories with over two million readers ran a fair second to the traditional westerns of Wister and Grey (Yates, p. 18). Bower's stories tend to revolve around the usual themes: East versus West, citizens versus outlaws, cattlemen versus sheepmen or nesters, or protagonists versus mysterious forces, such as the phony miners in *The Trail of the White Mule* (1922). But her most significant work is the fifteen-book series about domestic life at the Flying U Ranch, starting with *Chip of the Flying U* (1908) and ending with the posthumously published *The Family Failing* (1941), with some of the novels made into movies and at least two reprinted in 1951, 1952, and 1971 (Meyer, p. 26). One of the main protagonists is Dr. Della Whitmore, a capable and resolute woman who practices from her office in the ranch house. The ranch hands are a rowdy bunch who indulge in more horseplay than gunplay, and who participate like family members in doing domestic chores—even the cook is male. Bower's theme that occupations are not gender-specific shows in her other women characters, such as Della's physician friend Dr. Granthum, law-smart Georgie Howard in *Good Indian* (1912), and ranch wife cum movie star Jean Avery Lite in *Jean of the Lazy A* (1915) and *The Phantom Herd* (1916). Although some of the women remain contentedly single, like Dr. Granthum, most are or get married in keeping with the times, reader expectations, and the conventions of the domestic romance, and virtually all of them remain equal or superior to men in competence, intelligence, and determination. In a similar vein are the seven domestic westerns by journalist, editor, and rancher June Lockhart; her heroines are composed, courageous, and resilient, such as orphaned teenager Suzie MacDonald in *Me—Smith!* (1911), who skillfully manages a ranch while "hero" Smith sneak-thieves under the motto "to do what you aim to do and make a clean getaway—that was the successful life" (p. 60). Katharine Newlin Burt is another writer of domestic westerns, such as *Hidden Creek* (1920), *Snow Blind* (1921), and *The Tall Ladder* (1932), featuring independent and self-possessed heroines who earn their successes through their own power rather than by the help of men—in *A Man's Own Country* (1931), for instance, the heroine operates the ranch while her husband practices law, and in *Moon Mountain* (1938), the heroine is both wife and surrogate mother to her dependent husband.

In general, domestic westerns express the social belief that women should be wife-companions to their husbands and homemakers for their children, but that concept was altered by World War II as "some 6.5 million women entered the work force, over half for the first time. . . . Patriotism alone could not explain their willingness to leave families and homes for the factories. Rising war wages were a powerful inducement . . . many women preferred the relative freedom of work and wages to the confines of home" (Davidson et al., p. 1058). Westerns in turn began reflecting the war-inspired change in economic and social roles for women. The shift is well illustrated by the works of Vingie E. Roe, who between 1912 and 1957 wrote over thirty novels, the majority of which are domestic westerns starring heroines as adept at shooting, riding, roping, guiding wagon trains (e.g., *The Maid of Whispering Hills*, 1912; *The Splendid Road*, 1925; film, 1925), and ramrodding ranches (e.g., *Tharon of Lost Valley*, 1919; *Black Belle Rides the Uplands*, 1935) as they are at cooking, housekeeping, and child rearing. Then, in 1940, Roe published *The Golden Tide* (film, *The Perilous Journey*, 1953), wherein "Mother" Elizabeth Farnham and forty-two eligible young women band together in a female collective to go into business as seamstresses and cooks and to promote themselves as marriage material: "All desirous of finding decent husbands. (No others need apply.) Also no hurry. . . . We are respectable, self-sufficient, and mean to stay so" (p. 80). Not all marry; some choose business careers, a few choose to be prostitutes or mistresses. Clearly, Roe is sending the message that not only can women do what men do without losing their femininity, they have the same right as men to be on their own, taking chances and making errors and being promiscuous if they so desire, and that in their relationships with men they can stay separate and whole individuals who retain their uniqueness and equality even as they unite. In *The Golden Tide* Roe initiates "an authorial interest in women's rights as a social movement" (Yates, p. 59), which parallels the view of a real war worker who said, "They were hammering away that the women who went to work did it to help her man, and when he came back, she cheerfully leaped back to the home. . . . We were sold a bill of goods" (Davidson et al., pp. 1058–1059). Roe repeats this point in *Wild Harvest* (1941), in which the protagonist is an unmarried homesteader who one man fears is "one of those Woman's Rights females" (p. 87).

Following Roe's example with growing frequency, writers depicted women as independent individuals in their own right, often through their own eyes. In Lillian Bos Ross's *The Stranger* (1942; film *Zandy's Bride,* 1974), mail-order bride Hannah Martin refuses to knuckle under to her husband Zande Allen, and in due course it is Allen who bends, a better and stronger man for it. In John Ford's rendering of *The Searchers,* the abducted Debbie wishes to remain with the Comanches and refuses to see herself as a victim. In Nevin Busch's *Duel in the Sun* (1944; film, 1946), the protagonist is Pearl Chavez, a half-breed seductress who is smarter and deadlier than the two men who vie for her, and in Busch's *The Furies* (1948; film, 1950), rancher T. C. Jeffords's daughter Vance is his match in vitality and ambition. Women are shown as enigmatic, their strength lying in their mystery, like Lola Manners in *Winchester 73* (1950), who may or may not be a prostitute or in cahoots with the villain Waco Jonny Dean, and whose ambivalent status is not entirely settled at the end. Or they are shown as infuriatingly contrary, like Josie Minick in *The Ballad of Josie* (1967), who, after accidentally shooting her husband, starts importing sheep into Wyoming cattle country. Or they are shown as duplicitous bitches, like Marlene Dietrich's saloon-owner Altar Keane in *Rancho Notorious* (1952), Jeanne Crain's unbalanced ranch baronness in *Man Without a Star* (1955), Barbara Stanwyck's vicious outlaw leader in *Forty Guns* (1957), and Joan Crawford's promiscuous Vienna feuding with Mercedes McCambridge's ruthless cattle queen Emma Small in *Johnny Guitar* (1952). Women are shown as steadfastly capable, like Genevieve Bujold's immigrant widow in *Another Man, Another Chance* (1977), and as courageous, selfless, loving caregivers, like Sacajawea in *Sacajawea of the Shoshones* (1955; film, *The Far Horizons*, 1955) and in Henry Allen's *The Gates of the Mountain* (as Will Henry, 1963), as well as similar Indian heroines by Allen like "Light of Morning" Meyui in *From Where the Sun Now Stands*, Star of the North in *No Survivors* (as Will Henry, 1950), Crow Girl in *Yellowstone Kelly* (as Clay Fisher, 1957), Graywing Teal in *The Feleen Brand* (as Will Henry, 1962), and Monaseetah in *Yellow Hair* (as Clay Fisher, 1953). And women are shown as determined and even headstrong, even humorously so, like the two feisty teenage girls who run off to join the Doolin-Dalton gang in *Cattle Annie and Little Britches* (1980), and Jane Fonda's spitfire Cat Ballou in *Cat Ballou* (1965), which so deliciously and good-naturedly spoofs the conventions of the formula western. These are the types of female protagonists that, as late as 1993, revisionist Patricia Limerick was chastising western fiction for not providing, demanding more than women characters "whose genteel, white presence represents the final defeat of wilderness. . . . Capable of starting the shooting as well as stopping it, women [must] regain their legitimate claim on greed, envy, anger, desperation, and sin" (p. 32).

Meanwhile, white males were being shown not as courageous and determined, but as pigheaded, like Thursday in *Fort Apache* and rancher Tom Dunson in Borden Chase's *The Chisholm Trail* (*Post* serial, 1946; novel, *Blazing Guns on the Chisholm Trail*, 1947; film, *Red River*, 1948). And they were shown as inept, like the two cowhands who are fleeing a posse in *Ride in the Whirlwind* (1972) and the two wranglers in Max Evans's *The Rounders* (1960; film, 1965) whose moneymaking schemes invariably backfire on them. And they were shown as alienated, like the escapee Jubal in *Jubal Troop*, gunman Reb Kittredge in Norman A. Fox's *Roughshod* (1951; film, *Gunsmoke*, 1953), orphan Jed Cosgrave in Todhunter Ballard's *Two Edged Vengeance* (1952; film, *The Outcast*, 1954), and loner Jim Garry in *Gunman's Chance* by Frederick Glidden (as Luke Short, 1941; film, *Blood on the Moon*, 1948). And men were often shown as mentally disturbed in so-called psychological westerns, like Robert Mitchum's obsessed cowboy in *Pursued* (1947), Glenn Ford's sadistic judge in *The Man from Colorado* (1948), Glenn Ford's memory-plagued storekeeper facing Broderick Crawford's paranoid gunslinger in *The Fastest Gun Alive* (1956), and Glenn Ford's tormented husband teaming with Arthur Kennedy's psychopathic rancher and Dean Jagger's near-insane simpleton to track down his wife in *Day of the Evil Gun* (1968).

With more realistic characters and situations, relationships between men and women and attitudes toward sex began to be explored, just as they were beginning to be explored by mainstream authors and the population at large. One factor encouraging this development was the fact that, as book publisher Karl Edward Wagner observes, "the aftermath of war is characterized by a definite aura of moral permissiveness and thrill-seeking, just as the reverse characterizes a society on the brink of war" (quoted in Jones, p. 212). World War II also fostered a significant migration to America of Viennese and German psychologists. "Within a decade, they had succeeded in introducing the use of psychology in the analysis of the West as myth, and provided a new dimension in its perception" (Nash, p. 224). The result was not only psychological westerns whose characters are mentally unstable, but also more romantically inclined westerns whose characters are enmeshed in circumstances steamy with Freudian symbolism, victims of their childhood and environment. "Broadly, the old belief in the pastoral ideal, with its connection to renewal and rebirth, has been transformed into an obsession with changing relationships: movement, escape, spatiality (being spaced out), divorce, reformation of family structures, remarriage, proliferating affairs. . . . Sex, under such conditions, loses guilt, confinement, inhibition" (Karl, p. 19). It is carnal jealousy in *Johnny Guitar* that pits the sexually repressed Emma against the sexually unabashed Vienna, who, when asked how many men she has forgotten, replies: "As many women as you remember." Nevin Busch's *Duel in the Sun*, with its seductress heroine, was called by some critics "Lust in the Dust," and his *The Furies* dealt less with the feud between father and daughter than with their sexual conflicts and neurotic compulsions. Other writers such as Frank Fenton, Frederick Manfred, Henry Allen, and Samuel Fuller increasingly examined the sexual struggles and psychological weaknesses of their characters, broaching taboo subjects such as homosexuality in the Fenton-scripted *Ride Vaquero* (1953), interracial sex in *Yellowstone Kelly* by Allen (as Clay Fisher), incest in Manfred's *King of Spades* (1966), and sadism and perversion in director/writer Fuller's *Forty Guns*, although times still demanded that lust be implied rather than explicit.

Another form of relationship westerns investigated was that of the western protagonist in a post-western society, an anachronism, a troubled and disappointed character who has lived to see the crumbling of the Old West and the verities for which it stood. Like domestic westerns, westerns with anachronistic overtones had appeared years earlier, such as Willa Cather's *A Lost Lady* (1923), B. M. Bower's *Rodeo* (1928), and Eugene Manlove Rhodes's "Pasó por Aqui" (1927; film, *Four Faces West*, 1948), but during the postwar period, anachronistic personae and situations started to proliferate. Arguably the first anachronistic western is Jack Schaefer's *Shane*, serialized as "Ride to Nowhere" in *Argosy* in 1946, novelized as *Shane* in 1949, and filmed in 1952. On one level, the story is a mythic confrontation between Good and Evil, Shane the knight errant gunfighter siding with sodbuster farmers against Wilson the black-clad killer hired by a land-grabbing rancher. The story is the boyhood memory of the narrator, Bob Starrett, who recalls events surrounding the clash which suggest a passionate attraction between his mother and Shane, unmentioned yet nonetheless noticed by his father, and resulting in subtle tensions and unstated maneuverings among the three adults. Shane must leave at the end, of course, personally because to remain risks temptation and ruin of the family, and socially because his having saved the farmers effectively ends his way of life, now superseded by the lives of farmers and townsfolk. The boy Starrett is torn, liking Shane and wanting him to stay, yet so distressed by the domestic events that as an adult he keeps insisting he doesn't wish to remember them. To remember reality is to destroy the myth. This crucial point is somewhat lost in the film, unfortunately, for on a deeper and more sustained level *Shane* signifies that not only is the rugged individualist hero an anachronism, but that the classic western legend of home and heroism is itself an anachronism. As Robert Redford said in an interview (MSNBC, *Time Again*, August 8, 1997), "You become so mythologized that you cease to exist."

Following *Shane* was *The Gunfighter* (1950), a rueful *film noir*ish statement about a notorious but weary gunman out of his time, unable to find peace in a changing world until ignobly shot in the back by the "town squirt." The theme was copied extensively by a cycle of gunfighter westerns, such as *Gun Glory* (1957) in which a reformed gunman is rejected by his community, the mediocre *The Gun Hawk* (1963) in which a veteran gunman tries to prevent a glory-hunting youth from taking up his career, and *Gun for a Coward* (1957) in which one of two sons is a fast-draw braggart who causes chaos and death, a plot repeated in *Gunman's Walk* (1958) with the father forced to kill his son at the end, symbolically killing part of himself. The deaths of the horses featured in Tom Lea's *The Wonderful Country* and Frederick Manfred's *Conquering Horse* (1959) represent the death of the cowboy, whose life was dependent on horses for survival. In a number of westerns, cowboys are portrayed as hoary defenders of outmoded standards, like the veteran rodeo champions in Nicholas Ray's *The Lusty Men* (1952) and Bud Boetticher's *Bronco Buster* (1952), and Randolph Scott's and Joel McCrea's hapless exlawmen in Sam Peckinpah's *Ride the High Country* (1962), about which Cawelti observes, "The two heroes move once more toward their redemptive gunfight, but in the end they fight not to save the decent townspeople from outlaws but as the result of an almost accidental explosion of violence. The antagonists they destroy are not evil threats to a better society, and their victory does not purge society of anything. Joel McRea's heroic death redeems his own image of moral action; but it is also clear that, however admirable, this style of heroism is archaic —almost obsolescent—in a world where the Old West is dead" (pp. 253–254).

Ironically, one western that started out as anachronistic wound up as a quintessential reaffirmation of the mythic western and its traditional ethos. In the 1946 *Saturday Evening Post* serial "The Chisholm Trail" (1946) and its revision as the novel *Blazing Guns on the Chisholm Trail* (1947), author Borden Chase tells of a cattle drive from Missouri to Kansas headed by Thomas Dunson, a brutal, reckless rancher who becomes so obsessed with the commercial enterprise that his adopted son Matthew Garth and his crew mutiny, taking over the herd and leaving him behind. Dunson, accompanied by Garth's love interest Tess Millay, catches up with them in Kansas, where he is wounded in a shoot-out with the gunman Cherry before he has his showdown with Garth. Adamantly determined to kill Garth for his betrayal, Dunson draws to shoot but collapses from the wound, and dies shortly after Garth and Tess return him to his Texas ranch. When Howard Hawks directed the classic film based on the story, retitled *Red River* (1948), he insisted that Chase, who was writing the screenplay, change the showdown to a Hollywood ending wherein Dunson does not die. Consequently, in *Red River* Dunson is not wounded by Cherry, and his confrontation with Garth is halted by Tess in a climax lifted from *The Outlaw* (1943). As initially written, the showdown derives from the events leading up to it, and connotes that Old Westerners like Dunson must give way for the New Westerners. As filmed, the showdown seems disconnected, and Dunson appears not as anachronistic but as indomitable, stalwart, and proudly independent, a personal testament to the Code of the Old West. Because of *Red River*'s dramatic power and lasting popularity, the film ending with its reversed message is the version known world-wide, and to a large extent is responsible for making John Wayne the actor into John Wayne the icon.

Wayne achieved minor stardom through *Stagecoach* and gradually built his reputation over the next nine years, but his breakthrough came when he played the part of the much older Tom Dunson, western patriarch. It is one of his best performances, and the timing of the film's release could not have been more fortunate. The previous year, President Truman launched his campaign against Soviet influence in Greece and Turkey, and the House Committee on Un-American Activities (HUAC) held hearings on the Communist influence in the film industry. In 1948 the Soviets pushed back in Berlin and Prague, and "not only was the Cold War in full swing, but many Americans had hopes that the United States could win it . . . [fighting] not only across the globe but right in America, but unseen agents using underhanded means. In this way, the cold war mentality soon came to shape the lives of Americans at home" (Davidson et al., pp. 1096–1097). Chastened by the HUAC investigations, Hollywood produced anti-Soviet films like *The Iron Curtain* (1948), *Red Menace* (1949), and *I Was a Communist for the FBI* (1950), and pro-American films that confirmed the traditional ideals contained in the Western myth. "Perpetuation of the myth fitted the mood of Americans seeking an escape from their own uncertain world into one which was eminently predictable. In this universe, they also found a reaffirmation of basic American values—many of which were being questioned at home while they were challenged in the ideological conflict with the Soviet Union abroad" (Nash, p. 233). As the embodiment of these virtues following *Red River*, Wayne expressed Tom Dunsun's Code of the Old West in almost three decades of westerns starting with *3 Godfathers* (1949), *The Fighting Kentuckian* (1949), and *She Wore a Yellow Ribbon* (1949), as well as invading Mexico in *Rio Grande* (1950) and triumphing over Communists as an investigator for HUAC in *Big Jim McClain* (1952).

The formulaic western with its reassuring traditions continued to appeal to Americans through the 1950s. This was a period of unparalleled affluence and national accord as a "pent-up demand for consumer goods fueled a steady industrial expansion, and heavy government spending during the Cold War added an extra stimulus to the economy" (Divine et al., p. 493), and a social consensus "reflected the triumph of the melting pot and an agreement among the wide majority of Americans about fundamental values" (Davidson et al., p. 112). Despite the tensions of the Cold War and nuclear weapons, the political mood settled into a complacent conservatism resistant to reform and radicalism. This mood, "spring[ing] naturally from the team-spirit feelings, the powerful impulse to hang together as a people and frown on divisiveness and criticism" (Kelley, p. 707), was represented by the personality and administration of President Dwight Eisenhower, who in a 1953 speech accepting a civil rights award recalled that his home town of Abilene, Kansas, once had a marshal named Wild Bill Hickok. "If you don't know him read your Westerns more. Now, that town had a code, and I was raised as a boy to prize that code" (Barnouw, p. 18). That code is the Code of the Old West, which, as Max Westbrook says of John Wayne, "ignores protocol, debate, and the odds, kicks the door down, and gets the job done" (pp. 31–32). During the Eisenhower years, then, "to be an intellectual, a questioner, and a critic, was unpopular" (Kelley, p. 707), whereas formulaic westerns with their good and evil moral dualism gained an audience precisely because they tend to be anti-intellectual. "Things should be simple," Guy Madison declares in *The Hard Man* (1957), "things should be right or wrong, not someplace in between." Indeed, westerns with complex characterization and psychological motivation were denounced by contemporary critics, such as John Larner: "The signs of Byzantine decay are unmistakable" (p. 97); cowboy actor Johnny Mack Brown: "All you got is talk. You got New York actors in Western hats who don't know what a cow is standing around talking"; and another cowboy actor, Clint Walker: "We are a nation of hero-worshippers.... The kind of heroism that makes it possible for a man to live alone and at peace with himself, or to do what seems right whether it comes easy or comes hard, to stand up for what he believes in, even if it's going to be the last time he stands up" (quoted in MacDonald, pp. 50, 51).

Such western heroes, uncompromising in their own virtue and unquestioning in loyalty to national ideals, were played by actors like Audie Murphy, Cameron Mitchell, Dennis Morgan, John Lund, Jeff Chandler, Rex Allen, Rory Calhoun, John Hodiak, Richard Dix, and especially Randolph Scott. On occasion, Scott is less than honorable, such as his corrupt ex-lawman in *Ride the High Country* (1962), but in the main he portrays an outwardly debonair, inwardly steely man of conscience who, through suffering and loss, has matured to a rectitude "more unswerving if usually more concealed than Wayne's" (French, p. 58), most notably when seeking revenge as in *Coroner Creek* (1948), *Fighting Man of the Plains* (1949), *Tall Man Riding* (1955), the gritty *Decision at Sundown* (1957) in which the wife whose death he avenges had been a slut, and *Comanche Station* (1960), Scott's last picture until he emerged from retirement to play Gil Westrum in *Ride the High Country*.

Another popular purveyor of formula westerns was prolific writer Louis L'Amour. His first novel, *Hondo* (1952), focuses on the humanizing process undergone by half-breed Hondo Lane, embittered cavalry dispatch rider, as he falls in love with frontier widow Angie Lowe and her son Johnny, and comes to terms with Chief Vittoro and his Mescalero Apaches. L'Amour depicts Vittoro as a cruel yet honorable defender of his homeland, worthy of Hondo's respect—solid characterization which L'Amour fails to provide in subsequent stories about Indians, such as *The Burning Hills* (1956; film, 1956) and *Last Stand at Papago Wells* (1957; film, *Apache Territory*, 1958). In those stories, the Indians are relegated to little better than plot devices cropping up to explain and motivate the sequence of events, a fate shared by many of L'Amour's men and women. With the exception of *Hondo*, L'Amour's stories tend to be standard fare containing superior heroes, spunky heroines, simple plots emphasizing action, and the moral reiteration of Good victorious over Evil, all wrapped in a veneer of informational details and historical authenticity. His recipe worked; backed by strong promotion from his publisher Bantam Books, L'Amour became and has remained the top seller of westerns, with a number of his works adapted for films, and book sales currently estimated to exceed fifty million copies (Buscombe, p. 165). According to Richard Wheeler, western writer and past board member of the Western Writers of America, L'Amour's domination of the field for so many years "was both an asset and liability to the Western story. At one point in the early 80's, he was virtually the only author of single-title Westerns being published, and he kept the category alive at a time when publishers had largely abandoned it . . . . But if he was the rescuer of the category, he was also unwittingly responsible for leaving it in a straitjacket. His very success at writing the mythic, romantic Western ensured that the mass market houses would rarely deviate from his formula stories about a frontier West that never really existed" (p. 21).

The renaissance of the formula western reached its peak in the new medium of television. "From a shaky start after the war, TV boomed in the fifties. By 1957, the three networks controlled the airways, reaching 40 million sets over nearly 500 stations" (Divine et al., p. 504), and "greatly extended the scope of the Western myth even more extensively than books, radio, and moving pictures had done in earlier years" (Nash, p. 225). Early on, television programmers learned the adaptability of motion pictures when edited for commercials and dropped into specific time slots, and vintage B westerns shot in black and white and full of outdoor action worked particularly well in the small-screen format. Such sagebrush stars as Ken Maynard, Bob Steele, Tex Ritter, Hoot Gibson, and the Three Mesquiteers satisfied a loyal adult constituency and garnered a new young audience with Depression-made flicks like *The Land of the Missing Men* (1930), *Tombstone Canyon* (1932), *The Riding Avenger* (1936), *Hittin' the Trail* (1937), and *Santa Fe Stampede* (1938), in which one of the Mesquiteers is John Wayne. Soon original productions were being aired, some for the juvenile market like *Hopalong Cassidy, Annie Oakley,* and *The Adventures of Wild Bill Hickok,* and some for the prime-time adult market like *Frontier Doctor, Gunsmoke,* and *Tales of the Texas Rangers,* programs currying such favor that "Westerns ranked second only to Milton Berle's *Texaco Star Theater* as TV fare viewed together by parents and children. . . . By April 1951 Westerns were viewed at least once a week by 66.3 percent of homes with children, and by 39.2 percent of those without children. As late as 1955 such popularity continued as 58.3 percent of those responding admitted watching cowboy feature films on TV—and 60.5 percent of these viewers considered such motion pictures to be 'as good as, or better than other types of TV movies'" (MacDonald, pp. 17–18).

"Whenever Americans feel good about their country," writer Dick House asserts, "you'll see the reemergence of the western novel" (p. 9). Indeed, the general mood during the postwar Truman and early Eisenhower administrations was one of contentment. Yet beneath the bland surface of suburban affluence and optimism flowed a dark current of distrust and insecurity. Nuclear holocaust was a frighteningly real possibility. Rivalry with the Soviet Union led to a new Communist scare, and demagogues like Senator Joseph McCarthy hunted for the enemy at home rather than abroad, leveling accusations of treason and betrayal that unjustly ruined many loyal Americans. The insecurity that underlay American life increased during the second Eisenhower administration and surfaced in October 1957, when the Soviets sent the satellite Sputnik into orbit around the earth. "The public's reaction to this impressive scientific feat was panic. The declining rate of economic growth; the recession of 1957–1958; the growing concern that American schools were lagging behind their Russian counterparts—all contributed to the conviction that the nation had somehow lost its previously unquestioned primacy in the eyes of the world" (Divine et al., p. 493). The entertainment industry could also reflect this political temper, conveying more subtle nuances within American culture. Television westerns began providing recognizably human characters and more realistic settings in stories tinged with ambiguous grays. "Nowadays on TV westerns," critic Cleveland Amory noted, "there are not only good guys and bad guys, but also in-between guys" (p. 1). Series stars played poker, drank hard liquor, and chatted up the bargirls in saloons, like James Garner and Jack Kelly of *Maverick*—who followed their "Pappy's" advice that "work is all right for killin' time, but it's a shaky way to make a livin'"—and Gene Barry of *Bat Masterson*, who said that his Bat was "a familiar figure in all the bars and gambling joints—and numerous romances indicate he was not one to shun the ladies" (quoted in MacDonald, p. 52). Some were mercenary gunfighters, like Richard Boone of *Have Gun—Will Travel* and the one-armed gunman in *Tate*, or bounty hunters like the former slave of *The Outlaws* and Steve McQueen of *Wanted—Dead or Alive*, who said of his character Josh Randall, "There's a certain honesty and realism in this series. . . . The hero isn't always a nice guy" (quoted in MacDonald, p. 52). Other protagonists who had started as flawless one-dimensional heroes were altered to display more of their inner constitution, like Matt Dillon of *Gunsmoke*, about whom CBS vice-president Hubbell Robinson remarked in 1959, "We made him a man with doubts, confused about the job he had to do. He wondered whether he really had to do that job. We did the same for Chester and Doc. They're not just stooges for Matt" (Morse, p. 50).

Western novels and feature films already were offering characters psychologically more complex, but—unrestricted by production codes as television was and is—their stories became even darker and more abstract, dealing in pessimistic and existential themes. Existentialism, rooted in the writings of Søren Kierkegaard, Jean-Paul Sartre, and Albert Camus, was a bleak, cheerless outlook for humanity that attained enormous vogue among intellectuals and others who were voicing reservations about postwar conformity. "Life, existentialists said, is a terrible riddle in which we cannot find meaning, no matter how hard we try. The conditions of existence are such that fear and anxiety are built into us. Thus all persons are entirely on their own" (Kelley, p. 708). The psychological and anachronistic westerns of a few years earlier had already introduced audiences to a world of violence and disorder, but the new entries were more disturbing, portraying life as an ironic and paradoxical scene in which existential protagonists confront their fate alone, unable to do much to genuinely improve their conditions. The first existentialist western, however, is a 1943 novel by Wallace Stegner, *The Big Rock Candy Mountain* (1943), which won the Pulitzer Prize and the National Book Award, but remained alone in its category until the mid 1950s. In this singular work, protagonist Bo Mason attempts to achieve the American Dream, only to learn that the Myth is a fraud as he inexorably slides into violence, poverty, criminality, and eventually suicide.

Not all existentialist westerns are as tragic or fatalistic. Some existentialist philosophers such as Reinhold Niebuhr asserted that although humanity cannot achieve sweeping changes in its condition, it can "proximate" improvements; hence, while existentialist heroes must live unto themselves in a meaningless universe, they are not precluded from making meaning or achieving success. An example of this approach is Fred Zinnemann's *High Noon* (1952), which is derived from John Cunningham's Collier short story "The Tin Star" (1947). In Cunningham's rather pat story, Sheriff Doane is aided in his showdown with the gunmen by his young deputy Toby. In the classic film, written by blacklisted screenwriter Carl Foreman, Marshal Will Kane is not only on his own against the three killers, but is refused help by everyone in town, including his Quaker bride—in effect, he is alienated by the very society that he has sworn to protect. At the end, his wife shoots one of the killers, which saves Kane but leaves her bereft of faith in her pacifist religion, and Kane too is shorn of his belief in social values as he tosses his badge into the dust and rides off with his wife. Still, Kane achieves success in that he is alive and the killers are dead. Meaning is made as well, because *High Noon* is a typical western in the sense that it is about the forming and testing of personal character. *High Noon* explores the character of Kane, his dedication versus his fear; the character of his bride, her loyalty versus her religious faith; and the character of the hypocritical townsfolk and even of the killers, who are driven by their own warped brand of justice. Reading more into *High Noon* is debatable. For instance, Philip French notes that it "initially [was] an allegory about existential man standing alone in the McCarthy era" (p. 34), and critic Harry Schein likens it to American foreign policy: "The little community seems to be crippled with fear before the approaching villains; seems to be timid, neutral, and half-hearted like the United Nations before the Soviet Union, China, and North Korea; moral courage is apparent only in the very American sheriff " (p. 309). However, Foreman rejected such political analyses, insisting that *High Noon* was "about what was happening in Hollywood and nothing else but that" (quoted in Christian, p. 93), referring to the cowardice displayed by filmmakers in face of the HUAC investigations. And Jon Tuska argues that Foreman intended no more than to tell a good story by "making a picture that narrated the events of an hour and forty minutes and which took exactly an hour and forty minutes to narrate" (p. 539). As Emmert concludes, "Ultimately, then, Foreman's intentions may not be clear" (p. 20).

High Noon spawned a series of imitations, such as *Silver Lode* (1954) and *Star in the Dust* (1956), but a more common manifestation of existentialism was in conjunction with anachronism, as in Oakley Hall's memorable *Warlock* (1958; film, 1959). Warlock is a frontier town not unlike Tombstone, Arizona, and the events that pit the citizenry against rancher and rustler Abe McQuown are drawn on the mythic encounters between the Earp brothers and the Clantons, "combining," as Hall writes in a prefatory note, "what did happen with what might have happened . . . to show what should have happened." The townsfolk, corroded by moral anarchy, guilt-ridden by their failure to back their own symbols of law and order, hire gunfighter Clyde Blaisedell to bring "Peace and Safety" (p. 8). A man with a conscience and sense of sin, Blaisedell succeeds at the cost of his own soul, killing a man who does not deserve it and then setting a saloon on fire in an act of rage and contrition. An existentialist hero with an anachronistic occupation, Blaisedell declares, "I have got no friends" (p. 478), while the townsfolk turn against him and Deputy Pike goes to arrest him because "a town full of buildings is more important than a man is" (p. 482). Blaisedell beats Pike to the draw, but then throws his revolvers away and rides off, like Shane, a woman calling after him.

The sense of alienation and distaste for society that permeate *Warlock* captured the national mood of dissatisfaction and reform that arose with the Kennedy administration in the 1960s. The placid, expansive years of the 1950s "made it possible for several reform movements to emerge during the 1960s. The economic boom made minorities aware of the possibilities of economic opportunity. National liberation movements sweeping Africa and other Third World areas gave broader meaning to reforms at home. And the baby-boomers of the middle class came of age at a time when they had enough wealth and leisure to question the prosperity their parents had gained. These social forces, more than politicians or any of society's traditional leaders, were at the root of the decade's change" (Davidson et al., p. 115–6). The status quo, then, is untrustworthy and in need of change, yet reform for the existentialist comes to nothing, as shown in Edward Abbey's *The Brave Cowboy* (1958; film, *Lonely Are the Brave*, 1962). Protagonist Jack Burns, a misfit cowboy still living by the Code of the Old West, runs afoul of the modern technological age by trying to free a draft-resisting friend, and is forced to flee on horseback, eluding police jeeps and Air Force helicopters until he is accidentally squashed under a truck carrying a load of newfangled toilet pans. Another existentialist western set in modern times is *The Misfits* (1961), in which an elderly cowboy partners with a rodeo loser, a cynical aviator, and an emotionally numb divorcee to hunt wild horses for tinned pet food. The film ends with the cowboy and the divorcee "driving beneath the stars, having apparently discovered some peace in nothingness" (French, p. 144). Placing his trilogy *Trask* (1960), *Moontrap* (1962), and *To Build a Ship* (1963) in the mid-nineteenth century, Don Berry sees the natural world as a source of spiritual sustenance, and deplores the forces within our "civilized" selves which drive us to destroy it along with ourselves. The futility of creating civilized society also propels the action in E. L. Doctorow's *Welcome to Hard Times* (1960; film, 1967); as the protagonist Blue chronicles the destruction, rebuilding, and destruction anew of his frontier settlement, he sits dying in the street with the corpses of the prostitute Molly and the killer-rapist Turner, accompanied only by Helga, the insane wife of the Swede, and he realizes that "no matter what I've done it has failed" (p. 212). The inevitable failure to halt the corruption of society is the theme of Larry McMurtry's *Horseman, Pass By* (1960; film, *Hud*, 1963), in which the honorable rancher Bannon cannot stop his son Hud from becoming the decadent perversion of his western ideals. Those who live by anachronistic values are also portrayed as vulnerable and pathetic, like the aging cowboys in Jack Schaefer's *Monte Walsh* (1963; film, 1970), who are pawns in the plans of the corporate ranch owners; the exploited cowboys in J. P. S. Brown's *The Outfit* (1971), who work on a ranch that is just a hobby for its Hollywood owner; and the cowboy dreamer in Robert Flynn's *North to Yesterday* (1967), who after gathering a cattle herd discovers that the cattle trail is closed and nobody wants his beef. As the late Leland Sonnichsen points out, "Most of the time the man in the foreground . . . is ineffectual, frustrated, or unlucky. No matter how hard he climbs, he winds up back in the ditch" (p. 121).

Clearly, western fiction expanded in vitality, complexity, and seriousness through the 1960s, even while remaining an allegory for the American Dream. "We created this dream as we were growing up as people," notes historian Robert Athearn, "though we realized it only dimly as it was happening, and in turn the dream has continued to give us back a sense of who we are" (p. 274). With the approach of the 1970s, America grew disillusioned, cynical, and rebellious from the Vietnam War, the Watergate scandal, ghetto turmoil, campus uprisings, and political assassinations. The agitation that swept the nation was "wrenching to most people. From the schoolrooms and lunch counters of the South to the college campuses of the North, from eastern slums to western migrant labor camps, American society was in ferment" (Davidson et al., p. 155). The turmoil "reached a crescendo as the American people responded to two dominant events of the decade—the war in Vietnam and the cultural insurgency at home" (Divine et al., p. 531), and, I would contend, to a third event, that of Nixon's downfall and resignation, which revealed "the abuse of presidential power [and] involved a lust for power" (Divine et al., p. 542). Unavoidably, the American Dream began to tarnish, becoming subject to derision and condemnation. As Peter Goldman observed in 1970, "What seems now to have corroded is America's ancient faith that she can not only endure but prevail. . . . The riptides of contemporary history have estranged Americans one from another by age, by race, even by class in ways Karl Marx could not have imagined. The System against its own mutinous children. The flag itself, the very symbol of America's indivisibility, has become for some of her citizens a weapon of controversy" (p. 15). Inextricably tied to the Dream, confirming the Dream's values and aspirations by reflecting the more transitory assumptions, prejudices, and major issues of the day, the western inevitably fell from grace as the Dream fell from grace.

"For the first time, the country faces a massive breakdown, manifested in every section, class and stratum, in faith in its ideals, institutions and prospects," wrote Eugene Genovese, chairman of the department of history at the University of Rochester. "The disillusionment with the war . . . intersected with the racial crisis, decay of our cities, the rising tide of official and popular violence, and other manifestations of having to contend with a ruling class" (pp. 21, 22). One consequence was the demise of the television western. "For the Western to have continued to inundate network TV, or even to have survived as a viable video diversion, the mass audience would have had to maintain its taste for the mentality fundamental to this entertainment formation. This did not happen. . . . Where no outlaw's bullet could fell the Cartwrights of *Bonanza,* mass cynicism caused it to vanish from NBC in January 1973.

Although Matt Dillon and *Gunsmoke* survived on CBS for two decades, they died unceremoniously in 1975, anachronisms in an era of social re-evaluation" (MacDonald, pp. 117–118). Another consequence was that western novels and films began mirroring this society in which "our celebrated sense of national virtue and omnipotence is crumbling so quickly" (Genovese, p. 21). Where before stories of gritty realism tended to be about nonconformist individuals protecting themselves against the conformist crowd, now stories projected a West that was physically and spiritually soiled, a hostile milieu in which social outcasts fought to survive.

Blacks, Indians, and especially half-breeds grew in popularity as characters, for they were cut off from society and thus in a unique position to deliver scathing criticism. "Many Westerners saw in [the Vietnam War] parallels with our westering experience, marked as it was by our nearly genocidal treatment of Native Americans and by our oppression and exploitation of minorities and women" (Maguire, p. 453). In *Buck and the Preacher* (1972), Sidney Poitier is a frontier scout who fights rabid bigotry while guiding ex-slaves West. *The Legend of Nigger Charley* (1972) tells of slaves escaping professional slave catchers; its sequel, *The Soul of Nigger Charley* (1973), tells of the slaves' battles out West. Richard Roundtree in *Charley One-Eye* (1973) is an army deserter pursued by a white bounty hunter, and Fred Williamson in *Adios, Amigo* (1976) is an honest rancher who loses his spread to corrupt whites. Half-breed protagonists, such as those in *100 Rifles* (1969), *The Scalphunters* (1968), *Blue* (1968), Elmore Leonard's *Valdez Is Coming* (1970; film, 1971), and *Chato's Land* (1972), tend to struggle between two ways of life while wreaking revenge against a brutal, corrupt society. Westerns with Indian protagonists, such as Theodore Olson's *Arrow in the Sun* (1969; film, *Soldier Blue*, 1970), *Journey Through Rosebud* (1972), *Cheyenne Autumn*, *Windwalker* (1981), N. Scott Momaday's Pulitzer Prize-winning *House Made of Dawn* (1968), Frederick Manfred's *Manly-Hearted Woman* (1975), Denton Bedford's *Tsali* (1972), Dee Brown's *Creek Mary's Blood* (1980), Michael Blake's *Dances with Wolves* (1980), and James Welch's *Winter in the Blood* (1974), *The Death of Jim Loney* (1979), and most recently *Fools Crow* (1986), essentially are revisionist polemics on the mistreatment of Native Americans, who are cast as more civilized and thus morally superior to the whites who massacre them—although *Ulzana's*

Raid (1972) depicts the Apaches as no less brutal than the cavalrymen; and Thomas Sanchez's *Rabbit Boss* (1973) explores the weaknesses of the Washo Indians and, by implication, the similar abandonment by contemporary America of its heritage and promise.

Civilization's portrayal in westerns as the oppressive enemy paralleled the country's disgust at the war and disdain for the government. Staughton Lynd reports "the growing sense on the part of the American people (left and right) that government in Washington is almost a foreign power, an invader rather than a protector" (p. 28). In westerns, lawmen who before had upheld justice now blindly enforced the dictates of the legal system. In Harry Lawton's *Willy Boy: A Desert Manhunt* (1960; film, *Tell Them Willie Boy Is Here*, 1969), Willie Boy follows the Paiute law of "marriage by capture" by eloping with his girlfriend after killing her father, but white man's law calls it murder and a posse hunts him down, murdering him. Sometimes the lawman is as corrupt as the system, like the prison warden in *There Was a Crooked Man* (1970) and the ambitious lawman in *Posse* (1975), who hunts a criminal gang solely to gain election to Congress. "We have rightly come to feel," Lynd asserts, "not that we run the government, but that it runs us and we protect ourselves as best we can . . . taking the best page from our history and responding: Don't tread on me" (p. 28). Accordingly, the legal system is shunned by protagonists who pursue criminals on their own in such westerns as *The Revengers* (1972), *Hannie Caulder* (1972), *The Deadly Trackers* (1973), *Santee* (1973), and Brian Garfield's *Gundown* (1971; film, *The Last Hard Men*, 1976). Or the protagonists simply "drop out," as was the wont of "a growing portion of the nation's youth [who] loudly proclaims its defection from everything" (Genovese, p. 21), such as backwoodsman Johnson in Vardis Fisher's *Mountain Man* (1965; film, *Jeremiah Johnson*, 1973) who retreats to the remote Rockies, soured on civilization.

In contrast, the character who strives to work legally and morally within the system continues to be an anachronism in the existentialist vein, unable to cope and desperate to escape contemporary life—a reflection of the pervasive self-doubts and pessimism of Americans that were, according to Arthur Schlesinger, due less to the war and social unrest than to the intrinsic instability of the modern world: "Science and technology make, dissolve, rebuild and enlarge our environment every week; and the world alters more in a decade than it used to alter in centuries. This has meant the disappearance of familiar landmarks and guideposts that stabilized life for earlier generations" (pp. 28–29). Contrasting the simple life in the fictional West with the disruptive life in "the crises of modernity" (p. 28) produced anachronistic stories laden with mordant irony, such as Stuart Rosenberg's depressing *Pocket Money* (1972), C. W. Smith's Chicano novel *Thin Men of Haddam* (1973), and Elmer Kelton's elegiac *The Time It Never Rained* (1973). In Sergio Leone's *Once Upon a Time in the West* (1969), the arrival of technology in the form of a railroad results in the death of such western stereotypes as the hired gunslinger, the railroad boss, and the heroic outlaw, all passing to make room for a new America whose immigrants will be fed by the surviving reformed whore—all the more ironic because Italian director Leone had set out to create the definitive epic about the opening of the West, only to be thwarted by his ignorance of the fundamental ethos of the western myth. Similarly, John Wayne had starred in a trio of films about elderly lawmen supported by eccentrics and drunks against powerful, venal opponents (*Rio Bravo*, 1959; *El Dorado*, 1967; *Rio Lobo*, 1970), and as an elderly rancher who teaches children to carry on his Code (*The Cowboys*, 1972), all which are metaphors for the Vietnam experience, displaying "a profound pessimism, as if the aging [was] being equated with the aging, the loss of energy, of America itself" (French, p. 152)— and then in the 1975 film *The Shootist*, based on Glendon Swarthout's 1971 novel, Wayne plays aging gunman J. B. Books, who rejects dying slowly of cancer in favor of going down in a gunfight against a trio of villains; the film is John Wayne's last, and an ironic memorial, for Wayne was cancer-ridden and his screen persona had become as much an anachronism as the gunman, the gunfight, and the villains.

Kid Blue (1970), in which a failed train robber bungles his attempt to go straight in the early twentieth century, is a comedy version of the anachronistic and existentialist western. Not to be confused with lampoons and farces like *Support Your Local Sheriff* (1969), David Morboro's *Dirty Dingus Magee* (1969; film, 1970), *From Noon Till Three* (1976), and *The Duchess and the Dirtwater Fox* (1976), satires portraying the West of the western as extinct tend to be black and sardonic, like Frank Perry's *Rancho Deluxe* (1975), in which two anachronistic outlaws malfunction in the dehumanized corporate world of today, and Howard Zieff's *Hearts* of the West (1975), in which a western writer in the 1930s winds up acting in low-budget western movies. Or they are savage parodies like Mel Brooks's *Blazing Saddles: Never Give a Saga an Even Break* (1974), which punctured the conventions and symbols of the genre with such devastating accuracy that it alone almost killed off the formula western. But in their mocking of westerns as anachronistic, these comedies mock the hopes, ideals, and scruples of our forebears and their belief in the apparently anachronistic American Dream. They could do so because the "landmarks and signposts that stabilized life for earlier generations" were no longer relevant, no longer to be taken seriously, and "children, knowing how different their own lives will be, can no longer look to parents as models and authorities" (Schlesinger, p. 29). In a word, contemporary society had lost a sense of history. In 1970, Daniel Boorstein, director of the National Museum of Science and Technology at the Smithsoniam Institution, argued, "Without the materials of historical comparison, having lost our traditional respect for the wisdom of ancestors and the culture of kindred nations . . . we forget where we come from and how we got here [and lose] interest in the real examples from the human past which alone can help us shaping the standard of the humanly possible" (p. 24). Agreeing with Boorstein was Cornell professor of government Andrew Hacker: "We can no longer be a single nation, possessed of a common struggle. . . . We have, in short, become a loose aggregation of private persons who give higher priority to our personal pleasures than to collective endeavors" (p. 20). Consequently, heroes with their mythical interpretation of a period of history now considered anachronistic could no longer survive, for heroes were no longer acceptable to a mass audience grown skeptical or scornful of those who did what had to be done for the benefit of others.

In place of heroic stories came revisionist treatments like the squalid *Dirty Little Billy* (1972), whose ads declared, "Billy the Kid was a Punk." There is nobody to champion in Arthur Penn's *The Missouri Breaks* (1976), for Marlon Brando's psychotic "regulator" is contemptible and Jack Nicholson's grubby rustler possesses the ethics of a weasel. *Bad Company* (1972) depicts the making of bandits in a barren West peopled by nasty outlaws, nastier homesteaders, and ruined pioneers heading East—one of whom offers his wife for a dollar to the young protagonists. Jesse James of Philip Kaufman's *The Great Northfield Minnesota*

Raid (1972) is a homicidal maniac who dreams up robberies while sitting in the outhouse, and the Bill Cody of Robert Altman's *Buffalo Bill and the Indians, or: Sitting Bull's History Lesson* (1976) is a charlatan bent on promoting his own fallacious legend. The Earps and Doc Holliday of *Doc* (1971) are sleazy opportunists who frame the Clantons for crimes and provoke them into the notorious shoot-out, the film suggesting that western heroes were actually sick, violent, decadent, and responsible for undermining the nation's values. Other than Gentle Ben–type mountain men who ran off and befriended bears, there were no heroes, and realism degenerated into crudism as westerns ignored the horses and focused on the horseshit—literally. The streets of Tombstone in *Doc* are littered with manure. A stagecoach driver in Sam Peckinpah's *Ballad of Cable Hogue* (1970) urinates in the desert, and a fight in *There Was a Crooked Man* results in the loser being dunked in a full latrine.

"Americans can no longer display that spirit which transforms a people into a citizenry and turns territory into a nation," Hacker asserts. "Suffice it to say that increasingly we will encounter one another as enemies, that as individuals we stand more vulnerable to the abrasions we effect on each other" (p. 21).The western responded by rejecting the concept of community as either a place or a spirit. The once moral hero was shorn of community ties and values, and in his stead came the questionably moral protagonist—Edge, Lassiter, Slade, Steele; whatever his name, he is a ruthless, embittered loner with weapons, hell-bent on some mission of vengeance. There also came the outright immoral protagonists who are killers and renegades by choice rather than misfortune and who remain unrepentant to the end. Although presented with much charm, Cassidy and Henry Longbaugh in *Butch Cassidy and the Sundance Kid* (1969) are confirmed, if anachronistic, outlaws done in not by justice or decency but by technology. Manhunters whose missions are supported by the law and society succeed not because of superior morals but of superior skills, as in *The Professionals* (1966); or they fail because their level of savagery sickens a lead character who is only a bit less callous than they, as in *The Hunting Party* (1971), *The Revengers*, and *Joe Kidd* (1972). Or the protagonists constitute a disparate band of outlaws only a bit less vicious than the mangy lawmen or bounty hunters after them, as in Sam Peckinpah's inspired *The Wild Bunch* (1969)—wherein a gang of aging crooks are chased by thuggish bounty hunters until, as in *Butch*

Cassidy, the future catches up with them and modern weaponry brings them down. "It ain't like it used to be," Old Man Sykes says at the end, "but it'll do."

Such westerns proved very popular because of, not despite, their violence and moral drift, for they were metaphoric reflections of the conditions and moral confusion engendered by the war and domestic politics. Unfortunately, replacing the banished, anachronistic cowboy heroes were protagonists ill suited as role models for boys, unless the boy wished to become a freeway sniper or mass murderer. Virtuous role models for girls also became scarcer, westerns mimicking the feminist movement's aggressive agenda for social and sexual liberation. For many women, liberation meant "to open up the full range of employment outside the home," which translated into "being able to postpone or subordinate marriage to a full-time career" (Kelley, p. 806). Thus the girlfriend of the Sundance Kid, Etta Place, has no intention of marrying him, although she is not particularly fond of her respectable career either: "I teach school, and that's the bottom of the pit." For many other women, liberation meant casting aside old codes of conduct in favor of "the newer concept that the sexual appetites of men and women were equal, and that women had the same right to sexual experience as men" (Kelley, p. 809). For westerns, it meant stories like Marilyn Durham's *The Man Who Loved Cat Dancing* (1972; film, 1973), involving a discontented wife who runs off with an outlaw and finds fulfillment; and *Molly and Lawless John* (1972), involving a woman who kills her outlaw lover, then returns to her husband claiming she had been kidnapped and demanding the reward for the dead outlaw. It meant that in other westerns, like *Hang 'Em High* (1968), the heroine avoids sex not because she is chaste but because she has been traumatized by rape, a condition in due course cured by sex. It meant that liberation was not of prostitutes from their careers but of westerns from prior moral standards, such as in *The Cheyenne Social Club* (1970) and Edmund Naughton's *McCabe* (1970; film, *McCabe and Mrs. Miller*, 1971), a grim tale in which McCabe and Mrs. Miller run a bawdyhouse so prosperous that it helps clean up the town—customers have to wash in the new bathhouse before whoring— and in Altman's film, attracts a corporation whose offer to buy them out is refused and who then murders McCabe, thereby making McCabe an anachronistic victim of the future. It meant that as equals women stalked or held hostage by villains were more likely to be tortured as well as seduced, as in Diane Johnson's *The Shadow Knows* (1972), which depicts the terror of a victimized woman, or in *The Wild Bunch*, which portrays virtually all the women as whores and betrayers to be used as shields against gunfire. It meant the inspiration of a subgenre called "adult westerns," which author Jane Candia Coleman calls "shoot and screw" westerns (House, p. 6), wherein graphic sex is no longer used to enhance a relationship but is an end unto itself with no emotional involvement expected or welcomed. Most have male protagonists, such as Marshal Custis Long in the Longarm series, whose moniker "Longarm" did not originate because he extends the long arm of the law. A few adult westerns have female protagonists, such as Jessica Starbuck of the Lone Star series, who is a liberated lover of the 1880s: "Not a prude or hypocrite; she was pure woman, proud of her femininity" (Wesley Ellis, *Treachery Trail*, p. 102). The lustful lengths the protagonists go to could border on the absurd, as in Tom Cutter's *The Oklahoma Score* (1985) where the randy hero and a young woman manage to have sex while roped to the cowcatcher of a speeding locomotive.

Also beginning in the 1960s and continuing through the 1980s were westerns in which the protagonists were not just questionably moral or consciously immoral, but amoral—antiheroes who, like sociopaths, were oblivious of morality, honesty, or any other human sensibility. Although the values embodied in the heroic cowboy of legend had been largely discredited, and a more graphic and stylized violence was an integral component of "realistic" westerns like *The Wild Bunch*, the violence remained essential to the plot and was never itself the real point. "Cruel the Western is and violent, but rustling, fence-cutting, monopolizing the water supply, and such situations upon which script writers freely draw, were threats to human subsistence. Out of such great struggle all through history came the safety which allowed societies to flourish and to build" (Robert P. Ellis, p. 229). But representing the last stage in the breakdown of the genre's conventions and principles, the amoral western stripped away all vestiges of moral dimensions, its antiheroes winning out solely because they are more cold-bloodedly vicious and treacherous than their opponents. The three so-called spaghetti westerns by Sergio Leone that launched Clint Eastwood's film career (*A Fistful of Dollars*, 1964; *For a Few Dollars More*, 1966; *The Good, the Bad and the Ugly*, 1966) set the formula for these unromantic, corpse-strewn tales of blood and revenge, but the amoral western reached its nadir during the 1980s with subsequent Italian-, Spanish-, and American-made versions in the "Man With No Name" image. Their popularity, and the popularity of similar stories in other genres such as *Death Wish* (1974), *Dirty Harry* (1971), and *First Blood* (1982), attest to a public responsive to their themes, a public that in the real world gave voice to these themes by electing Ronald Reagan president.

Whether the Reagan agenda worked in practice, was successful in its goals, or created a "revolution" that bears his name is not germane here; the relevance lies in the roles President Reagan played as an image of popular culture and as an emblem of American national identity. After all, the election of presidents, akin to the choosing of westerns, is dependent on how citizens see themselves and those against whom they define themselves, and thus a president becomes symbolic of national self-perception. The perception in amoral westerns is that no one is secure or stable, no community in place or spirit is available "where," to quote Robert Frost, "it's safe to be known." The reason is the overabundance of villains: aberrant culprits of primal, unfathomable evil. The central tenet of Reagan's foreign policy was that the Soviet Union was an "evil empire" bent on "world revolution, ready to 'commit any crime, to lie, to cheat' to advance their cause" (Divine et al., p. 567). Villains don't come much bigger or badder than that. Such a threat calls for a strong authoritarian power, so one element of Reagan's agenda was a sharp increase in military outlays, his strategic goal "to provide the United States with the strength to act unilaterally anywhere in the world to beat back any communist threat" (Davidson et al., p. 1278). As already noted, however, public perception in the post-Watergate era was that institutions of government corrupted individuals who in turn corrupted society (sentiments that led to the passage of the War Powers Act, for example). Denying any suggestion of police-state control, Reagan promoted the authority of the individual. Fond of saying "Get the government off our backs," he strove to "reduce bureaucracy and to undermine agencies responsible for what seemed to him excessive meddling in the areas of civil rights, environmental and consumer protection, economic regulation, poverty programs, urban renewal, transportation, the arts, and education" (Davidson et al., p. 1278). The individual was on his own, operating like the antihero on the basis of the survival of the fittest. Survival in amoral westerns does not include villains, of course, nor the numerous misfits and dupes who are so easily divided, so weak and helpless, so useless to themselves and everyone else. Similarly, "the Reagan presidency, in conjunction with the New Right . . . equat[ed] individual actions with national actions in such a way that individual failings were seen as causes for national downfall (precisely its critique of Jimmy Carter and the 'cultural elite', but equally its justification for attacking single mothers, substance users, homosexuals, and welfare recipients)" (Jeffords, p. 12). Such an ideology proved divisive in a society already fragmented by race, religion, economics, location, and gender, although to many people Reagan's determined stance showed him to be firmly in charge, "walkin' tall" and "stickin' by his guns"—just like Eastwood in *High Plains Drifter* (1973) and *The Outlaw Josey Wales* (1976). Even after people learned that he "couldn't remember" Iran-Contra and that Nancy Reagan and her astrologer helped advise him on major issues, most thought approvingly of their president as a strong and decisive man. He was, like the westerns, what audiences wanted to see.

To be sure, Ronald Reagan and his administration considered themselves to be ethical patriots, defenders of the American Dream's principles of individualism, enterprise, and liberty. Still, his "ideological approach, as one analyst pointed out, tended to give Reagan policymakers an 'absolute certainty of their own rightness.' Since they were operating with 'pure hearts,' they found it all too easy to justify working with 'dirty hands.' In some cases, noble ends were used to justify dubious tactics" as in their dealings with Grenada, Lebanon, Libya, and Iran-Contra (Davidson et al., p. 1285). This "ends justify the means" philosophy operates in amoral westerns as well, except that in them the motive for violence is professional and abstract, shorn of any moral rationale. The antihero, as critic Pauline Kael said of the Clint Eastwood character, "expresses a new emotionlessness about killing that people think is the truth now. It used to be that the man who stood for high principles was also the best shot. Now we no longer believe that in order to be a great shot you need principles at all" (quoted in Johnstone, pp. 50–51). Lacking emotion, principles, or a motive that is socially or personally specific, the anti-hero is a shell, empty of human identity or history. "I looked at Eastwood," Sergio Leone told an interviewer, "and I didn't see any character, just a physical figure" (quoted in Cumbow, p. 154). The focal character in Cormac McCarthy's *Blood Meridian* leaves Tennessee because he has no family or patrimony, but in searching for a new homeland he only discovers an actual and metaphysical horror of blood, sex, and feuds. Similar horrors and orphan loners rule such westerns as *Cost of Dying* (1968), in which fleeing rustlers take refuge in a small Colorado town; *Get the Coffin Ready* (1968), in which antihero Django wreaks revenge by machine-gunning not only rival gang members but his own as well; *Cut-Throats Nine* (1973), which as a publicity gimmick, supplied the audience with "terror masks" to "hide your eyes when the violence became too much"; and the dreadful 3-D *Comin' At Ya!* (1981), in which the plot of a wounded groom seeking his abducted bride (both ex-bandits) serves as an excuse for rapine and massacre, for spurting blood and slinging bats, rats, and body parts at the audience.

Not unexpectedly, such senseless violence in mindless westerns became a favorite target of protesters. Behavioral researchers, the PTA, Congress, religious task forces, and similar groups singled out the western "as a major contributor to juvenile delinquency, a brutalizing reflection of a violence-prone society, an offender of civilized values" (MacDonald, p. 90). Revisionists such as Jane Tompkins concluded that the western exists "in order to provide a justification for violence" (p. 227). Protesters and critics seem either unaware or uncaring that, whereas the amoral western is callous, the classic western is compassionate, that the endless slaughter in *Pale Rider* (1985) and the heroic showdown in *High Noon* are virtually moral opposites. Indeed, if a story dispenses with the conventions and limitations of the western and depends on brutal violence for its *raison d'être*, then even if it is filled with horses, guns, saloons, and dust, it cannot rightly be called a western. Overlooked by Tompkins and others is that violence has no genre. When in the late 1960s the persistent criticism of violence led to the replacement of aggressive cowboy dramas with family westerns like *Bonanza*, violence persisted in police, detective, and other dramas. "As late as November 1984 one interest group, the National Coalition on TV Violence, could claim that video violence had risen 75 percent since 1980 and was now at record levels" (MacDonald, p. 100).

The current moribund state of the western, then, cannot be blamed on violence alone, but is the result of multiple causes, some self-inflicted, some due to factors outside the purview of the genre. For example, fewer people seem to have time to read these days. The pressures of work or the complexities of family life impinge on the time formerly spent curled beneath a lamp, a novel spread comfortably across one's lap. The Internet, computer games, and interactive TV have further encroached on that time-honored tradition of the printed text. Consequently, demand for books is down, including the demand by public libraries. "In recent years, library budgets shrank and paper prices soared," relates Jacqueline Johnson, editor at Walker and Company, a major supplier of westerns to libraries. "So we trimmed our list" (House, p. 16). Also, because westerns, more than other genres, are bought in places other than bookstores, such as drug and grocery stores, western publishers rely more on independent and magazine distributors, yet these distributors have been undergoing a process of conglomeration. As veteran literary agent Nat Sobel points out, "in less than a year, many wholesalers have been forced to sell their companies to the large agencies still surviving. In a few years there may be less than a dozen IDs [independent distributors] left in the game" (House, p. 15). The crunch of higher costs, lower demand, and fewer distributors has forced a number of paperback houses, particularly marginal ones catering to western audiences, to go out of business. An equally damaging development beginning in the 1980s has been the mergers and takeovers by large communications corporations "driven by illusions of media 'synergy' . . . to 'become more vertically integrated'" (Auletta, p. 54). As with the independent distributors, media giants such as Time/Warner/Turner have been created at the expense of smaller film and television studios, production companies, and especially book publishers and dealers. The consequence is described by western writer Clay Reynolds as "a serious industry-wide downsizing, a bloodletting .. . . In some cases, the [publishing] houses were bought to close down; in others, they were bought to lose money deliberately. . . . 'Mom and Pop' book-selling operations are being systematically squeezed out. Even well-heeled local or regional chains are pulling in their horns, closing stores, regrouping in the face of barracuda-like competition from mega-corporations which increasingly are controlling the retail end of the book business" (House, pp. 13, 15).

The heads of these mega-corporations, many of which have no relationship to books whatsoever, are after large profits quickly to justify their acquisitions. As has been the case with large film studios and commercial television, "publishing companies are being looked at simply for the money they make. And they don't look good—certainly not when they are compared with other companies in the content business" (Auletta, p. 54). Richard House recalls attending an editor's panel at the 1996 Western Writers of America convention when "someone asked what kind of surveys were done by publishers to determine what people wanted to read. One of the editors said that the only surveys they do is to look at the cash register receipts and sales figures" (p. 12). And as has been the case with large film studios and commercial television, the corporate heads seek to generate quick profits through blockbuster movies, ratings supershows, and now with publishing through sensational bestsellers. When the strategy works (*Independence Day, Seinfeld*), often the huge profits are swallowed by the staggering losses of the bombs. "One can see the craving for such [bestseller] titles in some recent celebrated failures: the more than four million dollars that Viking Penguin reportedly paid Marcia Clark for her account of the O. J. Simpson trial and the estimated three million dollars that Ballantine paid Simpson's attorney Johnnie L. Cochran, Jr. . . . The consequences of such extravagance can make for some startling numbers. Simon & Schuster according to a Viacom executive wrote off about thirty-five million dollars' worth of unearned advances in 1996." Random House, wrote off "well in excess of fifty million dollars. . . . Penguin Putnam, according to a senior executive there, wrote off unearned advances of about twenty million dollars" (Auletta, p. 56). These are millions that could have been invested in publishing more modest, yet well-written, novels, including westerns. Instead, five years ago Bantam Books cut back thirty percent; in 1996 HarperCollins had to abrogate contracts, slashing 106 titles; and Simon & Schuster's Carolyn Reidy admitted that "over the course of the last two years, we have reduced the number of books we publish by fifteen percent" (Auletta, p. 62). Another tragic result has been that editorial numbers in New York have been slashed by a third, causing a decline in editorial integrity from the standpoints of acquisition and quality work (House, p. 13). As writer and editor Dale Walker notes, "when cutbacks are made, Westerns are the first to go. New York publishers assign raw and inexperienced editors to their Western line, give the books no marketing attention, often shove off old pulp art covers and find all manners of ways to cheapen the line" (House, p. 6). This is testified to by author Richard Wheeler:

> My story *Richard Lamb* was about an old man who has become an Indian trader after years as a mountain man. He has flowing white beard and hair, and wears beautiful golden buckskins, elaborately decorated by his Blackfeet wife. But on the cover of the Ballantine paperback, he has been transformed into a cowboy with a Levi jacket, jeans, boots and spurs, and a cowboy hat. . . . Another of my stories has a heroine who is something of a con artist. The Ballantine cover for that one features an Indian warrior on a rearing horse, waving a signal blanket. (p. 22)

Not surprisingly, readers do not find westerns congruent with contemporary social realities, and are "often faced with a tired tokenism in small, remote shelves of desiccated reprints from such deceased writers as Zane Grey, Max Brand, Ernest Haycox, and Louis L'Amour. Great authors all, in their time, but scarcely indicative of the quality product of many of today's Western writers" (House, p. 2). Moreover, those working in the field must admit that although there are quality westerns available, the sad fact is that much if not most recent work has been poorly written pulp yarns and quickie formula movies. For too long, too many writers have depended on variations, gimmicks, switcheroos, and all the other desperate dodges of those who have found themselves proficient at telling obsolete stories, in order to churn out formulaic westerns the way harvester combines chuck bales of hay—and with just about that same level of literary content. As a result of being fed a diet of clichés and cardboard, people by and large think of westerns as juvenile horse-operas. When, as an exception proving the rule, a contemporary western becomes a popular bestseller, it is treated as a rare survivor from a bygone era, possessing qualities incompatible with the traditional form. *Young Guns* (1988) was advertised as having "brat-pack appeal," and Larry McMurtry's Pulitzer Prize-winning *Lonesome Dove* (1985; TV serial, 1986) was promoted as "stripping the glamour from the Old West." Most common is the attitude experienced by novelist Gene Shelton: "Many times at book signings and personal lectures, I've endured the put-down

'Oh, you just write westerns.' We have become, it seems, the yardstick by which hacks are measured in the literary field" (House, p. 3).

Perhaps the most critical self-inflicted wound suffered by westerns is that, ironically, they succeeded in their function as expressions of popular attitudes. "From World War II through the troubled Cold War years," non-formulaic westerns "accommodated a variety of issues and ideas that echoed feelings of . . . alienation and disillusionment" (Nash, p. 249), degenerating into existential and amoral westerns which reflected disgust for the shoddy present by reviling the past and rejecting the conventions of morality, heroism, and belief in the American Dream. This, the production of inferior formula westerns, and the collapse of the mainstream publishing industry have "combined into a giant step toward the western novel's oblivion. Enlightened, inspiring western literature and its authors took a slamming, shocking body block, as the disdain grew for the western in general" (House, p. 6). The western is gone, partly killed off and partly committing suicide, according to conventional wisdom and the eulogies of critics and scholars; as MacDonald says of western television programming, "the generation that once made the Western the most prolific form . . . has lived to see a rare occurrence in American popular culture: the death of a genre" (p. 127). Its epitaph could well be the epigraph of *For A Few Dollars More:* "When life had no value, death, sometimes, had its price."

Ridin' It Out

Will the Western ever experience a resurgence in popularity and regain its centrality as the American popular genre? If the reflections I have offered are largely correct, that seems unlikely.
John G. Cawelti

John G. Cawelti's discouraging words conclude his introduction, "Reflections on the Western Since 1970," to the second edition of *The Six-Gun Mystique* (1984), his provocative study of the western as a form of social and cultural ritual. For causes chronicled in the last chapter, appearances would indicate that his prediction has proven accurate. However, I contend that, to recycle Mark Twain, the reports of the western's demise are greatly exaggerated. My reason is suggested in another Cawelti piece, "God's Country . . . Differing Visions of the West": "If the myth is to remain a vital one . . . the Western must confront our new understanding of ourselves and to begin to articulate and explore the conflicts of value and meaning which now dominate our lives" (p. 274). At the time, Cawelti was referring to the "more enigmatic and pessimistic view of America" (p. 274), but in the intervening twenty-five years America has changed and the western has changed with it, continuing to "help us to define who we are by carefully examining where we should have been, and by implication, where we should be headed. The West is national self-awareness" (Marsden, p. 208). If for no other reason than its capacity for expressing American concerns and values, the endangered western is not doomed to extinction.

As Patricia Janis Broder says of the artistic portrayal of the West, "The West is part of contemporary America. Fortunately, many American artists have accepted the challenge to paint a land and culture in transition" (p. 8). Writers W. Michael Gear and Kathleen O'Neal Gear, for example, note that "for those of us who write novels about the American frontier experience, the sobering reality is that the market hasn't been worse since the 1930s. The best advice we can give is to buckle down and write your way through it" (p. 10), and best-selling author Kat Martin declares that "the western is not dead and I doubt it ever will be. Great novels like *Lonesome Dove* will always rise to the surface. Other westerns with memorable characters and a down right good tale will appear on the *New York Times* Bestseller Lists" (p. 23). Hence, continuing in the vernacular, the western may have fallen off "like wormy apples in a high wind," but it persists in getting up and back in the saddle, which is why this chapter is called "Ridin' It Out," a cowboy expression for staying with a bucking horse until it is broken.

Ironically, one major change or adaptation stems from the sustaining and recurrent elements of myth—the unchanging elements—

transforming into stories that masquerade as belonging to other genres. Nowadays, westerns can come marketed as mystery stories, such as Sandra West Prowell's *The Killing of Monday Brown* (1994), which blends Crow Indian rituals with detective fiction; Wayne Barton and Stan Williams's *Shadow of a Doubt* (1995), which stars Texas Ranger Jeff King; W. W. Lee's *Cannon's Revenge* (1995), in which ex-Ranger Birch trades cowboying for sleuthing; Charles Hackenberry's *Friends* (1994), in which two lawmen must solve a series of murders before they can retire; and Tim Champlin's *Deadly Season* (1997), in which Wells Fargo express messenger Jay McGraw becomes a temporary San Francisco policeman to smash a Chinatown opium gang.

More common than mysteries are westerns disguised as romances. "In the marketplace," romance writer Kat Martin observes, "romance novels make up fifty-three percent of all mass market books sold. A good percentage of these romances are westerns" (p. 23). Aside from Kat Martin's romances, such as *Midnight Rider* (1996), typical of romantic westerns are Penelope Williamson's *Heart of the West* (1997), in which heroine Clementine falls in love with her husband's brother; Ellen Recknor's *Leaving Missouri* (1997), in which Clutie Mac Chestnut is wed against her will at twelve and shoots her husband at sixteen; Tracy Dunham's *The Long Trail Home* (1997), in which white woman Elizabeth McFarland searches for her adopted Kiowa family and her half-Comanche husband; and Suzann Ledbetter's *Klondike Fever* (1997), in which, as its back cover says, "beautiful and brave Megan O'Malley . . . could not resist the lure of finding the greatest mother lode of all in the vast north country. But she didn't count upon a man from her past reappearing in her life."

A close second to romantic westerns are historical novels. Richard House finds "that many books with 'Historical Fiction' on the spine were the same-old, same-old shoot-'em-ups" (p. 18). Some are fictionalized accounts of history, like those about Custer such as Judy Alter's *Libby: A Novel of Elizabeth Bacon Custer* (1994), Terry Johnston's *Trumpet on the Land* (1995), and Earl Murray's *Flaming Sky: A Novel of the Little Bighorn* (1995); and those of Kit Carson like Ray Hogan's *Soldier in Buckskin* (1996) and Norman Zollinger's *Meridian: A Novel of Kit Carson's West* (1997); while other historical novels are purely fictional exploits like Cynthia Haselhoff's *The Chains of Sarai Stone* (1995) and Dawn Miller's *The Journal of Callie Wade* (1996).

A growing segment of the youth market is westerns, such as A. J. Arnold's *Diamond Buckow* (1994), about a teenager struggling to overcome abuse; Robert J. Conley's *The Dark Island* (1995), about a Spanish-Cherokee boy who feels that he is not accepted by either people; Elmer Kelton's *Cloudy in the West* (1997), in which a twelve-year-old is involved in murder and greed; and Stella Gipson Polk's *Glory Girl* (1997), in which pubescent Eve runs away from an orphanage to live in the East Texas hill country. Another popular subgenre is children's stories about and often by Indians, such as Natachee Scott Momaday's *Owl in the Cedar Tree* (1994), Lucille Mulcahy's *Dark Arrow* (1995), and Virginia Driving Hawk Sneve's *Chichi Hoohoo Bogeyman* (1993) and *When Thunders Spoke* (1993). The Gears report that in a Washington, D. C. super-bookstore they found seven copies of their *People of the Mist* "on an endcap in the 'Nature' section" (p. 9). There are Civil War gothics with plantations instead of ranches, Eastern westerns situated in rolling woodlands and cultivated hedgerows, "modernist" or "post-modernist" fiction where present-day lawmen, rodeo riders, and Cadillac-driving ranchers act out frontier myths, and even western horror stories, such as Richard Matheson's *Shadow on the Sun* (1995), which melds the supernatural into the western setting near Fort Apache, and Loren Paine's *The Devil on Horseback* (1995), which features a hired killer who never sleeps and rarely eats. There are Japanese, Russian, Australian, and South African "para-westerns" that resemble horse-operas in a style clearly influenced by the American model. They are all westerns because they are about personal character striving to overcome perilous circumstances in adventure stories which could not happen anywhere else but on a western or pseudo-western frontier. A recent review of Elmore Leonard's *Cuba Libre* notes that "Leonard's first novels were Westerns, that most stylized of genres, and his latest book could be mistaken for one—what with the horses, the Colt revolvers, the frontier towns—if it didn't take place in turn of the century Cuba" (Gates, p. 83). This is no mistake; *Cuba Libre* is a western, as are the books by the Gears, whose "fresh and compelling literary style(s) in prehistory and later period novels and sagas, co-authored or separately, are hailed as inventive proof that 'the Western'—or by whatever euphemism it shall survive—is far from dead" (House, p. 4).

This is not to argue that everything is a western, that tales of the Foreign Legion and medieval knights, say, are just cowboy yarns in different costumes. Nor is this to suggest that like grave robbers, other genres and narratives have simply appropriated the western's conventions, mythology, and social purposes. Media critic Larry Michie was incorrect when he asserted in 1976 that "this is the era of the new western, the cop show" (p. 101). So was Stan Steiner in claiming that "in Peckinpah's *Convoy*, truckers became 'the new cowboys'" (p. 99). So, too, was Pauline Kael in writing that "the Western cowboy hero hasn't disappeared; he's moved from the mythological purity of the wide-open spaces into the corrupt modern cities and towns ('Dirty Harry')" (p. 100). Granted, aspects of the western's themes, style, and social relevance have been co-opted by detective stories, police procedurals, trucker films, situation comedies, and even science fiction like *Star Wars* and *Star Trek*. But the totality of these features exists only in the western, and it differs from the totality of features which fashion other genres. The seedy criminality resolved in *Dirty Harry* or *NYPD Blue* is not the equivalent of the outlawry confronted in *Gunfight at the OK Corral* or *The Lone Ranger*, and no amount of rhetoric can make Sonny Crockett of *Miami Vice* into Marshall Matt Dillon or an eighteen-wheel Freightliner into Trigger. The realm of science fiction lies in the speculation of ideas like time travel and alien contact projected into the future, whereas the province of the western is in the dramatizations of contemporary concerns about character and community within an historical framework. Simply put, "The western speaks to Americans in ways other fictional forms do not" (Walker, p. 21).

So westerns still thrive, albeit somewhat in disguise. Recognizing this fact is surely the first step in rehabilitating the genre as a genre, for only when publishers, producers, and others in the entertainment field become convinced that the genre is both durable and flexible will they produce and promote stories that have the unmistakable stamp of westerns. Unfortunately, television remains lukewarm to westerns, although two new series will be offered this fall, TNT continues to produce superior TV-movies such as 1997's *The Buffalo Soldiers* starring Danny Glover, and Dan Curtis Productions is developing a miniseries based on Richard Matheson's *The Journal of the Gun Tears*. As of 1998 a few feature films were still being made: *Daily Variety* reported that Ron Howard would direct *The Pretenders*, Kathryn Bigelow would direct the epic *Marching to Valhalla*, Richard Attenborough would direct *Grey Owl*, and Universal Pictures would produce Ang Lee's *To Live On* (Swarthout, p. 26).

The mainstream publishers are still struggling. "Book sales have fallen in each of the past three years, and chains like Borders and Barnes & Noble have been returning volumes to publishers at an alarming rate" (Marks, p. 55). Apparently, mergers and acquisitions remain the answer to profits. In 1997, Penguin Books, already a conglomerate of "New American Library, Hamish Hamilton, and a half-dozen smaller houses on both sides of the Atlantic," bought the Putnam Berkley Group, thereby creating "the second largest English-language publishing firm in the world" (Boynton, p. 49). In April 1998 the German media giant Bertelsmann paid an estimated $1.4 billion for Random House, which also includes Bantam, Doubleday, and Dell, and thus became "the most powerful publisher of English-language books in the world, controlling a third of the consumer books in this country" (Marks, p. 55). These once proud, independent, and progressive publishing houses are predicted to continue their downward slide to the bottom line, their shrinking midlists including fewer westerns, their categories and literary styles increasingly homogenized. For instance, after twelve years of publishing hardback westerns, Walker & Co. ended its western line with Sam Brown's *Devil's Run* (1998), leaving as publishers of westerns on a regular basis only the relatively small St. Martin's Press and Tor/Forge, and the paperback house Leisure Books. According to editor Don A'Auria of Leisure, "We still publish classic authors and each month we publish a longer Historical Fiction novel . . . [and] we set aside two positions each month for shorter novels, as well as one for our continuing series-length novels" (p. 5). Leisure also established a western book club, which "surprised us with its quick growth. Response from our sales force was especially favorable," confirming their feeling that "there were still a significant number of western fans out there" (p. 5).

Tor/Forge publisher Tom Doherty is of similar opinion, believing that the current stagnation relates more to marketing than to demand. "I don't think it is stagnated by the lack of readers. I think it's stagnated by the distribution" (Moulton, p. 4). Doherty is referring to the consolidations and bankruptcies of independent distributors (IDs), accelerated in the past three years by national grocery store chains demanding that the IDs bid on regional and even national distribution. As a result, one chain is now dealing with eight instead of 108 IDs, and the bid-losing IDs have lost "as much as eighty percent of their value as major chains canceled accounts" (Gear, p. 8). The "changes in book distribution, combined with competition from superstores, have led to closure of about 1,200 mall stores" (Moulton, p. 4), and, according to the American Booksellers Association, a drop in member shops from 5,100 in 1993 to 3,427 today (Noah, p. 49). Doherty predicts that "publishers and authors should prepare for another three to five year slump, because it'll likely take that long for the wholesale distribution system to correct itself" (Moulton, p. 4). In the meantime, Tor/Forge continued to publish western fiction like Earl Murray's *The River at Sundown* (1998) and Loren Estleman's *Journey of the Dead* (1998), and western nonfiction like Dale Walker's *Legend and Lies* (1998) and *Boys of '98: Theodore Roosevelt and the Rough Riders* (1998). Clearly, as far as Leisure Books and Tor/Forge are concerned, the rumors of the western's demise have been proven wrong.

Fortunately, "the New York publishing monopoly has been severely —and effectively—challenged by literally thousands of smaller, independent presses that have sprung up all over the country. New ones—by the score—fire up business with every passing year. They range from 'mom and pop' enterprises where the layout is performed on the kitchen table, to more sizable organizations that hire scores of artists, editors, and marketing folks" (Crutchfield, p. 13). Known as 'niche' publishers, such operations focus on a particular narrow segment of the market with limited press runs and often but not always regional distribution. For instance, Northland Publishing is located in Flagstaff, Arizona, and concentrates on fact and fiction of the Southwestern Indian cultures, as in its *Neon Pow-Wow: New Native American Voices of the Southwest* (1995). To respectable reviews and sales, Laurel Press has produced the western anthologies *Dreamers and Desperadoes* and *Talking Leaves: Contemporary Native American Short Stories* (1991); Swallow/Ohio has put out *A Writer's Forum Anthology* (1993), *Higher Elevations: Stories from the West* (1993), and *The Interior Country: Stories of the Modern West* (1987); Cinco Puntos Press has published Laverne Harrell Clark's *Keepers of the Earth* (1997); Red Deer College Press has published *Don't Fence Me In: A Romance of the New West* (1995); and Wordware Publishing has put out

Western Horse Tales (1994), a collection of short stories edited by Don Worster.

Along with niche publishers is an impressive network of academic presses, "ranging from the giant Universities of California, Oklahoma, and Nebraska, each of which has hundreds of titles in print, to smaller, yet equally capable concerns such as the University of Idaho Press and the multi-school cooperative University Press of Colorado" (Crutchfield, p. 13). Southern Methodist University Press has published *Texas Bound: 19 Texas Stories* (1994); University of North Texas Press has published *Reflections in Dark Glass: The Life and Times of John Wesley Hardin* (1996); the University Press of Colorado has published two new novels by Wister Award winner Max Evans; and the University of Nevada Press has published Robert Laxalt's *A Lean Year and Other Stories* (1994) and *The Governor's Mansion* (1995). In 1997 alone it published Oakley Hall's *Separations,* Gailmarie Pahmeier's *The House on Breakaheart Road,* Emily Hammond's *Breathe Something Nice,* and Adrian Louis's *Wild Indians and Other Creatures,* and in 1998 it released Ernest Finney's *California Time* and Kate Braverman's collection of short stories *Small Craft Warning.*

Not only "is it time to look at presses and publishers that are located outside New York," states Greg Tobin, formerly of The Book of the Month Club, but "there's also self-publishing. I sometimes think if Tom Clancy decided to self-publish, he would make a hell of a lot more money" (House, p. 6A). At the moment, regional and university presses cannot afford to pay writers very well—although that may be changing —and what promotion they do is strictly shoestring. Still, even a little hype can pay off handsomely; meagerly promoted, the *Real West* series hosted by Kenny Rogers proved one of the highest-rated original series ever to appear on the Arts & Entertainment channel (Cunningham, p. 5). More could be done, though, by publisher and writer alike. Book signings at bookstores can be effective in selling books and building careers, and author Larry Martin also advises writers to take a book buyer to lunch. "You've only got to concentrate on selling one person, who is in your business, who may actually remember you until time for the next book buy—and he or she can buy thousands" (p. 12). Suzann Ledbetter suggests that a city's library, park board, or community center could be approached to arrange a free children's program, perhaps with storytelling, music, and faux shoot-outs. Art galleries and decor shops could have showings of original artwork used on book jackets, historic to the present, in conjunction with the publication of westerns. At nearly any sort of event, bookmarks, publishers' catalogues, even flyers publicizing autograph parties could be on hand for giveaways. "Spawn an interest in the West and you spawn folks clamoring to read about it" (House, pp. 20–21).

More crucial than promotion to the revival of westerns as a popular genre, however, is that the issues addressed within its historical and geographical context be relevant for the public. Such issues as starvation wages, exploited labor, ignorance, and epidemics which were commonplace in the 1890s seem like fantasies in the 1990s, and more recent controversies like the Cold War and the budget deficit seem largely to have disappeared, or at least to have lost their former force. Now relevant topics include the role of the military, the need for racial harmony, the place of new immigrants, and the depletion of resources. So, for instance, considering the public concern for the environment, westerns that extol conspicuous consumption or employ a Horatio Alger–type rags-to-riches plot would be passé, while westerns that involve ways of conserving rather than exploiting nature would find a market because they embody what is considered to be right and proper and good for the general welfare. Chances for success would likely be heightened if such westerns took a page from the news and promoted cooperation over confrontation: "Longtime Enemies Agree United Front Necessary To Tackle Ecological Issues" is the headline to a February 1998 newspaper story. "Ranchers and rural environmentalists should work together to help maintain the land they love and need, the two groups agreed Saturday" (Steele, p. 1B).

Another issue currently debated is the influx of women into the workplace, with its ramifications of male bias and sexual harassment. In response, the one popular western now on television, *Dr. Quinn, Medicine Woman*, depicts Dr. Quinn (Jane Seymour) in an 1870s Colorado frontier town, stirring much consternation and hostility among the chauvinist locals because she is a female doctor. This is historically absurd; doctors were so scarce that they were welcomed whatever their gender or color, and by 1890 there were 452 women doctors and surgeons, comprising 14 percent of the profession in the West (Steiner,

p. 85). Quinn also takes on a lover (and eventual husband) who has lived among the Indians so long that he is more Indian than the Indians —and he is not a warrior, either, but the sort of sharing, caring, sensitive man women say they want these days. That such a relationship would actually have flourished, much less been countenanced in a frontier hamlet, is ludicrous as well. Nor does this matter, because as a result of how Dr. Quinn is characterized, and how her lover/husband and the others are characterized and interact, such issues as sexism, racism, and similar "isms" so topical today are discussed and solved in the politically correct ways currently in vogue.

Still, however relevant the issues may be, mass revival of the genre cannot occur as long as the public is dismissive of the values associated with westerns—intrepidity, courage, justice, hope, the values once considered eternal verities. But there are signs that such values are beginning to emerge from the nihilistic 1980s and resonate once again with audiences. One example is the newspaper account quoted above, indicating that the bitterest of adversaries are operating less from self-interest and more for the common good. Another is suggested by historian Robert Kelley: "[F]or the first time since 1964, a long decline in confidence in government was reversed. While in 1964 a total of 76 percent of Americans had said the government in Washington could be trusted to do what was right 'just about always' or 'most of the time,' by 1980 this figure had dropped to 25 percent. By 1988, a modest upward trend was appearing, for the proportion had risen to 33 percent . . . [and] in that same year *Time's* cover story celebrated the rebirth of American patriotism" (p. 854). Regaining credence are such values as perseverance, responsibility, and integrity. Baltimore Orioles shortstop Cal Ripken, Jr., advises that "it's easy to do something day after day if you love what you're doing. Perseverance means doing it when it's not always easy . . . and it requires responsibility and integrity and compassion" (pp. 12–13). Responsibility for Detroit Pistons forward Grant Hill means that "if you work hard and are responsible for your actions, if you play by the rules, you can accomplish anything" (p. 8). Following the Oklahoma City bombing, firefighter Chris Fields found that "the outpouring of compassion renewed my belief that Americans still care for their fellow man. . . . You have never seen such giving people. They were the heroes—the ones who worked their jobs from 8 to 5 and then served meals to rescuers until 2 A.M. That's love for your fellow man. We were doing our duty —they were going way above" (p. 4). The most important factor for integrity, according to Dr. Walter Turnbull, director of the forty-member Boys Choir of Harlem and four-hundred-student Choir Academy of Harlem, "is providing an environment in which children can learn integrity—an environment where discipline is important, where honesty is important, where courage is important, where love is important" (p. 10). And after the polarizing antagonisms of the 1970s and 1980s, there is a refreshing emphasis on people's being tolerant, "modest in defending their own beliefs and generous in allowing others to differ," writes Mary Fisher, who electrified the Republican National Convention with an address about her AIDS infection. "[W]hen they are grown, my sons will know there is no difference of race or creed, gender or nationality, that makes us more or less worthy of life and its promises" (p. 5). Typical of the approach education is now taking is this final passage in a children's book called *The Battle of Little Big Horn*:

> People often look for good guys and bad guys, guys in a conflict like the Battle of Little Big-Horn. Some might think that Custer and his men, in their greed for victory, were all bad—that Crazy Horse and the Sioux in their defense of their villages, were all good. But for the most part Custer and his men were just soldiers following orders that were given to them by the U. S. Government. And Crazy Horse and the other Indians were trying to protect a way of life that could not withstand the westward movement of the white people.
>
> In the end, the real meaning of Custer's last stand can't be measured in terms of good guys and bad guys. It's just one part of a story about two very different peoples who had two very different ways of life. (Henckle Highlights, p. 29)

The regeneration of values and ethics is reflected in current westerns which, like the serious westerns of the postwar period, define the strength of their protagonists internally rather than externally, as a matter of moral rather than muscular fiber. For example, in Frank Burleson's *Devil Dance* (1997), protagonist Nathaniel Barrington confronts the wreckage of his life, hoping to redeem himself by caring for Gloria, a street urchin; in Frances Hurst's *High Mountain Winter* (1996), young pioneer Maryl Stoner perseveres through hunger and hardship during winter on the Oregon Trail; and in Mike Blakely's *Shortgrass Song* (1995), protagonist Caleb Holcomb is an itinerant musician and odd-jobber who acts as a bridge from the Old West to the present, taking responsibility for those changes that make him unhappy. The fundamental theme, then, is still one of character: what individual choices and acts mean in an environment where weakness can be fatal. "And where there is no choice, there is no morality" (Schlessinger, p. 5); thus for questions of character to be significant and even portentous requires that protagonists be severely tested but have a fighting chance of overcoming their challenge, rather than face the inevitable defeat by cruel men in amoral westerns or by crueler fate in revisionist westerns such as John Nichols's *American Blood* (1989) and Thomas McGuane's *Something to be Desired* (1985)—westerns whose settings "are dotted by what a 1989 *U. S. News & World Report* story referred to as 'brutal men, used and disappointing women, decaying families, suffocating small towns and a loneliness that bears little resemblance to that of Zane Grey's lonesome cowboy'" (Hart, p. 14). In such a desolate West of anti-social outcasts, there can be no community in spirit or place worth striving for. In current westerns, however, no matter how alone and independent protagonists may be, they resolve their inner conflicts in terms of the community because, as Sigmund Freud pointed out, no matter how independent each of us may act, the question still arises as to who or what one is acting independent of.

That, paradoxically, independence requires relationships even by loners is illustrated by such mountain man westerns as R. C. House's *Buckskinner* (1996) and Terry Johnston's *Crack in the Sky* (1997), both thematically about unfettered freedom versus confining civilization. The revival of community as a concept in westerns is in response to social change over the past decade, as Americans have grown increasingly anxious over how they became such a lonely people—how mass society dehumanized and cut individuals off from one another—and the need to survive in a splintering culture, to somehow get along and sustain secure communities in a nation lacking the safety valve of the frontier. This shift in the aftermath of the existentialist 1970s and 1980s coincided with the shift by the Bush administration away from the cold-warrior image of Reagan to a "kinder, gentler" government of men reluctant to kill, pledged to their families, yet firm and decisive. The election and reelection of Bill Clinton indicates a further shift in the public's sense of its national identity, as voters rejected first the foreign-policy issues offered by Bush and then the austere message touted by Bob Dole in favor of domestic concerns about jobs, crime, education, and social services. On the grass-roots level, moreover, citizens have been volunteering for charitable work in their neighborhoods, and collecting into manageably sized town meetings, neighborhood committees, and civic service groups such as the Goodenough Communities, which "incorporate the security and long-term commitment of traditional community—members take care of each other's practical needs through good times and bad—yet also embody the flexibility and psychological sophistication characteristic of contemporary American culture" (Shaffer, p. 89). There has been a growing community-based orientation in mental health, corrections, and especially education, which has "come to believe that incorporating and building on cultural and spiritual teachings is the surest way to ensure that ignorance on the part of one ethnic group doesn't result in the ridicule, or misunderstanding, of another's way" (Devlin, p. 36). Coalitions of minority executive and program directors from nonprofit service agencies, such as Seattle's Minority Executive Directors Coalition of King County, encourage cooperation among newly arriving Koreans, Vietnamese, Cambodians, and Samoans. "Seattle's challenge today: to include everyone, have enough to go around, and ensure equitable distribution" (Williamson, p. 32). Susan McCormick, chair of the Oats Park restoration committee in small Fallon, Nevada, reports that "people here have a real sense of community. They see beyond their own immediate needs and can focus on the community needs" (Burghart, p. 15). Community organizing is the subject of Maritza Pick's *How to Save Your Neighborhood, City, or Town*, and a favorite topic of Bill Clinton, who declared in a speech as president-elect on November 3, 1992, "We need a new spirit of community, a sense that we're all in this together. If we have no sense of community, the American dream will continue to wither" (Stiehm, p. 87).

Responsive western fiction is redefining its forms to project this communal awakening into the legendary past, and because its focus is on who instead of what the protagonist is, its stories are striving, like society, to be more inclusive of alternative points of view. Clancy Carlile's *Children of the Dust* (1997) intertwines the Oklahoma land rush of the

1880s with a story of revenge, racism, and love. Greg Tobin's saga *Prairie: An Epic of the West* (1997) traces hundreds of years of the Crane band of Indians dealing with archenemy Red Horn people, intrusive French colonists, and missionary Jesuits. G. G. Boyer's *Winchester Affidavit* (1997) depicts the relationships between Anglo ranchers, Mexican farmers, Jicarilla Apaches, outlaw gangs, and foreign syndicates. Frontier towns and other communal groups are more likely to be shown as home to complex relationships, as in Richard Wheeler's tale of a boomtown *Cashbox* (1994), and they are less likely to be depicted as simplemindedly weak or corrupt, as in Elmer Kelton's *Honor at Daybreak* (1992), in which the townsfolk come together to help the sheriff in a reversal of the *High Noon* format.

Over the next decade or two, ranching as a community effort will be stressed; already Don Coldsmith's *Spanish Bit* series interweaves personal adventures with the outfit working as a unit, and in J. P. S. Brown's *Native Born* (1994), a fifth-generation cattleman organizes his ranch against individual banditry and a corrupt power structure. The theme of Larry McMurtry's *Lonesome Dove* (1985) is that of bonding, of cowhands growing closer together in friendship, loyalty, and sacrifice as they endure the hardships of ranch life and of a long trail drive to Montana. There will be an increasing number of strong female characters, such as those found in *Lonesome Dove*, Diane Carey's *Distant Drum* series, the exceptional films *Thousand Pieces of Gold* (1991) and *The Ballad of Little Jo* (1993), and Kate Cameron's *Orenda: A Novel of the Iroquois Nation* (1991), in which "Morning Song, daughter of an Iroquois and a violent French trader, learns to be stubborn, brave, and spirited." Yvonne Adamson's *Bridey's Mountain* (1994) traces four generations of women who fight to hold a piece of land called Bridey's Mountain; Irene Bennett Brown's *The Plainswoman* (1995) relates the struggles of a woman homesteading in Kansas circa 1880; and Sandra Dallas's *The Diary of Mattie Spenser* (1997) draws on actual journals to create the life of a young woman in the 1860s Colorado frontier. Woman, after all, traditionally symbolizes the values and morality of community, while the explorations of what it was like to be a woman on the frontier provide insights into contemporary male and female interactions.

The Indian story is rapidly moving beyond the plight of the individual toward a portrayal of the minority group experience—the *Spanish Bit* saga again comes to mind, as well as *Dances with Wolves;* Frank Bergon's *Shoshone Mike* (1987) about a Northwest Indian rodeo contestant; James Welch's *Fools Crow* (1989) about the world of the Blackfeet in 1870s Montana; Terry Johnston's *Reap the Whirlwind: The Battle of the Rosebud* (1994) about Chief Crazy Horse and his side of the famous battle; and Geo. W. Proctor's *Blood of My Blood: A Novel of Quanah Parker* (1996) about the capture of Cynthia Ann Parker by the Comanches to the death of her son Quanah. Like the Indians, Chicanos and half-breeds will be shown struggling against an Anglo culture intent on denying them their own communal sense of identity, as in Lucha Corpi's *Delia's Song* (1989), and resisting the tensions and divisions within mixed-blood families, as in Arturo Islas's *The Rain God* (1991) and Norman Zollinger's *Chapultepec* (1995), set in Mexico during the era of Maximilian. In a 1994 interview on National Public Radio's *Morning Edition*, the writer and director of the recently-released *Geronimo*, Walter Hill, spoke of how westerns are changing in terms of ethnic minorities: "What illustrated the American myth was how we came west and they were there, and we did this and they did that, and what followed was heroic or tragic or whatever. But it was very much we and they. What is different about [Geronimo] is that there is no we or they, but all of us together as Americans, and if you destroy one part, then we're all the losers."

Whether western fiction regains broad popularity, then, depends largely on whether American society continues its recent trend toward renewed belief in the values, virtues, and optimism that characterize the American Dream. Even though, as critic Kent Steckmesser observes, "these traits may seem anachronistic in a settled and industrialized society [and] much of the hero's appeal seems to be connected with a sentimental nostalgia for the freedom of the vanished frontier" (p. 241), Americans are feeling more confident and optimistic about their country than they have in two decades, and as Scott Emmert points out, are once again "pursu[ing] the Dream. Like a will-o'-wisp, or an insistently recurring mirage, the allure of the Dream remains, tantalizing, potentially destructive, yet undefined" (p. 29). Hence, as allegories of the Dream, current westerns appeal to more than mere nostalgia. They symbolize "America's belief in personal integrity and ingenuity ... the cowboy travels the land, making amends in an unbalanced world; and selling the

American landscape and personality to the rest of the world" (Fishwick, pp. 91, 92). Few people will ever again know the kind of total community that intermingled place and kin, work and friends, as presented in the traditional western, but the need for community nonetheless remains. Also expressed by westerns is a cluster of values held by the majority stressing domestic concerns, peace over combat, environmental preservation over exploitation, and cooperation over competition. Present as well are legacies of the Reagan Revolution, such as the creation of a national debate over what constitutes family values, the calls for restoring public and private morality and for replacing self-gratification with self-restraint, and the premise that "regardless of emotional angst or tremendous temptation, to be fully human and to benefit maximally from the life experience, you must get back to the 3 C's: Character, Courage, and Conscience" (Schlessinger, p. 5)—although sometimes the crusade seems more reactionary than traditional, as in the Washington State Republican party platform banning witchcraft and yoga. "But the very conflicts and divisions that these different and vocal strains of U. S. political culture exhibit will undoubtedly yield new definitions of national identity," as Jeffords suggests (p. 23).

Most likely the debate over national identity will never be resolved, but the effort to understand who Americans are as a people is the essence of westerns, both those which present ideas and issues that challenge the status quo, and those which supply social critiques about ideas and modes of behavior that should be retained. In this the western is a unique medium for seeking out connections between people and institutions, and for working out balances between surface and strata, the observed and the unseen. Thus, at its best, the western gives the lie to those who try to reduce it to popular entertainment or castigate it for lacking weight. As Philip French notes, "The Western is a great grab bag, a hungry cuckoo of a genre, a voracious bastard of a form, open equally to visionaries and opportunists, ready to seize anything that's in the air from juvenile delinquency to ecology. Yet despite this, or in some ways because of it, one of the things the Western is always about is America rewriting and reinterpreting her own past, however honestly or dishonestly it may be done" (p. 24).

In America, especially during the last forty years, no field of literature has acted more responsibly as a means of making us see ourselves, and in years to come western fiction will create a new mythology, or rather, a revision of the frontier myth that will reflect—as westerns always have—prevailing cultural beliefs, goals, and dreams. It will be told in a modern narrative blend which employs more realism, yet keeps to the tradition of relating frontier adventures about personal character striving to overcome perilous circumstances. And all the while the western will be making meaning, will be as current as tomorrow's newspaper.

Bibliography

Abel, Darrel. *American Literature*. Woodbury, N.Y.: Barron's, 1963.

Adams, James Truslow. *The Epic of America*. Boston: Little, Brown, 1931.

Adams, Les, and Buck Rainey. *Shoot-'em-up: The Complete Guide to Westerns of the Sound Era*. New Rochelle, N.Y.: Arlington House, 1978.

Alexander, Fred. *Moving Frontiers*. Port Washington, N.Y.: Kennikat Press, 1947.

Amory, Cleveland. "Review: *The Dakotas*." *TV Guide* (April 6, 1963): p. 1.

Arber, Edward, ed. *The Story of the Pilgrim Fathers, 1606–1623 a.d. as told by Themselves, Their Friends, and Their Enemies*. n.p., 1897. Reprint, New York: Kraus, 1969.

Athearn, Robert G. *The Mythic West in Twentieth Century America*. Lawrence: University Press of Kansas, 1986.

Auletta, Ken. "The Impossible Business." *The New Yorker* (October 6, 1997): 50, 52, 54–56, 59–60, 62–63.

Averill, Charles E. *Kit Carson, the Prince of the Gold Hunters, or, The Adventures of the Sacramento. A Tale of the New Eldorado, Founded on Actual Facts.* Boston: G. H. Williams, 1849.

Badger, Joseph E. *Mountain Kate; or, Love in the Trapping Grounds. A Tale of the Powder River Country.* New York: Beadle and Adams, 1872.

Bakeless, John. *Master of the Wilderness: Daniel Boone.* New York: William Morrow, 1939.

Bannister, Robert C. *Social Darwinism: Science and Myth in Anglo-American Social Thought.* Philadelphia: Temple University Press, 1979.

Barbour, Alan G. *Saturday Afternoon at the Movies.* New York: Bonanza Books, 1986.

Baritz, Loren. "The Idea of the West." *American Historical Review* LXVI/3 (April 1961): 618–640.

Barnouw, Erik. *Tube of Plenty: The Evolution of American Television.* New York: Oxford University Press, 1975.

Bartram, William. *Travels in Georgia and Florida, 1773–1774: A Report to Dr. John Fothergill.* Ed. Francis Harper. Philadelphia: American Philosophical Society, 1944.

Baym, Nina. *Novels, Readers, and Reviewers: Responses to Fiction in Antebellum America.* Ithaca, N.Y.: Cornell University Press, 1984.

Beauman, Nicola. *A Very Great Profession: The Woman's Novel, 1914–39.* London: Virago Press, 1981.

Becker, Carl L. *Everyman His Own Historian.* New York: F. S. Crofts & Co., 1935.

Bold, Christine. *Selling the Wild West: Popular Western Fiction, 1860 to 1960.* Bloomington: Indiana University Press, 1987.

Boorstein, Daniel J. "A Case of Hypochondria." *Newsweek* (July 6, 1970): 23–25.

Boynton, Robert S. "The Hollywood Way." *The New Yorker* (March 30, 1998).

Branch, Douglas. *The Cowboy and His Interpreters.* New York: D. Appleton and Co., 1926.

Bredahl, A. Carl. *New Ground: Western American Narrative and the Literary Canon.* Chapel Hill: University of North Carolina Press, 1989.

Broder, Patricia Janis. *The American West: The Modern Vision.* Boston: Bulfinch Press, 1984.

Brown, Bill. "Popular Forms II." In Emory Elliott, ed., *The Columbia History of the American Novel,* pp. 357–379. New York: Columbia University Press, 1991.

Brown, Charles Brockden. *Edgar Huntly: Or, Memoirs of a Sleepwalker.* Ed. David Lee Brown. New York: Macmillan, 1928.

Brown, Richard Maxwell. *No Duty to Retreat: Violence and Values in American History and Society.* New York: Oxford University Press, 1991.

Buscombe, Edward. *The BFI Complete Companion to the Western.* New York: Atheneum, 1988.

Calder, Jeni. *There Must Be a Lone Ranger: The American West in Film and Reality.* New York: McGraw-Hill, 1974.

Campbell, Joseph. *The Hero with a Thousand Faces.* Princeton, N.J.: Princeton University Press, 1949.

Carnegie, Andrew. *The Gospel of Wealth and Other Timely Essays.* Ed. Edward C. Kirkland. Cambridge, Mass.: Harvard University Press, 1962.

Carpenter, Frederic I. *American Literature and Dream.* New York: Philosophical Library, 1955.

Carver, Jonathan. *Travels through the Interior Parts of North America in the Years 1766, 1767, and 1768*, 3rd ed. 1781. Reprint, Minneapolis: Ross & Haines, 1956.

Cary, Max, and E. H. Warmington. *The Ancient Explorers*. New York: Doubleday, 1929.

Cawelti, John G. "God's Country . . . Differing Visions of the West." *Western American Literature* 9 (Winter 1975): 273–283.

———. *Adventure, Mystery and Romance: Formula Stories as Art and Popular Culture*. Chicago: University of Chicago Press, 1976.

———. *The Six-Gun Mystique* 2nd ed. Bowling Green, Ohio: Bowling Green University Press, 1984.

Chandler, Raymond. *The Simple Art of Murder*. New York: Pocket Books, 1964.

Chase, Richard Volney. *The American Novel and its Tradition*. Garden City, N.Y.: Doubleday, 1957.

Christian, Terry. *Reel Politics: American Political Movies from Birth of a Nation to Platoon*. New York: Basic Blackwell, 1987.

Clark, Thomas D. "Virgins, Villains & Varmints." *American Heritage* (Spring 1952): 42–72.

Clark, Walter Van Tilberg. *The Ox-Bow Incident*. 1940; New York: Signet Classics, 1960.

Cloud, Barbara. *The Business of Newspapers on the Western Frontier*. Reno: University of Nevada Press, 1992.

Clough, Wilson. *The Necessary Earth: Nature and Solitude in American Literature*. Austin: University of Texas Press, 1964.

Cobbs, John L. *Owen Wister*. Boston: Twayne, 1984.

Coburn, Walt. "Satan's Saddle Mates." *.44 Western* 31/3 (May 1954): 16–35, 88–100.

Cook, Nancy S. "Investment in Place: Thomas McGuane in Montana." In Barbara Howard Meldrum, ed., *Old West—New West: Centennial Essays*, pp. 213–229. Moscow: University of Idaho Press, 1993.

Cook, William Wallace [John Milton Edwards]. *The Fiction Factory*. Ridgewood, N.J.: The Editor Company, 1912.

Cooper, Edgar L. "Queen of Gunsmoke Range." *Lariet Story Magazine* 10/4 (October 1936): 3–23.

Cooper, James Fenimore. *Leather Stocking Tales*. New York: Houghton Mifflin, 1898.

Crutchfield, James A. "Getting in the Groove with the 'Niche' Publishers." *The Roundup Magazine* 5/4 (April 1998): 13–14.

Cumbow, Robert C. *Once Upon a Time: The Films of Sergio Leone*. Metuchen, N.J.: Scarecrow Press, 1987.

Cunningham, Chet. "Comments on Spur Awards." *The Roundup Magazine* 5/4 (March–April 1993): 4–5.

Curti, Merle. "Dime Novels and the American Tradition." *Yale Review* 26 (Summer 1937): 761–778.

Cushman, Dan. "She-Wolf of the Rio Grande." *Lariet Story Magazine* 16/6 (March 1949): 74–128.

Darwin, Charles. *On the Origin of Species*. 1859; New York: Modern Library, 1936.

D'Auria, Don. "Leisure Books: Still a Western Believer." *The Roundup Magazine* V/4 (April 1998): 5–6.

Davidson, James West, William E. Gienapp, Christine Leigh Heyrman, Mark H. Lytle, and Michael B. Stoff. *Nation of Nations*. New York: Alfred A. Knopf; 1991.

Davis, Robert Murray. "Review: *West of Everything*." *Western American Literature* XXVII/3 (November 1992): 241.

————. *Playing Cowboys: Low Culture and High Art in the Western*. Norman: University of Oklahoma Press, 1992.

Dekker, George. *The American Historical Romance*. New York: Cambridge University Press, 1987.

Denning, Michael. *Mechanic Accents: Dime Novels and Working-Class Culture in America*. New York: Verso, 1987.

Deverell, William. "Fighting Words." *Western Historical Quarterly* (Summer 1994): 185–206.

Devlin, Jeanne M. "Where the Wind Comes Sweeping . . ." *Modern Maturity* (June–July 1997): 36.

DeVoto, Bernard. "Birth of an Art." *Harper's Magazine* CCXI (December 1955): 8–9, 12, 14, 16.

————. "Horizon Land (1)." *Saturday Review of Literature* (October 17, 1936): 8.

Didion, Joan. "Thinking about Western Thinking." *Esquire* 85/2 (February 1976): 10–14.

Dinan, John A. *The Pulp Western: A Popular History of the Western Fiction Magazine in America*. San Bernardino, Calif.: Borgo Press, 1983.

Dinnerstein, Leonard, and David M. Reimers. *Ethnic Americans: A History of Immigration and Assimilation*. New York: Dodd, Mead, 1975.

Divine, Robert A., T. H. Breen, George M. Fredrickson, R. Hal Williams, and Randy Roberts. *America Past and Present*. New York: HarperCollins, 1990.

Doctorow, E. L. *Welcome to Hard Times*. New York: Random House, 1960.

Dodd, Samuel Calvin Tait. *Combinations: Their Uses and Abuses, with a History of the Standard Oil Trust*. New York: G. F. Nesbitt, 1888.

Douglass, Amanda Hart. *Jamaica!* New York: Norton, 1977.

Drake, Benjamin. *Life of Tecumsah and of His Brother the Prophet: With a Historical Sketch of the Shawanoe Indians*. Cincinnati: Anderson, Gates, and Wright, 1858.

Dundes, Allen. *Sacred Narrative: Readings in the Theory of Myth*. Berkeley: University of California Press, 1984.

DuPlessis, Rachel Blau. *Writing beyond the Ending: Narrative Strategies of Twentieth-Century Women Writers*. Bloomington: Indiana University Press, 1983.

Dupree, A. Hunter. *Asa Gray 1810–1888*. Cambridge, Mass.: Harvard University Press, 1959.

Durham, Philip. "A General Classification of 1,531 Dime Novels." *Huntington Library Quarterly* (May 1954): 287–291.

————. "Dime Novels: An American Heritage." *Western Humanities Review* (Winter 1954–55): 33–43.

————. *Seth Jones by Edward S. Ellis and Deadwood Dick on Deck by Edward L. Wheeler: Dime Novels*. New York: Odyssey Press, 1966.

Eckhardt, C. F. "Saddle Horses, Sixguns and Historical Accuracy." *Roundup Magazine* 1/5 (May–June 1994): 20–21.

Elkin, Frederick. "Psychological Appeal of the Hollywood Western." *Journal of Educational Sociology* 24 (October 1950): 72–86.

Elliott, John Huxtable. *The Old World and the New 1492–1650*. Cambridge: Cambridge University Press, 1970.

Ellis, Edward S. *Seth Jones; or, the Captives of the Frontier*. New York: Beadle & Adams, 1860.

Ellis, Robert P. "The Appeal of the Western Movie Thriller." *America* (May 17, 1958): 228–229.

Ellis, Wesley. *Lone Star and the Phantom Gunmen.* New York: Jove, 1987.

———. *Lone Star on the Treachery Trail.* New York: Jove, 1982.

Emmert, Scott. *Loaded Fictions: Social Criticism in the Twentieth-Century Western.* Moscow: University of Idaho Press, 1996.

Estleman, Loren D. *The Wister Trace: Classic Novels of the American Frontier.* Ottawa, Ill.: Jameson, 1987.

Etulain, Richard W. "The Historical Development of the Western." *Journal of Popular Culture* 7/3 (1973): 717–726.

Everett, William. "Critical Notices: Beadle's Dime Books." *North American Review* 99 (July 1864): 303–309.

Faragher, John Mack, ed. *Rereading Frederick Jackson Turner.* New York: Henry Holt, 1994.

Fiedler, Leslie A. *Love and Death in the American Novel.* New York: Dell, 1966.

———. *The Return of the Vanishing American.* New York: Stein & Day, 1968.

Fields, Chris. "Compassion." *USA Weekend* (November 17–19, 1995): 4–5.

Filsen, John. *The Discovery, Settlement, and Present State of Kentuckte: and an Essay Towards the Topography, and Natural History of that Important Country.* Reprint, *Filsen's Kentucke,* Filsen Club Publications No. 35. Louisville, Kentucky: John P. Morton & Company, 1930.

Fisher, Mary. "Tolerance." *USA Weekend* (November 17–19, 1995): 5.

Fishwick, Marshall W. "The Cowboy: America's Contribution to the World's Mythology." *Western Folklore* 11 (1951–52): 77–92.

———. "Billy the Kid: Faust in America." *Saturday Review of Literature* XXXV (October 11, 1952): 35–36.

Flint, Timothy. *Biographical Memoire of Daniel Boone: The First Settler of Kentucky, Interspersed with Incidents in the Early Annals of the Country.* Ed. James K. Folsom. New Haven, Conn.: Yale University Press, 1967.

———. *The Shoshonee Valley.* Cincinnati: E. H. Fleet, 1830.

Folsom, James K. *The American Western Novel.* New Haven, Conn.: College and University Press, 1966.

Fradkin, Philip L. *Sagebrush Country: Land and the American West.* Tucson: University of Arizona Press, 1989.

Franz, Joe B., and Julian Ernest Coathe, Jr. *The American Cowboy: The Myth and the Reality.* Norman: University of Oklahoma Press, 1955.

Frazer, Sir James George. *The Golden Bough: A Study of Magic and Religion.* London: Macmillan, 1961.

Frémont, John Charles. "'California' 1. Geographical Memoir of Upper California, in illustration of his Map of Oregon and California." *Southern Quarterly Review* 16/31 (October 1849): 82–114.

French, Philip. *Westerns: Aspects of a Movie Genre.* New York: Oxford University Press, 1977.

Freneau, Philip. "The Indian Student, or, Force of Nature." In *The Poems (1786) and Miscellaneous Works (1788) of Philip Freneau.* Ed. Lewis Leary. Delmar, N.Y.: Scholars' Facsimiles & Reprints, 1975.

Frye, Northrop. *The Educated Imagination.* Bloomington: Indiana University Press, 1964.

Fuller, Margaret. *Writings.* Ed. Mason Wade. New York: Doubleday, 1941.

Fuller, Robert C. *American Religious Life*. New York: Oxford University Press, 1989.

Fussell, Edwin S. *Frontier: American Literature and the American West*. Princeton, N.J.: Princeton University Press, 1965.

Garland, Hamlin. "Passing of the Frontier." *Dial* VXVII (October 4, 1919): 285–286.

Garvey, Ellen Gruber. *The Adman in the Parlor: Magazine and the Gendering of Consumer Culture, 1880s to 1910s*. New York: Oxford University Press, 1996.

Gates, Henry Louis, Jr. "Time Bandits." *The New Yorker* (October 17, 1997): 83–84.

Gear, W. Michael, and Kathleen O'Neal Gear. "The Western Fiction Market: Surviving the Worst of Times." *The Roundup Magazine* V/4 (April 1998): 7–10.

Genovese, Eugene D. "A Massive Breakdown." *Newsweek* (July 6, 1970): 21–22.

Gerstner, Patrick, and Nicholas Cords, eds. *Myth and Southern History*. Chicago: Rand McNally, 1974.

Gillespie, Charles C. "Lamark and Darwin in the History of Science." In Hiram Bentley Glass, Owsei Tempkin, and William L. Straus, Jr., eds., *Forerunners of Darwin*, pp. 265–291. Baltimore: Johns Hopkins University Press, 1959.

Goetzmann, William H. "The Mountain Man as Jacksonian Man." *American Quarterly* 15 (Fall 1963): 402–415.

Goldman, Eric. *Rendezvous with Destiny*. New York: Knopf, 1963.

Goldman, Peter. "The Spirit of '70." *Newsweek* (July 6, 1970): 15–16.

Goodrum, Charles, and Helen Dalrymple. *Advertising in America: The First 200 Years*. New York: Abrams, 1990.

Goodstone, Tony. *The Pulps: Fifty Years of American Pop Culture*. New York: Chelsea House, 1970.

Goulart, Ron. *Cheap Thrills: An Informal History of the Pulp Magazines*. New Rochelle, N.Y.: Arlington House, 1972.

Green, John C. "The Concept of Order in Darwinism." In Paul G. Kuntz, ed., *The Concept of Order*, pp. 89–103. Seattle: University of Washington Press, 1968.

Grey, Loren, ed. *Zane Grey's Indian Tales*. London: New English Library, 1977.

Grey, Zane. *The Border Legion*. 1916; Roslyn, N.Y.: Walter J. Black, 1944.

———. "Breaking Through: The Story of My Own Life." *American Magazine* XCVII (July 1924): 11–13, 76, 78, 80.

———. *Call of the Canyon*. 1924; Roslyn, N.Y.: Walter J. Black, 1952.

———. *Captives of the Desert*. 1952; Roslyn, N.Y.: Walter J. Black, 1954.

———. *Code of the West*. 1934; New York: Grosset & Dunlap, 1962.

———. *The Deer Stalker*. 1949; Roslyn, N.Y.: Walter J. Black, 1953.

———. *The Heritage of the Desert*. 1910; New York: Pocket Books, 1968.

———. *The Light of the Western Stars*. 1914; New York: Grosset & Dunlap, 1942.

———. *The Lone Star Ranger*. 1915; Roslyn, N.Y.: Walter J. Black, 1943.

———. *The Man of the Forest*. New York: Grosset & Dunlap, 1920.

———. *The Rainbow Trail*. New York: Harper & Brothers, 1915.

———. *Riders of the Purple Sage*. 1912; New York: Pocket Books, 1980.

———. *Robber's Roost*. 1932; Roslyn, N.Y.: Walter J. Black, 1960.

———. *Stairs of Sand*. 1943; Roslyn, N.Y.: Walter J. Black, 1956.

———. *Thunder Mountain*. 1935; Roslyn, N.Y.: Walter J. Black, 1963.

———. *The Valley of Wild Horses*. 1947; Roslyn, N.Y.: Walter J. Black, 1955.

———. *The Vanishing American*. 1925; New York: Grosset, 1953.

———. *Wanderer of the Wasteland*. 1923; New York: Harper & Row, 1990.

Gruber, Frank. *Zane Grey: A Biography*. New York: World Publishing Company, 1970.

Hacker, Andrew. "We Will Meet As Enemies." *Newsweek* (July 6, 1970): 20–21.

Hall, James. *Letters from the West: Containing Sketches of Scenery, Manners, and Customs; and Anecdotes Connected with the First Settlements of the Western Sections of the United States.* 1828; reprint, Gainesville, Fla.: Scholars' Facsimiles & Reprints, 1967.

Hall, Oakley. *Warlock.* 1958; New York, Bantam Books, 1970.

Hamilton, Cynthia S. *Western and Hard-Boiled Detective Fiction in America.* Iowa City: University of Iowa Press, 1987.

Hancock, W. K. *Survey of British Commonwealth Affairs.* Oxford: Oxford University Press, 1940.

Harmon, Jim. *The Great Radio Comedians.* Garden City, N.Y.: Doubleday, 1970.

Hart, Heidi, and Larry Henry. "Goin' Out West (Where They'll Appreciate Me)." *Nevada Weekly* (January 18–24, 1995): 14–15.

Hart, James D. *The Popular Book: A History of America's Literary Taste.* New York: Oxford University Press, 1950.

Hart, Sue. "Dorothy Johnson and Recycling Cinema." *The Roundup Quarterly* 4/2 (Winter 1991): 15–26.

Harvey, Charles M. "The Dime Novel in American Life." *Atlantic Monthly* 100 (July 1947): 37–45.

Hatab, Lawrence J. *Myth & Philosophy: A Contest of Truths.* La Salle, Ill.: Open Court, 1990.

Haycox, Ernest. *Return of a Fighter.* New York: Signet, 1980.

Henckle Highlights from American History Series. *The Battle of Little Big Horn.* Billings, Mont.: Falcon Press, 1992.

Henry, Will. "Let's Tell It Like It Was." *The Roundup* XXIV/12 (December 1976): 1–4.

Heuman, William. "The Fur Brigade." *North-West Romances* 17/10 (Spring 1933): 72–96.

Hill, Grant. "Responsibility." *USA Weekend* (November 17–19): 8.

Hines, Robert V. *Community on the American Frontier: Separate But Not Alone.* Norman: University of Oklahoma Press, 1980.

Hitt, Jim. *The American West from Fiction (1823–1976) into Film (1909–1986).* Jefferson, N.C.: McFarland & Company, 1990.

Hofstader, Richard. *Social Darwinism in American Thought.* Boston: Beacon Press, 1955.

Horowitz, James. *They Went Thataway.* New York: E. P. Dutton, 1976

House, Richard C. "Western Fiction Survey." Unpublished manuscript.

Hoveland, Roxanne, and Gary B. Wilcox. *Advertising in Society.* Lincolnwood, Ill.: MIC Business Books, 1989.

Hutton, Paul A. "From Little Big Horn to Little Big Man: The Changing Image of a Western Hero in Popular Culture." *Western Historical Quarterly* 7 (January 1976): 19–46.

Hyde, Anne Farrar. *An American Vision: Far Western Landscape and National Culture, 1820–1920.* New York: New York University Press, 1990.

Ingraham, Prentiss. *Buck Taylor, The Saddle King; or, The Lasso Rangers' League. A Romance of the Border Heroes of To-day.* New York: Beadle and Adams, 1891.

———. *Gold Plume, the Boy Bandit.* New York: Beadle and Adams, 1881.

Jackson, Carlton. *Zane Grey.* Boston: Twayne, 1989.

Jakes, John. "Bantam/Doubleday WWA Anthology." *The Roundup Magazine* 1/2 (November–December 1993): 16.

James, William. *The Varieties of Religious Experience*. New York: Collier, 1961.

Jeffords, Susan. *Hard Bodies: Hollywood Masculinity in the Reagan Era*. New Brunswick, N.J.: Rutgers University Press, 1994.

Jenks, George C. "Dime Novel Makers." *The Bookman* 20 (October 1904): 108–114.

Johannsen, Albert. *The House of Beadle and Adams and Its Dime and Nickel Novels: The Story of a Vanished Literature*. Norman: University of Oklahoma Press, 1950.

Johnson, Laura Winthrop. "Eight Hundred Miles in an Ambulance." *Lippincott's* XV (June 1875): 691–698.

Johnstone, Iain. *The Man with No Name: The Biography of Clint Eastwood*. New York: Morrow Quill, 1981.

Jones, Daryl. *The Dime Novel Western*. Bowling Green, Ohio: Bowling Green State University Popular Press, 1978.

Kael, Pauline. "The Street Western." *The New Yorker* (February 25, 1974): 101–102, 105–106.

Karl, Frederick R. *American Fictions 1940/1980*. New York: Harper & Row, 1983.

Karr, Jean. *Zane Grey: Man of the West*. Kingswood Surrey, England: World's Work, 1951.

Katz, William Loren. *The Black West*. Seattle: Open Hand, 1987.

Kaufmann, Donald L. "The Indian as Media Hand-Me-Down." *Colorado Quarterly* XXIII/3 (Winter 1975): 489–504.

Kazin, Alfred. *On Native Ground: An Interpretation of Modern American Prose Literature*. New York: Reynal & Hitchcock, 1942.

Kelley, Robert. *The Shaping of American Past*. Englewood Cliffs, N.J.: Prentice Hall, 1990.

Kellogg, John H. *The Living Temple*. Battle Creek, Mich.: Good Health Publishing Company, 1903.

Kelton, Elmer. "Rancher Use of Range Resource." *The Roundup Quarterly* 5/3 (Spring 1993): 6–16.

Kennerly, William Clark [as told to Elizabeth Russell]. *Persimmon Hill: A Narrative of Old St. Louis and the Far West*. Norman: University of Oklahoma Press, 1948.

Kimball, Arthur G. *Ace of Hearts: The Westerns of Zane Grey*. Fort Worth: Texas Christian University Press, 1993.

King, Henry. "Picturesque Features of Kansas Farming." *Scribner's* XIX (November 1879): 132–140.

Kirk, G. S. *Myth: Its Meaning and Functions in Ancient and Other Cultures*. Berkeley: University of California Press, 1970.

Klein, Marcus. *Easterns, Westerns, and Private Eyes: American Matters, 1870–1900*. Madison: University of Wisconsin Press, 1994.

Knight, Arthur. *The Liveliest Art: A Panoramic History of the Movies*. New York: New American Library, 1959.

Lackmann, Ron. *I Remember Radio*. New York: G. P. Putnam's Sons, 1970.

Lawlor, Mary. *Desert, Garden, Margin, Range: Literature on the American Frontier*. New York: Twayne, 1992.

Lears, Jackson. *No Place of Grace: Antimodernism and the Transformation of American Culture, 1880–1920*. New York: Pantheon, 1981.

Lee, Robert Edson. *From West to East: Studies in the Literature of the American West*. Urbana: University of Illinois Press, 1966.

Leeming, David. *Mythology*. New York: Newsweek Books, 1976.

Levinson, Daniel J. *The Seasons of A Man's Life*. New York: Knopf, 1978.

Lévi-Strauss, Claude. *Structural Anthropology.* New York: Penguin, 1972.

Lewis, Ethel Clark. "A Weaver of Romances." *Dime Novel Roundup* 110 (October 1941): 1–4.

Limerick, Patricia Nelson. *The Legacy of Conquest: The Unbroken Past of the American West.* New York: Norton, 1987.

———. "What Raymond Chandler Knew and Western Historians Forgot." In Barbara Howard Meldrum, ed., *Old West—New West,* pp. 28–39. Moscow: University of Idaho Press, 1993.

Lockhart, Caroline. "*Me—Smith.*" Philadelphia: J. B. Lippincott Co., 1911.

Long, Robert Emmet. *James Fenimore Cooper.* New York: Continuum, 1990.

Longfellow, Henry Wadsworth. "Hiawatha." *The Complete Poetical Works of Longfellow.* Boston: Houghton Mifflin, 1893.

Lovell, Alan. "The Western." *Screen Education* 41 (September–October 1967): 88–114.

Luebke, Frederick C. "Ethnic Group Settlement in the Great Plains." *Western Historical Quarterly* VIII (1977): 405–430.

Lynd, Staughton. "Again—Don't Tread on Me." *Newsweek* (July 6, 1970): 26–28.

MacDonald, J. Fred. *Who Shot the Sheriff? The Rise and Fall of the Television Western.* New York: Praeger, 1987.

Maguire, James H. "Fiction in the West." In Emory Elliott, ed., *The Columbia History of the American Novel,* pp. 437–464. New York: Columbia University Press, 1991.

Mann, Peter H. *A New Survey: The Facts about Romantic Fiction.* London: Mills and Boon, 1974.

Marks, John. "A New Microsoft of American Publishing." *U. S. News & World Report* (April 6, 1998): 55.

Marsden, Michael. "The Popular Western Novel as a Cultural Artifact." *Arizona and the West* 20 (Autumn 1978): 203–208.

Martin, Charles M. *Gun Law.* New York: Arcadia House, 1941.

Martin, Kat. "Is The Western Really Dead? An Optimist's Point of View." *The Roundup Magazine* V/4 (April 1998): 23.

Martin, Larry Jay. "Capturing the Elusive Bookseller!" *The Roundup Magazine* V/4 (April 1998): 11–12.

McGregor, Gaile. *The Noble Savage in the New World Garden: Notes Toward a Syntactics of Place.* Bowling Green, Ohio: Bowling Green State University Press, 1988.

McWilliams, Carey. "Myths of the West." *North American Review* CCXXXII (1931): 424–432.

Meyer, Roy W. "B. M. Bower: The Poor Man's Wister." In Richard W. Etulain and Michael T. Marsden, eds., *The Popular Western: Essays Toward a Definition,* pp. 25–38. Bowling Green, Ohio: Bowling Green University Press, 1974.

Michie, Larry. "Television Forecast." *Variety* (January 7, 1976): 101.

Milton, John R. *The Novel of the American West.* Lincoln: University of Nebraska Press, 1980.

Minow, Newton M. "The Broadcasters Are Public Trustees." In Allen Kirschner and Linda Kirschner, eds., *Radio and Television: Readings in the Mass Media,* pp. 207–217. Indianapolis: Bobbs-Merrill, 1971.

Minter, David. *A Cultural History of the American Novel: Henry James to William Faulkner.* New York: Cambridge University Press, 1994.

Mitchell, Lee Clark. *Westerns: Making the Man in Fiction and Film.* Chicago: University of Chicago Press, 1996.

Mogen, David, Mark Busby, and Paul Bryant. *The Frontier Experience and the American Dream*. College Station: Texas A & M University Press, 1989.

Morse, Leon. "Hubbell Robinson Evaluates TV Programming Today." *Television Magazine* (December 1959): 48–54.

Mott, Frank Luther. *A History of American Magazines*, Vol. 2. Cambridge, Mass.: Harvard University Press, 1938.

Moulton, Candy. "Book Industry Faces Continued Market Slump." *The Roundup Magazine* V/4 (April 1998): 4.

Nash, Gerald D. *Creating the West: Historical Interpretations 1890–1990*. Albuquerque: University of New Mexico Press, 1991.

Nichols, George Ward. "Wild Bill." *Harper's New Monthly Magazine* XXXIV (February 1867): 273–285.

Noah, Timothy. "Big Bookstores: Octopi in Tweed?" *The U. S. News & World Report* (March 30, 1998): 49.

Norris, Frank. "The Frontier Gone At Last." *World's Work* III (February 1902): 1728–1729.

Old Family Letters: Copied from the Originals for Alexander Biddle, Series A. Philadelphia: Lippincott, 1892.

Parks, Rita. *The Western Hero in Film and Television: Mass Media Mythology*. Ann Arbor, Mich.: Books On Demand, 1982.

Patch, Howard Rollin. *The Other World, According to Descriptions in Medieval Literature*. Cambridge, Mass.: Harvard University Press, 1950.

Paul, Rodman W. *The Far West and the Great Plains in Transition, 1859–1900*. New York: Harper & Row, 1988.

Pearson, Edmund. *Dime Novels; or, Following an Old Trail in Popular Literature*. Port Washington, N.Y.: Kennikat Press, 1929.

Pomeroy, Earl. "Rediscovering the West." *American Quarterly* 12 (Spring 1960): 20–30.

Presbrey, Frank. *The History and Development of Advertising*. 1929; New York: Greenwood Press, 1968.

Quinlan, James Eldridge. *The Original Life and Adventures of Tom Quick, the Indian Slayer (1851, as Tom Quick, the Indian Slayer)*. Deposit, N.Y.: M. J. Ivers & Co., 1894.

Radway, Janice A. *Reading the Romance: Women, Patriarchy, and Popular Literature*. Chapel Hill: University of North Carolina Press, 1984.

Reddy, John. "TV Westerns: The Shots Heard Round the World." *Reader's Digest* (January 1959): 134–136.

Reynolds, John Murray. "Tomahawk Valley." *Frontier Stories* 16/2 (Spring 1945): 2–15.

Ripken, Cal, Jr. "Perseverance." *USA Weekend* (November 17–19, 1995): 12–13.

Roan, Tom. "The Devil Comes Back to Forty Mile." *10 Story Magazine* 10/2 (February 1939): 7–24.

———. *Gun Lord of Silver City*. London: Wright & Brown, 1943.

Roe, Vingie E. *The Golden Tide*. London: Cassell, 1940.

———. *The Splendid Road*. New York: Duffield & Company, 1925.

———. *Wild Harvest*. New York: Grossett & Dunlap, 1941.

Rogers, Roger. *Ponteach: Or the Savages of America*. 1766; reprint, New York: Burt Franklin Publisher, 1971.

Rojas, Arnold L. *California Vaquero*. Fresno, Calif.: Library Guild, 1953.

Ronald, Ann. *Zane Grey*. Boise, Idaho: Boise State University, 1975.

———. *The New West of Edward Abbey*. Reno: University of Nevada Press, 1982.

Roosevelt, Theodore. *Hunting Trips of a Ranchman: Sketches of Sport on the Northern Cattle Plains.* 1885; New York: Scribner's, 1927.

Ross, Edward A. *The Foundations of Sociology.* New York: Macmillan, 1905.

Rubin-Dorsky, Jeffrey. "The Early American Novel." In Emory Elliott, ed., *The Columbia History of the American Novel*, pp. 6–25. New York: Columbia University Press, 1991.

Ruland, Richard, and Malcolm Bradbury. *From Puritanism to Postmodernism: A History of American Literature.* New York: Viking Penguin, 1991.

Russell, Charles M. *Trails Plowed Under.* 1927; New York: Garden City Publishing Co., 1941.

Schackel, Sandra Kay. "Women in Western Films: The Civilizer, The Saloon Singer, and their Modern Sister." In Archer C. McDonald, ed., *Shooting Stars: Heroes and Heroines of Western Film*, pp. 196–217. Bloomington: Indiana University Press, 1987.

Schaefer, Jack. *Shane: The Critical Edition.* Ed. James C. Work. Lincoln: University of Nebraska Press, 1984.

Schein, Harry. "The Olympian Cowboy." *American Scholar* 24 (Summer 1955): 309–317.

Schick, Frank L. *The Paperbound Book in America.* New York: R. R. Bowker, 1958.

Schlesinger, Arthur M., Jr. "The Velocity of History." *Newsweek* (July 6, 1970): 28–30.

Schlessinger, Dr. Laura. *How Could You Do That?!: The Abdication of Character, Courage, and Conscience.* New York: HarperCollins, 1996.

Schudson, Michael. *Advertising, the Uneasy Persuasion: Its Dubious Impact on American Society.* New York: Basic Books, 1984.

Schwartz, Joel S. "Charles Darwin's Debt to Malthus and Edward Blyth." *Journal of the History of Biology* 7 (1974): 301–318.

Scott, Harvey W. *History of the Oregon Country.* Ed. Leslie M. Scott. Six volumes. Cambridge, Mass.: Harvard University Press, 1924.

Sedgwick, Catharine Maria. *Hope Leslie; or, Early Times in Massachusetts.* 1827; reprint, New Brunswick, N.J.: Rutgers University Press, 1987.

Settle, William A., Jr. *Jesse James Was His Name.* Columbia: University of Missouri Press, 1966.

Shaffer, Caroline, and Kristin Anundsen. "Creating Community Anywhere." *Open Exchange* (September 1993): 8, 89.

Shapin, Steven, and Barry Barnes. "Darwinism and Social Darwinism." In Steven Shapin and Barry Barnes, ed., *Natural Order: Historical Studies of Scientific Culture*, pp. 125–142. Beverly Hills, Calif.: Sage Publications, 1979.

Showalter, Elaine. *A Literature of Their Own.* Princeton, N.J.: Princeton University Press, 1977.

Simms, William Gilmore. *The Cassique of Kiawah.* New York: A. C. Armstrong and Son, 1859.

Slotkin, Richard. *The Fatal Environment: The Myth of the Frontier in the Age of Industrialization, 1800–1890.* New York: Atheneum, 1985.

———. *Gunfighter Nation: The Myth of the Frontier in Twentieth-Century America.* New York: HarperCollins, 1993.

———. *Regeneration through Violence: The Myth of the American Frontier, 1600–1860.* Middletown, Conn.: Wesleyan University Press, 1973.

Smith, Helena Huntington. *The War on Powder River.* New York: McGraw-Hill, 1966.

Smith, Henry Nash. "The West as an Image of the American Past." *University of Kansas Review* 18 (Autumn 1951): 29–40.

———. *Virgin Land: The American West as Symbol and Myth.* Cambridge, Mass.: Harvard University Press, 1950.

Sonnichsen, C. L. *From Hopalong to Hud: Thoughts on Western Fiction.* College Station: Texas A & M University Press, 1978.

Spiller, Robert E. *Late Harvest: Essays and Addresses in American Literature and Culture.* Westport, Conn.: Greenwood, 1981.

Steckmesser, Kent L. *The Western Hero in History and Legend.* Norman: University of Oklahoma Press, 1965.

Steele, Patti. "Longtime Enemies Agree United Front Necessary to Tackle Ecological Issues." *Reno Gazette-Journal* (February 9, 1998): 1B.

Steffen, Jerome O. *Comparative Frontiers: A Proposal for Studying the American West.* Norman: University of Oklahoma Press, 1980.

Stegner, Wallace. *The Sound of Mountain Water.* New York: E. P. Dutton, 1980.

Steiner, Stan. *The Waning of the West.* New York: St. Martin's, 1979.

Stephens, Ann S. *Malaeska: The Indian Wife of the White Hunter.* New York: Beadle and Adams, 1860.

Stern, Madeleine B. *Publishers for Mass Entertainment in Nineteenth Century America.* Boston: G. K. Hall, 1980.

Stiehm, Jamie. "Community and Communitarians." *The Nation* (July 18, 1994): 87–89.

Swarthout, Miles Hood. "Hollywood Westerns." *The Roundup Magazine* V/4 (April 1998): 26, 37.

Tanner, Stephen L. "Ernest Haycox's Short Fiction: Magazine Versions of the West, 1924–1948." *The Roundup Quarterly* 1/4 (Summer 1993): 7–13.

Tatch, Howard R. *The Other World According to Descriptions in Medieval Literature.* Cambridge, Massachusetts: Harvard University Press, 1950.

Tompkins, Jane. "West of Everything." *The South Atlantic Quarterly* 86/4 (Fall 1987): 357–378.

———. *West of Everything: The Inner Life of Westerns.* New York: Oxford University Press, 1992.

Topping, Gary. "Zane Grey: A Literary Reassessment." *American Literature* 13 (Spring 1978): 51–64.

Turnbull, Walter. "Integrity." *USA Weekend* (November 17–19, 1995): 10.

Turner, Frederick Jackson. *The Frontier in American History.* New York: Holt, Rinehart and Winston, 1962.

Turner, William O. "The Frontier in Print." *The Roundup* 4 (April 1968): 58–65.

Tuska, Jon. *The Filming of the West.* Garden City, N.Y.: Doubleday, 1976.

Viviani, Christopher. *Le Western.* Paris: Editions Henri Veyrier, 1982.

Walker, Dale. "On the Western: That-a-way, Now This-a-way." *The Roundup Magazine* 1/4 (May–April 1994): 6–7.

———. "The Candle Has Gone Out: Remembering Will Henry (1912–1991)." *The Roundup Quarterly* 4/3 (Spring 1992): 7–20.

Warne, Philip S. *A Hard Crowd; or, Gentleman Sam's Sister.* New York: Beadle and Adams, 1878.

Washburn, W. E. *The Indian and the White Man.* Garden City, N.Y.: Doubleday, 1964.

Westbrook, Max. "Flag and Family in John Wayne's Westerns: The Audience as Co-Conspirator." *Western American Literature* XXIX/1 (May 1994): 25–40.

Westland, Lynn. *Shootin' Iron*. New York: Phoenix Press, 1939.

Westland, Lynn. *Trail to Montana*. New York: Phoenix Press, 1941.

Wheeler, Edward L. *Deadwood Dick on Deck: or Calamity Jane the Heroine of Whoop-Up*. New York: Beadle and Adams, 1878.

Wheeler, Richard S. "Commentary: Grace Under Pressure: A Beleaguered Literary Genre." *The Roundup Quarterly* 5/2 (Winter 1992): 17–21.

Wilentz, Sean. *Chants Democratic: New York City and the Rise of the American Working Class, 1788–1850*. New York: Oxford University Press, 1984.

Wilkinson, Rupert. *American Tough*. Westport, Conn.: Greenwood, 1984.

Williams, Ioan, ed. *Sir Walter Scott on Novelists and Fiction*. London: Routledge & Kegan Paul, 1968.

Williamson, Don. "Seattle's Pacific Solution." *Modern Maturity* (July 18, 1997): 32.

Wilson, R Jackson, ed. *Darwinism and the American Intellectual: An Anthology*. Chicago: Dorsey Press, 1989.

Winokur, Jon. *Writers on Writing*. Philadelphia: Running Press, 1990.

Winslow, Edward. "Good News from New England." In Edward Arber, *The Story of The Pilgrim Fathers, 1606–1623 a.d., as told by Themselves, their Friends, and their Enemies*. 1897; New York: Kraus Reprint Co., 1969.

Wister, Owen. *The Virginian: A Horseman of the Plains*. 1902; New York: Grosset & Dunlap, 1911.

Workman, Chuck. "Impressions: Great Moments from the Movies." *Modern Maturity* (February–March 1993): 36–39.

Worster, Donald. *Under Western Skies: Nature and History in the American West*. New York: Oxford University Press, 1992.

Wright, Doris M. "The Making of Cosmopolitan California: An Analysis of Immigration, 1848–1870." *California Historical Quarterly* XX (1941): 65–79.

Wylder, Delbert E. "The Western Novel as Literature of the Last Frontier." In David Mogen, Mark Busky, and Paul Bryant, eds., *The Frontier Experience and the American Dream: Essays on American Culture*, pp. 120–131. College Station: Texas A & M University Press, 1989.

Wyllie, Irwin G. *The Self-Made Man: The Myth of Rags to Riches*. New Brunswick, N.J.: Rutgers University Press, 1954.

Yates, Norris. *Gender and Genre: An Introduction to Women Writers of Formula Westerns 1900–1950*. Albuquerque: University of New Mexico Press, 1995.

Ziff, Larzer. *Writing in the New Nation*. New Haven, Conn.: Yale University Press, 1991.

Index

A

"Dime Novel in American Life, The," 64
"Dime Novel Makers," 64
Dime Novel, 61
Dime Novel Western, The, 3, 65
"Dime Novels: An American Heritage," 65
"Dime Novels and the American Tradition," 64
Dime Novels; or, Following An Old Trail in Popular Literature, 64
Dime Novels: Popular American Escape Fiction of the Nineteenth Century, 65
Dime Song Book, The, 60
Dime Western Novel, The, 92
Dinan, John, 3
Dirty Dingus Magee (film), 164
Dirty Dingus Magee (novel), 164
Dirty Harry, 169
Dirty Little Billy, 165
Discovery, Settlement and Present State of Kentucke, The, 10, 43, 46
Distant Drum, 190
Dix, Richard, 154
Doc, 166
Doctorow, E.L., 12, 160
Dodd, Samuel, 109
Dodge City, Kansas
    death toll from gunfights, 25
"Don't Fence Me In," 35
Don't Fence Me In: A Romance of the New West, 183
Dr. Quinn, Medicine Woman, 185–186
Drake, Benjamin, 41
Dreamers and Desperadoes, 183
Drums Along the Mohawk, 21, 130
Dualities, 33, 37
    civil law versus natural law, 83
    civilization versus wilderness, 32–33, 38, 67, 91, 101
    community versus the individual, 31–32, 68, 75
    of gender, 30
    Indian as godless savage versus Indian as idealized man, 39
    justice versus injustice, 31
    the Law of Nature versus the Law of Man, 31
    West versus East, 30–31
Dude, The, 73
Duel in the Sun (novel), 147, 149
Duel in the Sun (film), 147
Dunham, Tracy, 179
DuPlessis, Rachel, 3
Durham, Marilyn, 167
Durham, Philip, 65
Dutchess and the Dirtwater Fox, The, 164
Dutchman's Fireside, 47

E

Earp brothers
    in film, 159, 166
Earp Brothers of Tombstone, The, 7
Earp, Wyatt, 7, 44
    movie character, 140
    portrayal in *My Darling Clementine*, 27
    revisionist view of, 7
Eastlake, William, 143
Eastwood, Clint, 23, 31, 170
    early career, 168–169
    in *Pale Rider*, 26
Eckhardt, Charlie, 138
Edgar Huntly; Or, Memoirs of a Sleepwalker, 41
Edmonds, Walter D., 130
Edwards, Amos, 26
El Dorado, 164
Elkin, Frederick
    in film, 144
Elliot, William, 132
Ellis, Edward S., 68